and Restraint

AND THE DESIGN OF INSTITUTIONS

David M. Primo

THE UNIVERSITY OF CHICAGO PRESS
CHICAGO & LONDON

DAVID M. PRIMO is assistant professor in the Department of Political
Science at the University of Rochester. He is the coauthor of
The Plane Truth: Airline Crashes, the Media, and Transportation Policy.

The University of Chicago Press, Chicago 60637
The University of Chicago Press, Ltd., London
© 2007 by The University of Chicago
All rights reserved. Published 2007
Printed in the United States of America

16 15 14 13 12 11 10 09 08 07   1 2 3 4 5

ISBN-13: 978-0-226-68259-4 (cloth)
ISBN-13: 978-0-226-68260-0 (paper)
ISBN-10: 0-226-68259-5 (cloth)
ISBN-10: 0-226-68260-9 (paper)

LIBRARY OF CONGRESS CATALOGING-IN-PUBLICATION DATA
Primo, David M.
Rules and restraint : government spending and the design of
    institutions / David M. Primo.
    p. cm.
Includes bibliographical references and index.
ISBN-13: 978-0-226-68259-4 (cloth : alk. paper)
ISBN-10: 0-226-68259-5 (cloth : alk. paper)
ISBN-13: 978-0-226-68260-0 (pbk. : alk. paper)
ISBN-10: 0-226-68260-9 (pbk. : alk. paper)
    1. Finance, Public — United States. 2. Budget — United
States. I. Title.
HJ257.3.P75 2007
352.4'973 — dc22

2007009845

*For my wife, Neeta
and my parents, Mauro and Elda*

AMERICAN POLITICS AND POLITICAL ECONOMY,
a series edited by Benjamin I. Page

CONTENTS

List of Illustrations   ix
Acknowledgments   xi

1 : Introduction   1
2 : Rule Design and Enforcement   23
3 : External Enforcement   42
4 : Internal Enforcement   61
5 : The U.S. States   82
6 : The Federal Government   105
7 : Conclusion   123

Appendix A. Technical Material for Chapter 3   141
Appendix B. Technical Material for Chapter 4   150
Appendix C. Technical Material for Chapter 5   156
Appendix D. Technical Material for Chapter 6   158
Notes   161
References   175
Index   189

ILLUSTRATIONS

FIGURES

1.1 Government spending, 1948–2004   2

1.2 Per capita spending, 1948–2004   2

1.3 Spending as a percentage of GDP, 1948–2004   3

2.1 Prisoner's Dilemma   26

3.1 Extensive form, baseline model   49

3.2 Extensive form, model with spending limit   52

4.1 Extensive form, closed rule model   67

4.2 Extensive form, open rule model   68

4.3 Open and closed rule model comparison, part 1   73

4.4 Open and closed rule model comparison, part 2   74

4.5 Open and closed rule model comparison, part 3   75

4.6 Extensive form, enforcement model   77

4.7 Net benefits, open rule vs. closed rule with spending limit   78

4.8 Implementation of the spending limit   79

6.1 Gramm-Rudman-Hollings and deficit reduction   112

6.2 Proposed Balanced Budget Amendment to the U.S. Constitution, as passed by the House (U.S. House 1995)   117

TABLES

4.1 Comparison of open and closed rule results   72

5.1 Summary statistics   90

5.2 Data sources   91

5.3 Spending in the U.S. states, regression results   94

D.1 Spending patterns under the 90 percent rule   159

In fiscal year 1999, the U.S. federal government balanced its budget (leaving aside social security, which is technically "off-budget" in a separate trust fund) for the first time since 1960. To some observers, this represented a major shift in American politics, even prompting then Federal Reserve Chairman Alan Greenspan to caution the Congress against private asset accumulation once the national debt was paid up and surpluses began building. We all know what has happened since: budget surpluses were short-lived and deficit spending returned with a vengeance. Politicians, like most people, are much better at spending than saving, and this book explores the ways in which rules do and do not affect government spending decisions.

My interest in budget rules developed during my time at Stanford. The intellectual environment there undoubtedly shaped who I am as a scholar, as it prompted me to consider the role of institutions in new ways. I owe a debt of gratitude to John Ferejohn, who, while offering me excellent advice on my research, also suggested turning this project into a book, and to David Baron, who has commented on my papers over the years and whose work on bargaining has had a tremendous influence on my thinking. Tim Groseclose was a terrific mentor, and his ability to ask interesting questions is a quality I strive to emulate in my own work. I also thank Keith Krehbiel for showing me how to articulate arguments clearly and challenge the conventional wisdom. Barry Weingast's work on self-enforcing constitutions and Terry Moe's work on agency design have changed my understanding of budget rules. Jonathan Bendor, Mo Fiorina, Simon Jackman, and Romain Wacziarg also offered valuable advice on my research in this area.

While this work began at Stanford, the book took shape at the University of Rochester. Gerald Gamm, the chair of the Political Science Department, works tirelessly on behalf of faculty and had confidence in this project. Larry Rothenberg read the entire manuscript closely and made many constructive suggestions for shaping my argument. I benefited, too, from my discussions with Dick Fenno during the course of this project. I also received helpful comments from Kevin Clarke, John Duggan, Mark Fey, Tasos Kalandrakis, and Dick Niemi. Matt Jacobsmeier, my research assistant, has read the manuscript more times than anybody should have to, pointing out errors and areas where the manuscript could use strengthening. I also want to acknowledge Karen Kopecky for all assistance with programming, Jon Sabella and Matt Stiffler for research assistance, and Rachel Sussman for her careful reading of early versions of the manuscript.

Although the research was conducted at Stanford and Rochester, I have received input from scholars across many schools and many conferences, so any attempt at a comprehensive list will inevitably fail. I apologize in advance to those who are inadvertently left out. Portions of this book have been presented at Cornell University, George Mason University, New York University, Stanford University, the University of Rochester, the annual meeting of the American Political Science Association, the annual meeting of the Midwest Political Science Association, and the annual meeting of the Public Choice Society. In addition, I had the opportunity to present this research and receive feedback at a Current Research Workshop sponsored by the Institute for Humane Studies (IHS). I want to thank John Gilmour, Bill Heniff, Nolan McCarty, and Antonio Merlo for their many useful comments on what became chapter 4 of this book. I also want to thank Nigel Ashford and Amanda Brand at IHS for making the event possible.

For their comments, I also thank Chris Achen, Jim Alt, Steve Ansolabehere, Neal Beck, Sarah Binder, Richard Briffault, Steve Callander, Brandice Canes-Wrone, Erwin Chemerinsky, Steve Coate, Mark Crain, John de Figueiredo, Bob Inman, John Jackson, Rod Kiewiet, George Krause, Bob Lowry, Andrew Martin, John Matsusaka, Ben Page, Jim Poterba, Mike Rappaport, John Samples, David Schoenbrod, Jim Snyder, Mario Villarreal, and Dick Winters.

I also wish to express my gratitude to two grant-making organizations for their generous support. The National Science Foundation supported this research from its initial stages (SES-0314786), and the Earhart Foundation provided the resources to enable me to complete the project. I hope that the quality of the scholarship in this book gives them an intellectual return on their investment.

I am grateful to Oxford University Press for its permission to reproduce and adapt sections of a published article in the book. A less-general version of the model presented in chapter 3, and much of the statistical analysis presented in chapter 5, appeared in "Stop Us before We Spend Again: Institutional Constraints on Government Spending," *Economics and Politics* 18 (2006): 269–312.

It is an honor to be working with Chicago, a press with a rich tradition of publishing important work in law and economics as well as political science. The acquisitions editors at Chicago, John Tryneski and Alex Schwartz, made me feel very welcome at the press and made the whole process as smooth as one could hope, and Parker Smathers and Rodney Powell have fielded my many questions about the process patiently and quickly. Yvonne Zipter's careful copyediting eye has improved the flow of the book. I also wish to thank three anonymous reviewers, whose suggestions strengthened the manuscript. Of course, I bear complete responsibility for the final product.

Finally, I wish to acknowledge my family, whose support has made the inevitable setbacks in academia less painful and the successes more rewarding. My parents, Mauro and Elda, have always maintained optimism in my work in a way that only parents can. My brothers, Luke and Mark, and their families have helped me keep my work in perspective. My in-laws, the Gandhi family, have offered much encouragement throughout the writing of this book.

Most of all, though, I want to thank my wife Neeta, who has not only been exceedingly supportive throughout the writing of this book but has also read and commented on the manuscript. My appreciation extends beyond her input on my research. Not long after we met, Neeta left sunny Palo Alto for snowy Rochester (a true sign of love, some might say), and we have built a great life together. I look forward each day to our conversations about work, the world, or nothing in particular. Love is in many ways about the little moments — talking about the day, cooking together, watching a movie. I treasure this time together, and I treasure her love.

CHAPTER I

Introduction

Rules are made to be broken.
PROVERB

The United States is in an era of political polarization and gridlock.[1] Finding common ground on most issues is all but impossible because policy stances of key players diverge so dramatically. A similar story can be told for the states.[2] For instance, New York State's legislative process is referred to as "dysfunctional" by reform groups (e.g., Creelan and Moulton 2004). Yet, one policy area is immune from the political paralysis lamented by so many. Local, state, and federal governments must authorize spending each year; inaction is not a viable option. On that point even hardened partisans can agree. The centrality of budgeting is magnified in an era of gridlock because under such circumstances, budgetary policymaking is the only game in town.

Given the primacy of budgeting in the legislative process, it should not be surprising that legislative rules are written specifically for the consideration of bills related to the budget. Like no other policy area, the budget process is governed by specific rules. These rules govern the timing of the budget process, the permissibility of amendments to bills once they leave a committee, the relationship between outlays and revenues, the size of majorities required for bill enactment, the number of votes required to override executive vetoes of spending and taxing legislation, and so on.

Spending levels appear, at first glance, to be unaffected by rules. Government outlays have risen dramatically at all levels of government in the post–World War II era. Per capita spending by the federal government, in constant fiscal year 2000 dollars, has increased from $1,596 in fiscal year 1948 to $7,150 in fiscal year 2004.[3] At the state and local levels combined, those figures are $760 in 1948 and $3,971 in 2004. All told, government spends much more today than it did a half century ago. Figures 1.1–1.3 depict government spending in total, at the federal level, and at the state and

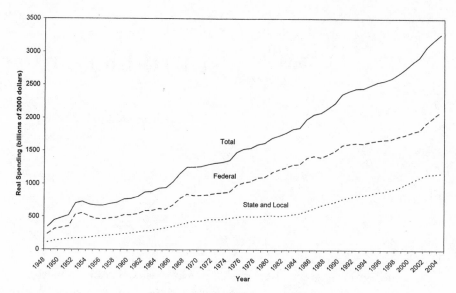

Figure 1.1 Government spending, 1948–2004

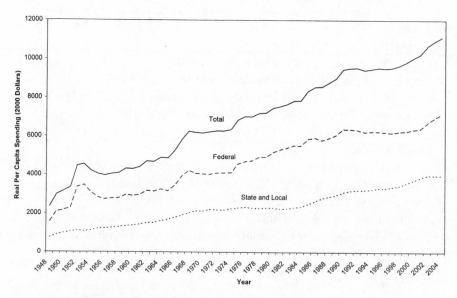

Figure 1.2 Per capita spending, 1948–2004

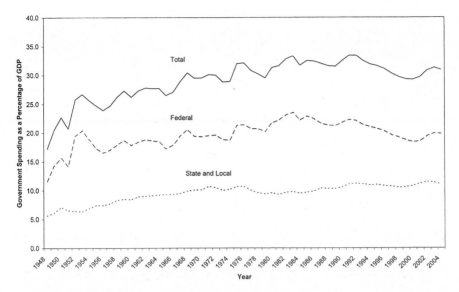

Figure 1.3 Spending as a percentage of GDP, 1948–2004

local levels in the post–World War II era. Whether we are measuring real total spending, real per capita spending, or spending as a percentage of gross domestic product (GDP), the postwar increase is unmistakable.

Numerous government services are viewed by many as untouchable, making downward movements in spending very difficult to achieve. Combined with the difficulties in rule design and enforcement that are the focus of this book, it seems natural to wonder whether budget rules can ever be effective. The answer is yes. For instance, spending has remained consistently lower in states with effective budget rules, and states with effective budget rules are more responsible in how they adjust their spending as state per capita income increases. In contrast, federal budget reform has, for the most part, failed. As we will see in this book, rules vary in their effectiveness and in their enforceability; the general spending trends discussed above mask underlying differences. Therefore, one must understand how rules shape outcomes in order to understand budgeting.

Moving from the big picture to a more fine-grained analysis, an examination of spending and taxing at the U.S. state and federal levels reveals several puzzles:

• In 1985, the U.S. Congress passed and President Ronald Reagan signed into law new budget rules designed to eliminate the deficit by the 1990 fiscal year (U.S. Congress 1985). While the deficit declined initially, by 1991 it had shot up to a level higher than before the law took effect, and the reform is widely considered to have been a colossal failure. On the surface it was deceptively simple, with clear guidelines and a straightforward enforcement procedure. Why did this law fail?

- Nearly all states have some form of a balanced budget requirement on the books, yet the magnitude of deficits and spending varies greatly across the states. What explains this variation?
- Some states have rules that shut down government if a budget deadline is missed; others do not. Why do states with shutdown provisions spend more than states without such laws?
- Why are certain legislative rules, like the Senate filibuster, treated as if they are sacrosanct, while budget rules are often ignored?
- Despite the success of constitutional balanced budget rules at the state level, a comparable amendment to the U.S. Constitution is unlikely to be successful at lowering spending or eliminating deficits. Why might we expect rules successful at the state level to falter at the federal level?

The dominance of budgeting in the legislative process makes it a topic of intrinsic interest, and understanding how rules shape outcomes is the focus of this book. In the course of developing a theory and examining its implications empirically, the above puzzles will be addressed. The theoretical models in this book rely on two components: an examination of how rules shape policy outcomes, and an examination of how the enforcement of rules influences their effectiveness. The impact of a rule depends both on its procedural details and on its enforcement. As I demonstrate, effective rule design is fraught with peril. Rules are designed via political processes, where effectiveness may not be a primary concern. Even if a well-designed rule is promulgated, such a rule will tend to be difficult to enforce within an organization because the incentive to ignore it may be too strong to overcome. Enforcement from outside the organization thus becomes an attractive option, yet even here problems arise. The most successful form of external enforcement, a constitutional amendment, runs the risk of locking in a poorly designed rule that is the product of political compromise.[4] Even rules that are enforced successfully may not accomplish their intended goals.

The central argument of this book is that the conditions required for effective budget rules — an appropriate design and appropriate enforcement mechanism — will rarely be met in practice. The models presented here demonstrate that effective rules can be designed in theory, but in practice rules are designed by individuals with interests. These interests may lead to the enactment of ineffective rules, or such outcomes may arise as the result of the political compromise necessary for almost any rule to be enacted. These tendencies are exacerbated in modern-day America because existing governmental commitments to multiple constituencies, ranging from seniors to homeowners to industry groups, make any sort of reform challenging. This is especially true at the national level, where effective federal budget reform is unlikely to be achieved via typical routes (e.g., legislation or constitutional amendments initiated by Congress). As we will see, state governments are in much better shape than the federal government, in part because a key rule, a balanced budget requirement, was enacted in most states at a time when preexisting commitments were not so prevalent. Still, modern-day reforms in the states face an uphill battle similar to what transpires at the federal level.

This study of budget rules also serves as a window into the issue of institutional design and rule enforcement more generally. By showing how fragile internally enforced budget rules are, I offer insight into why general rules of legislative procedure tend to be more stable. The answer is simple: neglecting to enforce a general rule of procedure has more significant long-term implications for a legislature since it has an impact on all future legislation rather than a subset of it. It is this contrast between the fragility of budget rules and the stability of more general rules that offers up a possibility for internal enforcement of budget rules. By tying a budget rule to an important, more general procedure of a legislature, the costs of failing to enforce the budget rule increase because an enforcement setback threatens the legislature's overall functioning. Before laying out the methodological approach and argument of the book in more detail, I discuss the environment in which budget rules are adopted, utilized, and enforced or not enforced.

The Environment of Budget Rules

Transaction Costs Loom Large

Designing and enforcing budget rules is not unlike facilitating economic transactions. As the literature spawned in economics by Coase (1937) argues, "it is costly to transact" (North 1990, 12). This paradigm challenges conventional neoclassical economic approaches, which assume frictionless bargaining. For an economic transaction to occur, the participating parties must have sufficient information and be aware of a credible enforcement mechanism. Since information and enforcement are costly to secure, most contracts governing agreements are by their very nature incomplete. One cannot specify all possible contingencies without incurring such great costs that the transaction is not worth pursuing. And in some cases, especially in political settings, contracts cannot be written down or enforced.

Rules and structures within an organization, by facilitating agreements and bargaining, reduce these transaction costs. For instance, Weingast and Marshall (1988) view the congressional committee system as providing a means of facilitating vote trading and bargaining that would not occur in the absence of tight control over proposal power. They view deals in Congress as suffering from at least two problems: nonsimultaneous exchange and noncontemporaneous benefit flows. The former refers to the fact that bills are often not considered in tandem. The latter refers to the fact that benefits passed today may not be awarded until a later date and that if the political environment changes in the meantime, there may be incentives to change the terms of the bargain ex post. However, if the legislators who receive those benefit flows run the committee that has jurisdiction over that area of spending, then they can block any attempt to make such a change. In sum, the purported blocking power of committees enables legislators to enforce bargains that would not be enforceable in a world where the floor median controlled the agenda.[5]

Still, rules can accomplish only so much. First, they must be enforced, which introduces another sort of transaction cost. The enforcer must be provided with incentives to make decisions in the interest of the organization he or she oversees. Second, designers must possess sufficient information in order to properly structure rules. While rules may minimize transaction costs by facilitating political bargaining, they will, of necessity, be imperfect because they cannot cover all possible contingencies. Budget rules, therefore, are designed in some cases to reduce transaction costs, but no rule (or contract) can contain provisions for all possible contingencies. The political economy approach in this book assumes that perfect contracts cannot be written and requires that agreements either be enforced by an external arbiter (who may or may not be a perfect enforcer) or be enforced endogenously within the organization. Third, most discussions of transaction costs assume that decision makers seek to minimize such costs. However, those who stand to lose from a particular organizational arrangement may want to increase transaction costs so as to make changes to the status quo more difficult. For instance, a member of Congress who is against wasteful spending on local boondoggles may want to make it more difficult for such transactions to occur. In this case, transaction costs may be used as a weapon to prevent outcomes that one prefers to avoid; this is especially true in the context of agency design (Moe 1989; Wood and Bohte 2004).

Rules Are Malleable and Potentially Unstable

Senator Ted Stevens (R-AK) is a fierce defender of his state's interests, and one of his long-standing policy goals is to enact legislation that permits drilling for oil in the Arctic National Wildlife Refuge (ANWR). Any stand-alone bill permitting exploration faces an uphill battle, so over the years Stevens has attempted, unsuccessfully, to secure passage by attaching the provision to must-pass spending legislation. In 2005 Stevens took a new tack. The House and the Senate passed different versions of a defense appropriations bill, resulting in the formation of a conference committee to reconcile the two pieces of legislation. Stevens was a member of the conference committee and inserted language permitting drilling in ANWR into the conference report. In doing so, Stevens (and the conference committee) violated Rule 28 of the Senate rules. Rule 28 prohibits new components of legislation from being inserted into a conference report. As a way to police this sort of violation, any Senator may raise a point of order against extraneous measures in conference reports. If the point of order is sustained by the presiding officer, the offending provisions are stricken from the legislation.

Stevens, a Senate veteran, was prepared for this and crafted a plan. If a point of order was raised and sustained, he would appeal the ruling. A simple majority vote in support of the appeal would be sufficient to overturn the chair's ruling and set a precedent that would effectively repeal Rule 28. Recognizing the importance of Rule 28 to the Senate, Stevens had inserted the following language into the provision: "Effective immediately, the Presiding Officer shall apply all of the precedents of the Senate under Rule XXVIII in effect at the beginning of the 109th Congress." In other words, as soon as the president signed the legislation, Rule 28 would be in force once more. Stevens had crafted a way to waive the rule just for his bill.

This tactic outraged Senator Robert Byrd (D-WV), a master of parliamentary procedure and a fierce defender of Senate traditions and norms. Byrd has mastered the intricacies of Senate procedure and has used them to great advantage during his forty-plus years in the Senate. When he takes to the well of the Senate, his colleagues listen.

On December 21, 2005, Byrd spoke out against Stevens's maneuvering: "I love this man from Alaska. I do, I love him. I feel my blood in my veins is with his blood. I love him, but I love the Senate more. I came here and swore an oath to uphold the Constitution of the United States, and I would die upholding that oath. . . . If permitted today, [Stevens's gambit] could be utilized again and again, with terrible consequences for the Senate rules. . . . Allowing this process to continue unfolding as it has in recent days would cause significant harm to the Senate as an institution" (Byrd 2005).

Byrd was not alone in his criticisms. Russell Feingold (D-WI) noted, "Some have said there is precedent for violating Rule XXVIII. My response is simple: Abusing the process and breaking the rules in the past does not justify doing so now, especially knowing it was a mistake. . . . We have a responsibility to respect the rules and traditions of the Senate" (Feingold 2005).

Despite the dramatic words, there was nothing particularly novel about Stevens's actions. Similar techniques had been used in the past to nullify a rule (although the attempt to reinstate the rule immediately was a novel twist). Moreover, Rule 28 violations have commonly gone unchallenged. Byrd's concern was not the violation of Rule 28 but that the means of violating it threatened the functioning of the Senate.

Stevens was ultimately unsuccessful, but not before the fragility of Senate rules was laid bare. Byrd's concern was well-founded; unless constitutionally mandated, legislative rules are essentially changeable at will. As Kettl has written, "Procedures simply cannot force elected officials to make decisions that they do not want to make" (2003a, 129). Stevens's actions may have been more brazen than most, but they were certainly not unprecedented.

Just because the rules *can* be changed does not mean that they *will* be changed. Decision makers must have an incentive to change them. Often they do, as a result of the "inheritability problem" identified by Riker (1980). To the extent that rules are determined as part of a collective choice process, the determination of what rules to enact will suffer from the same problems that plague policymaking. Decision-maker preferences over the rules depend on the expected influence of those rules, so we should expect to see the same sorts of instability in collective preferences over rules that we do over policy. Moreover, we should also observe the same sort of strategizing over rule choice that we do over policy choice.

Inheritability means that even if the theorist can identify the optimal rule for an organization, there is no guarantee that this rule will be selected from a menu of potential rules. The outcome will depend on the existing institutional arrangement, the procedure for selecting the rule, and the preferences of decision makers within the organization. To the extent that members of the organization have relatively similar preferences,

Riker's inheritability problem becomes less severe. In a body like the Congress, though, preferences are far from homogenous. Inheritability lurks in the background of discussions about rule design, suggesting why rule enforcement is so important. Legislators will frequently have incentives to circumvent, if not alter, rules. Given these challenges, what is remarkable is not that rules are sometimes violated but, rather, that procedural rules are typically followed so closely.[6] The creation of budget rules occurs in the shadow of these tensions.

In this book I will distinguish between exogenous (external) and endogenous (internal) rule enforcement, as this distinction is essential to understanding the puzzles raised above. With few exceptions, most rule enforcement at the federal level is endogenous, while at the state level many more rules are constitutionally mandated and therefore externally enforceable by the courts. The inability of Congress to follow its own budget rules is a direct consequence of weak internal enforcement. The juxtaposition of successful general procedural rules and unsuccessful budget rules will be explored in this book.

Long-Term/Short-Term and Micro-Macro Tensions Plague Budgeting

GOVERNMENT THE CONTORTIONIST. This phrase comes from Aaron Wildavsky, one of the leading scholars of the budget process in the twentieth century. He frames the micro-macro problem in budgeting perfectly:

> Congress is torn between two kinds of contradictory promises: to certain beneficiaries in particular or to people in general, in regard to budget balance. This conflict is resolved in the usual way by backing and filling, that is, by doing something that seems to satisfy each promise. . . . If government often resembles a contortionist, that is because it promises, in effect, to move simultaneously in two opposite directions. . . . [Consider] the conflict between individual and collective rationality. What makes sense to pursue individually may appear undesirable when these individual actions are viewed from a more general perspective. We see this conflict in budgeting: A desire for more programs conflicts with spending control (Wildavsky and Caiden 2004, 22, 23).

In one respect, members of Congress reflect the inconsistent preferences of their constituents. For example, in the midst of the 1995 congressional debate over a constitutional amendment to balance the federal budget, the American public was asked by CBS News and the *New York Times* to indicate their support or opposition to the amendment (CBS News and the *New York Times* 1995). A whopping 79 percent supported the amendment. However, when the question was reframed to note that a balanced budget may require "cuts in Social Security," only 36 percent were in favor of the rule change. A similar phenomenon plagues the legislative process. Namely, the desire for a macro-level goal, such as low spending or a balanced budget, may clash with a micro-level goal, such as preserving benefits targeting particular constituencies.[7]

The simple logic of majority rule and electoral incentives shows why spending often wins out over fiscal discipline. Before bargaining over specifics begins, it may be the case that all legislators prefer budgets to be balanced. In the abstract, a balanced budget is a wildly popular policy, though not one without its critics. In reality, the temptation of short-term gain often wins out. For example, suppose that the budget is currently in balance, but a new spending proposal will benefit a majority of legislators while leaving taxes unchanged, thereby implying deficit spending. If those benefits are sufficiently large relative to the costs of higher deficits, which have to be paid off in the future and are therefore discounted, then a majority of legislators will vote for the new spending. This logic applies to budget cuts as well. A government running a deficit will not balance its books if the cuts required to do so would confer tangible harms on key constituencies. Deficits are amorphous, their consequences not easily captured by a television news story. The consequences of cuts, in contrast, lend themselves to vivid portrayals of struggle and heartache for identifiable beneficiaries of a government program. Even if a package of large-scale cuts were agreed to, the agreement would be unstable. The next day, programs comprising a portion of the large-scale cuts, benefiting a majority but with costs spread out across the population, presumably could still be enacted by the legislature.

Put in electoral terms, new outlays confer tangible benefits that legislators may claim credit for at election time, while a balanced budget is an amorphous goal for which it is more difficult to claim credit. Meanwhile, spending cuts are harmful to a legislator just as spending increases are beneficial. Thus, a legislative majority has an incentive to approve deficit spending. Research by congressional scholar Douglas Arnold has found that members of Congress are much more inclined to approve additional federal spending than to vote for cuts in such spending. Conversely, they are also more likely to be fiscally conservative when dealing with votes on macro-level economic policy, compared with micro-level policy votes

(Arnold 1990). These patterns are consistent with the macro-micro tension described above.

This tension between short-term spending and long-term fiscal restraint creates the need for effectively enforced budget rules. If legislators could escape blame for budget cuts, then they would be more apt to focus on the macro level. Let us consider the example of tax code simplification, which comes in many forms: a flat tax with a straightforward standard deduction, the elimination of corporate taxation, the elimination of all tax credits and itemized deductions, and so on. The problem is that while tax code simplification has no strong constituency, tax breaks and deductions have very specific constituencies. To take one popular tax policy as an example, only a retiring — or exceptionally electorally secure — senator would call for the elimination of the tax deduction on mortgage interest.[8] President Reagan's 1986 tax reform, which streamlined deductions and simplified tax rates, was successful in part because it was considered as a package. By bundling several provisions together, Reagan and members of Congress made it more difficult for a group to challenge the reform on the basis of any specific provision.

The procedure for closing military bases, created in 1988, also illustrates this tension. Eliminating a military base is a risky proposition. Legislators whose districts contain bases will fight hard to protect them. Logrolls, as well as many procedural hurdles, were keeping outdated military bases alive. Legislators at the time collectively realized that bases imposing huge costs on the federal government needed to be closed. At the same time, they had a vested interest in avoiding blame for such closures. The answer, courtesy of Rep. Dick Armey (R-TX), was to establish a commission charged with determining which bases would be closed. The commission would present a list to the secretary of defense, who could either approve or disapprove of the list in its entirety. If he approved the list, the recommended bases would be closed unless Congress took action to veto the entire proposal. Through this procedure, bases could be closed without any further action by Congress, and if Congress chose to act, its only option would be to reject the recommendations in toto. This rule was successful because it allowed members to delegate the tough, specific decisions to a commission while being on record voting in favor of macro-level fiscal responsibility. By shifting agenda-setting power to an outside agent, making approval the default outcome, and preventing Congress from amending recommendations, the rule achieved its end.

TIME INCONSISTENCY. Even universal agreement on which fiscal policies maximize social welfare offers no guarantee of successful implementation without incentives at each decision point to undertake the optimal action. Imagine a world, lasting for two periods, as defined below, with a benevolent government setting fiscal policy that in turn affects the decisions of consumers.[9] At the beginning of period one, the government sets a fiscal policy, and consumers respond accordingly. Both consumers and government take into account expected behavior in period two when making decisions in period one. Then, in period two, the government again sets fiscal policy and consumers react accordingly. Policies must be consistent, meaning that at each decision point, the government maximizes social welfare given its information. Consumers respond to the actions of government similarly, maximizing their respective individual utilities.

The optimal set of fiscal policies maximizes the welfare of society totaled over both periods, but rarely do consistent and optimal policies intersect. Kydland and Prescott (1977) demonstrate that the only way for a consistent policy to be optimal is if one of two very demanding conditions holds: (*a*) consumers' expectations of government behavior in period two do not affect their decisions in period one; or (*b*) the net effect of consumer behavior in period one on overall welfare is zero. These conditions are rarely met in any economy where consumer behavior is conditioned on past experience and expectations about the future.

Kydland and Prescott advocate for rules rather than discretion, arguing that the presence of rules will constrain governmental action and induce consumers to behave in a way that generates optimal economic outcomes. This perspective assumes, however, that the correct rule will be both selected and enforced. As we will see, this is a strong assumption. Even a benevolent government interested only in the welfare of society will not achieve optimality unless it somehow convincingly pledges in advance to institute the optimal policy in both periods via a rule. Such a guarantee, of course, is unrealistic without some mechanism to ensure commitment (read: enforcement).

Rules Do Not Operate in a Vacuum

GOVERNMENT ORGANIZATION. When examining the impact of a rule, such as a supermajority requirement for budget passage, it is important to keep in mind that such a provision will be embedded in a larger electoral and governmental structure and that this structure influences outcomes. There is a large theoretical and empirical literature comparing the impact of single and multimember districts on spending outcomes. The foundation of this literature is the view that the electoral environment alters legislator incentives. Lizzeri and Persico (2001) have shown that winner-take-all systems tend to provide transfers instead of national public goods, with the opposite relationship holding in proportional representation (PR) systems. Milesi-Ferretti, Perotti, and Rostagno (2002) allow for a mix of transfers to groups and local public goods spending, and they find that majoritarian systems (with multiple districts) will emphasize local public goods, while PR systems (with one district) will have more group transfer spending. Persson and Tabellini (2004a) find that majoritarian elections lead to smaller government and smaller welfare systems than proportional elections do. The governmental structure, such as the distinction between presidential and parliamentary regimes, also alters outcomes (Inman and Fitts 1990; Fitts and Inman 1992; Chari, Jones, and Marimon 1997; Persson and Tabellini 1999).[10] In addition, bicameralism shapes policy outcomes since the impact of having two houses changes how governments form (Druckman and Thies 2002; Diermeier, Eraslan, and Merlo 2002), the nature of bargaining processes (Buchanan and Tullock 1962; Heller 1997; Tsebelis and Money 1997; Lee 2000; Ansolabehere, Snyder, and Ting 2003; Kalandrakis 2004; Cutrone and Mc-Carty 2006), legislative productivity (Rogers 2003), and even the selection of rules within a legislature (Diermeier and Myerson 1999).

Federalism, or power sharing at different governmental levels, is an important phenomenon that mediates the incentives of center and local governments in budgeting. The seminal work in the area of fiscal federalism includes Tiebout (1956) and Oates (1972). In recent years there has been an explosion of political economy research in this area (e.g., Persson and Tabellini 1996a, 1996b; Cremer and Palfrey 1999; Rodden 2002, 2005; Inman 2003; Rodden, Eskeland, and Litvack 2003; Bednar 2005, in press; de Figueiredo and Weingast 2005).

De Figueiredo and Weingast (2005) highlight the two key questions in the literature: How can the center be made strong (and credible) enough so that it prevents local governments from overspending? At the same time, how can it be kept from becoming so powerful that it obviates the benefits of decentralization? In the area of budgeting, this becomes especially important because localities want to secure benefits at the expense of the center and may adopt local policies that are fiscally irresponsible because they expect a bailout (Inman 2003). As Rodden (2002) shows, subnational governments that are limited in their borrowing ability tend to be more fiscally responsible than those governments that have significant borrowing authority and are dependent on funding from the national government.

Moreover, federalism is itself an endogenous phenomenon that may collapse if incentives to maintain it are not present (Bednar, in press). Many of federalism's benefits, such as a strong national defense, are public goods that, once provided, cannot be allocated only to those who contribute their "fair share" to their provision (Bednar 2005). This creates a classic free rider problem in which states have an incentive to act opportunistically. A fundamental challenge for federal systems, therefore, is to maintain the system despite the omnipresent temptations for states to free ride.

I hold government organization constant in my models, focusing on elected officials who are assumed to come from single-member districts, who operate in a unicameral setting, and who are embedded in a system that, while not explicitly federal, features many of the "common pool" problems inherent in such a system. Because I consider basic models where districts are assumed to be of equal size, adding an additional legislature will not change the results.[11] By limiting my attention to one governmental structure, I am able to home in on the impact of rules (and the interaction of rules) and limit the number of moving parts in the analysis.

INSTITUTIONAL INTERACTIONS. A lesson of institutional design is that rules are not applied in isolation. A new rule interacts with an existing set of institutional arrangements, sometimes creating unexpected outcomes. In a later chapter I demonstrate that introducing supermajority voting requirements for the passage of spending bills will lead to increased spending when spending limits are in place but will lead to decreased spending otherwise. The intuition is that proposers build coalitions differently when they are unconstrained by a spending limit than when such a rule is in place.

This sort of institutional interaction often occurs within the context of a single large-scale reform. For instance, many proposals for federal balanced budget rules require a three-fifths supermajority to increase taxes, thereby changing two key features of the bargaining process at once. Not only must budgets be balanced, but tax increases must receive the approval of a supermajority. The more complicated a reform, the more likely it is that unintended consequences will occur due to institutional interactions.[12]

Institutional interactions can never be fully accounted for because most organizations have hundreds, if not thousands, of rules. The advantage of the approach I have adopted in this book is that it isolates specific rules in the legislative process, thereby allowing an analysis of interactions that are expected to be of import for policy outcomes.

The Political Economy Approach

Foundations

How can the researcher or reformer understand the impact of rules and evaluate the likelihood of successful enforcement? The tools of political economy, such as game theory and econometrics, are ideally suited for tackling this challenging topic. By examining models that place strategic interactions at center stage, I will focus on the influence of rules and address all of the previously discussed challenges of budget rule design. These models will be supplemented by case studies that enable a more in-depth analysis of some particularly illuminating situations. This approach reflects the perspective that proper nouns and abstract models can be mutually reinforcing.

I will explore theoretical questions using game theory. Game theory and other political economy techniques account for the interactive, strategic nature of budgeting. These tools are also useful for understanding the emergence and development of institutions. Using large-n statistical techniques supplemented by in-depth case analyses, I will also examine how well my theory matches the data. Technical material is placed in appendices at the end of the book for readers interested in the mathematics behind the results.

In adopting the political economy approach and utilizing game theory, I am making several assumptions.[13]

1. *Political actors are rational, self-interested, and strategic.* Those involved in the budget process are not necessarily benevolent and concerned with the body politic. As with all rational individuals, they have preferences that guide their behavior. One concern with the analysis of proposed reforms is that they often ignore the strategic and self-interested components of politics and, implicitly, assume that a benevolent dictator will be implementing a rule.
2. *Advance contracting is not possible unless explicitly assumed.* In other words, a fundamental problem arises because a contract cannot be written to guide behavior. Furthermore, to explore the implications of this problem requires the use of tools that do not assume advance contracting. If legislators wrote down a contract in advance stipulating that they would be forced to give up their seats if they voted for deficit spending after agreeing to a balanced budget, such an agreement would solve the time inconsistency problem discussed above. Such contracts, of course, are not enforceable. In contrast, the public pledges legislators are often

asked to make on budgetary matters are a creative way to generate similar contractual effects, since voters have the power to sanction violators.

3. *All behavior must form an equilibrium, meaning that the actions of legislators must be optimal, given what other players will do (or are expected to do)*. Put another way, legislators take into account each other's behavior (or expected behavior) when determining their own actions. Hence, if a rule is enacted that requires a change in the behavior of proposers, this will in turn affect the behavior of those who have to decide whether to approve a bill.

There are many advantages to using the model-based approach adopted in this book. Formal models allow us to probe mechanisms and examine the impact of institutions independently, as well as observe how they interact. By changing particular rules or features of a model, we can observe how equilibrium behavior changes.[14] Game theoretic models are particularly advantageous because they often generate results that run counter to intuition and lead us in unanticipated directions.[15] Models also offer insight into how the analyst should structure and interpret data analysis. For example, a model that finds interaction effects among institutions may lead the researcher to cut the data in new ways. Finally, since they can be used to analyze the expected outcomes of policies, models have the potential to inform policymakers. While the rough-and-tumble of politics suggests caution in overstating the case, at the very least scientific analysis serves to present policymakers with a more informed basis for decision making.

Morton (1999) argues that models are subjected to empirical scrutiny in several ways, which range from testing hypotheses derived from the model to testing the assumptions of the model. A model with equilibria consistently in opposition to what the data show will not be held up as useful for very long, unless it serves some other purpose.[16] In this book, I present models that offer insights into how budget rules interact with other institutional features. Chapters 3 and 4 present arguments about how external and internal enforcement of budget rules plays out. These models are then used in the empirical chapters as the foundation for understanding budgeting in the U.S. states and U.S. federal government. In short, the models serve as tools for understanding the impact of state and federal budget rules on spending.

Normative and Positive Analysis

Any analysis of rule design must distinguish between normative and positive analysis. Normative analysis refers to what individuals ought to do, given some notion of welfare. In economics (and in this book), efficiency, defined as Pareto optimality, is used as the normative benchmark for evaluating outcomes. An allocation of resources is Pareto optimal if nobody can be made better off without making somebody else worse off. This standard is appropriate when evaluating models where resources are allocated across districts.

While efficiency is often viewed as a tool of positive analysis, it also implies a particular conception of what the best way to set up a society is. Another important normative criterion is equity. The efficient outcomes in this book's models will be equitable, so I will not focus directly on equity in my discussions. However, efficient allocations of resources are often inequitable, and equity considerations shape debates over government spending. For instance, some individuals might oppose the creation of a balanced budget rule if the spending cuts needed to achieve balance would hurt programs benefiting the poor.

In the context of discussions of fiscal federalism, Qian and Weingast (1997) and Oates (2005) distinguish between first and second generation theories, with the former referring to studies that presume that government acts as a "custodian of the public interest," and the latter referring to studies that are more positive in orientation. One drawback to early public finance models is that they do not incorporate political incentives into the analysis; instead, they assume that the decision maker is a benevolent central planner. The results of such models are useful for establishing a benchmark by which to evaluate outcomes that arise out of a political process, but they should not be considered in any sense predictions or expectations about the sorts of policies that we will observe in practice. Positive analysis refers to claims about what individuals actually do, given a set of alternatives, rules, and preferences. When analyzing the impact of a rule, positive analysis is concerned with learning how the rule alters behavior and outcomes, irrespective of any notion of what is best for society. An easy way to think about the distinction is that normative analysis is concerned with what is socially optimal while positive analysis is concerned with what is strategically optimal.

This book utilizes a normative benchmark, where appropriate, to evaluate rules. When analyzing how projects should be allocated across districts, I develop an efficient baseline for comparison with what occurs when legislators act strategically. This efficient baseline is developed by determining what actions maximize social welfare (a measure that coincides, in this book's models, with the economic concept of Pareto optimality). Similarly, when considering the impact of a rule on behavior, I assess its impact in terms of whether it moves outcomes closer to or farther away from the efficient outcome.[17] This step also enables one to assess how changes in rules alter outcomes more generally. For example, one can assess how a balanced budget rule would alter spending patterns, noting both whether it moves outcomes away from the efficient outcome and whether it leads to increased or decreased spending.

While I do not explicitly model how legislators design rules, normative and positive analysis guides this discussion. The study of how rules affect outcomes is useful for understanding the selection of rules. Normative analysis probes whether such rules improve social welfare, while positive analysis examines whether such rules would be adopted, given decision makers' views about their expected impact.

Because the two approaches are based on the same models, it would clutter the analysis to distinguish constantly between the two. Instead I summarize the distinction here. References to movement away from or toward the efficient outcome constitute normative analysis. References to how rules alter behavior reflect positive analysis. Normative analysis typically is a subset of positive analysis in that any understanding of the normative impact of a rule requires positive analysis. The same is true when considering rule adoption. To understand whether a rule is likely to be adopted, one needs to understand the consequences of the rule and the incentives of decision makers. This information also speaks to the normative desirability of any reform.

Illustration: Keynesianism and Deficit Politics

The rise of Keynesianism in the post–World War II era offers clear evidence of the benefits of the political economy approach. The political economy approach does not assume a benevolent dictator. Rather, politicians are assumed to be rational actors who are acting in their self-interest. As Buchanan and Wagner put it,

> The applicability of any set of policy rules or precepts is not invariant over alternative decision-making institutions. An idealized set of policy prescriptions may be formulated for a truly benevolent despotism. But this set may be far distant from the ideal prescriptions for the complex "game" of democratic politics, a game that involves the participation of citizens as voters who are simultaneously taxpayers and public-service beneficiaries, the activities of professional politicians whose electoral successes depend on pleasing these voters, the struggles of the sometimes fragile coalitions reflected in organized or unorganized political parties, and, finally, the machinations of bureaucrats who are employed

by government but who tend, indirectly, to control the details of government operation (Buchanan and Wagner 1977, 77–78).

Balanced budgets were the norm in U.S. federal politics until the postwar era (Buchanan and Wagner 1977; Savage 1988; Arnold 1990), when this norm was shattered by the Keynesian revolution. A central tenet of Keynesianism is that deficits are permissible in times of economic stagnation, while surpluses are expected in times of expansion. On average, then, budgets will be balanced, though in any given year the federal government will engage in a countercyclical fiscal policy that may result in deficit spending in bad times and surpluses in good times.

Even if Keynesianism was the "right" policy, it suffered from two problems. First, it required that economic activity be unaffected by government decision making and that business cycles occur in predictable ways (Buchanan and Wagner 1977). Second, it required legislators to commit to running surpluses in flush times, a step that often necessitates tax increases. With no formal rule to this effect, the temptation to run deficit spending in both good times and bad was too much to resist. Keynesianism provided a justification for deficit spending and thereby changed the nature of federal budgeting (Buchanan and Wagner 1977). The fragile "balanced budget equilibrium" was shattered.

In response to this change, many have proposed federal constitutional amendments to tamp deficits. But as I argue in this book, amendments that make it through the Congress would be the product of political compromise, and the effect of that compromise would be to entrench ineffective and routinely circumvented provisions. Any constitutional budget rule that has the potential for enactment in this way will almost surely prove ineffective, and potentially harmful, in the long run.

Illustration: The Family Budget Protection Act

Since 2003, Republicans have proposed the Family Budget Protection Act, a panoply of reforms including presidential line-item veto authority (subject to congressional approval to address concerns about the provision's constitutionality), caps on spending growth, and the elimination of baseline budgeting, under which spending is compared to estimates that incorporate expected spending increases.[18] Two provisions of the act are especially noteworthy: first, most federal programs would be subject to sunset provisions, meaning that their "status quo" levels would be set to zero every ten years. Second, the reversion level of spending if agreement is not reached on a budget would be the previous year's level, minus 1 percent. Currently, if agreement on the budget is not reached, the government shuts down unless continuing resolutions are enacted. In effect, then, the reversion level of spending is currently determined endogenously as part of bargaining, with zero being a possibility if an agreement is not reached.

These two rules work at cross-purposes. Sunset provisions, which were all the rage in the 1970s, advantage advocates of a program because the threat of program termination may result in higher levels of spending due to a fear of seeing the program end. Suppose that an agency had to propose and justify a budget for the upcoming fiscal year. Congress then either accepts its recommendation or rejects it. If the recommendation is rejected, the agency would be shut down. The agency, which wants to maximize its budget, should propose a spending level y that makes key legislators indifferent between seeing the agency remain open at a cost of y, and seeing it close. If the agency provides an important function, the value y will be very high, since only in cases of extremely high proposed budgets will key members of Congress prefer the agency be closed.

Using the same logic, moving the reversion level of spending from being endogenously determined to (essentially) last year's budget will dampen the bargaining advantage of a high-spending proposer (Romer and Rosenthal 1978; Primo 2002). If the offered level of spending is high, the receiver can reject it, knowing that the reversion level of spending will not be so bad (i.e., there is no possibility of a shutdown). While both of these rules may sound like they represent "fiscal discipline," only one has the potential to mitigate tendencies to overspend. Still, legislators may have an incentive to propose ineffective rules because citizens who perceive these rules as beneficial will reward them.

The Argument

This book examines the design and enforcement of budget rules. I argue that there are two components to a rule: (1) the procedures or requirements it lays out; and (2) the mechanisms for enforcing those procedures. I further divide enforcement into two categories: (1) external to the organization; and (2) internal to the organization. Internally enforced rules are effective only under a limited number of conditions. External enforcement mechanisms are more likely to be successful, but the problem of procedural effectiveness looms large. A complicating matter, explored in detail in chapter 6, is that rules designed via a political process are likely to be ineffectively designed. Preexisting commitments make the development of budget rules much more challenging than in previous eras, where governments, for better or worse, did less. External enforcement, in the form of courts monitoring adherence to a constitutional amendment, may therefore lock in bad rules.

Budget rules that are properly designed (i.e., those that can at least theoretically achieve desired ends) will achieve desired ends only if a credible external enforcer exists or endogenous enforcement is feasible. The challenge of rule design, therefore, is to create a rule that (*a*) is efficacious and (*b*) has a credible enforcement mechanism. As I demonstrate in this book, accomplishing both is a challenge. My thesis is that budget rules will rarely achieve any measure of success because problems of design and enforcement conspire to thwart the rules. These problems are rooted in the four areas mentioned earlier: transaction costs, rule malleability and instability, the clashing of long- versus short-term and macro- versus micro-level preferences, and the interconnectedness of budget rules with government organization.

A complete understanding of rules requires that design and enforcement be considered in tandem. In the existing literature, it is common to examine the impact of rules, assuming away the issue of enforcement. While this approach is appropriate for establishing a benchmark, any understanding of budget rules must take into account that enforcement is imperfect at best, and often nonexistent. Otherwise an analysis of the impact of a rule that says, "reduce the deficit by 100 million dollars every year until it reaches zero," would be trivial to analyze. At the other extreme, some scholars argue that in essence no rules are fixed (i.e., all rules are endogenous). While in the limit this is accurate, in order to conduct fruitful analysis it is useful to assume that some structures are exogenously given.[19] I argue later that it is precisely these (relatively) fixed, immutable aspects of organizations that allow for endogenous enforcement to succeed. This book advances the existing literature, therefore, by bridging the gap between studies that probe the impact of rules without regard to enforcement, and those that endogenize everything. These insights are also relevant for questions of institutional design beyond budgeting.

I proceed as follows. Chapter 2 discusses why institutions exist and the challenges encountered both in designing rules and enforcing them. I explain why exogenously enforced rules are more stable than those that must be enforced within an organization, but that both types of enforcement can succeed under certain conditions.

Chapter 3 analyzes the impact of spending limits, supermajority voting rules, and executive veto authority on budgetary bargaining under exogenous enforcement. Assuming perfect enforcement, I demonstrate that the impact of these rules is contingent on the institutional environment in which they operate. I then allow for imperfect enforcement and discuss the conditions under which this type of enforcement will be effective.

In chapter 4, I turn to endogenous enforcement, demonstrating the conditions under which a legislature can induce a proposer to abide by a spending limit that is enforced within the chamber. As it turns out, the problem is that legislators will often have an incentive to not enforce the rule. Only under limited conditions will this enforcement method be successful, including when the voting procedure is close to a simple majority.

Chapter 5 empirically explores the impact of balanced budget rules, reversion budgets, and other rules on spending in the U.S. states, building on the theory developed in chapter 3. I find that states with strict balanced budget rules enforced by an external arbiter—an elected court—spend less than states without such rules. In addition, states with harsh reversion budgets, which take effect in the event of a stalemate, spend more than states with less severe reversion budgets.

In chapter 6, I apply the theory from chapters 3 and 4 to the federal government. Through a series of case studies, including Gramm-Rudman-Hollings, the Budget Enforcement Act of 1990, and proposed constitutional balanced budget amendments, I demonstrate why existing reforms have failed and why proposed reforms face a perilous future.

Finally, chapter 7 addresses the prospects for future reforms, given the challenges of enforcement and the political problems associated with design. I discuss the hurdles facing constitutional budget reform, the implications of my argument for international agreements, and the ways in which the theoretical and empirical results presented in the book are useful for practitioners and policymakers.

This book is a cautionary tale about the potential for budget rules to have the desired effects on policy outcomes. For a rule to be both properly designed and successfully enforced, many factors must come together. Given modern commitments to powerful and varied constituencies, the promise of budget rules will rarely be fulfilled in practice.

CHAPTER 2 # Rule Design and Enforcement

If men were angels, no government would be necessary.
JAMES MADISON, *FEDERALIST 51*

In *Federalist* 51, Madison frames the challenge of determining the optimal level of government power. On the one hand, government needs to be strong enough to ensure a peaceful state. On the other hand, government cannot be made so commanding that it becomes oppressive. Madison's argument is persuasive but incomplete. Even if men (and women) were angels, a government would still be necessary, if only to serve as a preference aggregation device. The argument can be extended in another way: if men were angels, many major functions of institutions would be unnecessary.

An institution is a formal or informal rule (or set of rules), and the associated means of enforcement, that organizes interactions among individuals.[1] These rules may be given a corporeal existence by structures like the U.S. Capitol or the United Nations Building. North (1990, 3) refers to institutions as being "humanly-devised constraints." To truly capture the concept, though, the net should be cast wider. Norms guide our behavior each day, even though in many cases they are not the product of human design but, rather, are part of what Hayek terms a "spontaneous order" (1973). Such rules are as important as those that are the result of conscious action, though the latter will be my focus here. In what follows, I will use the term "institution" when referring to a rule (and its implicit or explicit enforcement procedures), and "organization" when referring to a body like Congress or a corporation. Such bodies are also commonly referred to as institutions, but I adopt different terminology to avoid confusion.

Institutions serve many functions. They facilitate preference aggregation and decision making. Institutions also mediate transactions among individuals, as in a stock market, or reduce transaction costs, as in a firm (Coase 1937). Put differently, "institutions reduce uncertainty by providing a structure to everyday life" (North 1990, 3). If men were angels, enforcement or monitoring would not be a crucial part of most institutions. If men were angels, insider trading would not occur. If men were angels, budget rules would bind behavior, even in the face of difficult choices. Men are not angels, of course, thus prompting a need for governmental and nongovernmental institutions to regulate as well as facilitate interactions among self-interested individuals. To be effective, institutions must be designed to account for the realities of self-interest, incentives to misrepresent preferences, and other deviations from the "angelic ideal."

This chapter begins by discussing some of the major purposes of institutions. Transaction costs, discussed in chapter 1, are in the background here, since the problems institutions set out to solve are the root causes of many sorts of transaction costs. Then, I address the issue of institutional formation by distinguishing between rule design and enforcement. The first question to ask about a rule is, if it is perfectly enforced, will it solve the problem it is designed to solve? The second question is, if so, what is necessary to ensure successful enforcement? Enforcement takes one of two forms — internal or external to the organization — and I discuss the pros and cons of each category. In doing so, I provide a foundation for the study of budget rules.

If Only Men and Women Were Angels . . .

What exactly does it mean to say that people are angels, and why do deviations from this ideal introduce a role for institutions? First, angels are other-regarding, and they internalize the utility of others. Given sufficient information, an individual who internalizes the utility of others when making a decision acts as a welfare-optimizing social planner.[2] Second, angels are an "open book." They truthfully reveal their preferences and any private information that may be of use to others involved in the decision-making process. In a bargaining setting, an angel would be willing to tell you the minimum payment that he would accept in exchange for an object. Similarly, when faced with the onset of a military dispute, truthful revelation by states about whether they are strong or weak would facilitate bargaining and avoid the costs of war. Third, angels adhere to organizational rules. There is no need for an enforcer because angels will "do the right thing."

Self-Interest

The realities of human interaction shape the design of institutions. While individuals are other-regarding in some circumstances, the self-interest assumption is necessary and reasonable when designing institutions. Institutions built on trust alone can crumble in the presence of even a smattering of self-interested behavior. Still, the assumption of other-regarding preferences creates a useful baseline for evaluating institutional effectiveness. A social planner who maximizes a social welfare function summing across the utility of all actors in a society represents the best-case scenario for institutional designers. In addition, designers must be prepared for misrepresentation and rule violations that arise when individuals have incentives to undertake these behaviors, given the self-interest assumption. For example, if town residents pay local taxes based on how much value they place on local public services, one should not be surprised if valuations are systematically underreported. Likewise, a weak political leader has an incentive to appear strong so as to emerge victorious in a political or military standoff. Finally, why follow an unenforced rule if the payoff from violating it is higher?

One of the most basic institutions is the laissez-faire economic market with enforceable contracts. Under certain assumptions, the free market harnesses self-interest and decentralized information for collectively beneficial outcomes, but only in cases where sufficient information is available and where contracts are enforceable. As Adam Smith famously writes in *The Wealth of Nations,* "But man has almost constant occasion for the help of his brethren, and it is in vain for him to expect it from their benevolence only. . . . It is not from the benevolence of the butcher, the brewer, or the baker that we expect our dinner, but from their regard to their own interest" (Smith [1776] 1999, 118–19). Smith's argument (formalized by Arrow and Debreu 1954, Walras 1954, and others) is that a free market with complete contracting leads to the "best" outcomes for society. Here best is defined as Pareto optimal, which means, as noted in chapter 1, that the allocation of resources cannot be altered to make somebody better off without making somebody else worse off. The many assumptions underlying this general equilibrium model are difficult to realize in practice. The free market relies on effective enforcement of contracts and the assumption of perfect competition, under which firms (and consumers) are price takers. Deviations from the free market ideal occur in the absence of these conditions. Since market mechanisms can often be utilized to correct deviations from Pareto optimality, one should not necessarily interpret the occurrence of "market failure" as a justification for government-mandated institutions. Decision making within governmental institutions introduces an entirely new set of issues that may exacerbate problems.[3] Still, even though the free market harnesses self-interest for productive ends and often has the power to correct itself, its success relies on formal or informal institutions that ensure contract enforcement.

Arguably the most famous of all collective action problems, the Prisoner's Dilemma illustrates the implications of self-interested behavior. In this game, two individuals must simultaneously choose from one of two actions: cooperation (*c*) or defection (*d*). The payoffs, shown in figure 2.1, depend on the actions of both players. For instance, if player P1 plays *c* and player P2 plays *d*, P1 receives a payoff of 3 while P2 receives 0. This matrix implies that each player should defect, regardless of what the other player does, making defection a dominant strategy. The reasoning is straightforward. No matter what the other player does, a higher payoff is achieved by playing defect than by playing cooperate. The outcome resulting from both players playing *d* is Pareto-dominated, as both would prefer the outcome resulting from mutual cooperation than the one occurring following mutual defection. Players who could trust one another would agree to cooperate, making both of them better off. Without some sort of endogenous enforcement mechanism (such as a punishment strategy implemented through repeated interactions), though, a suboptimal outcome will result, as a self-interested individual would renege on the agreement in this one-shot interaction. In this book I will focus primarily on problems that occur when self-interested behavior leads to collectively suboptimal outcomes and violations of rules. Next, I focus on informational issues and discuss the challenges facing institutional designers.

Information

In the realm of informational concerns, I focus on three areas: incentives to misrepresent preferences; informational asymmetries in bargaining; and principal-agent problems. The public goods literature provides a classic example of incentives to misrepresent preferences as well as a rule for inducing truthful preference revelation. Suppose that a government must determine the size and funding scheme for a pure public good, such as national defense, which has the features of nonexcludability and nonrivalry in consumption. Once a public good is provided, no citizen can be pre-

P2

		c	*d*
P1	*c*	2, 2	0, 3
	d	3, 0	1, 1

Figure 2.1 Prisoner's Dilemma

vented from receiving benefits from it, nor does any one citizen's consumption interfere with the ability of others to also consume the good. This situation creates problems in pricing and production. Because the public good cannot be withheld from anybody once it is provided, it becomes difficult to charge for it. The absence of sufficient revenues means that the public good will either be underproduced or not produced at all.

Because of this, government often intervenes to provide public goods. Under certain conditions, government involvement leads to the optimal level of the public good being provided. Specifically, the government could tax citizens such that for each individual, the marginal benefit of the public good equaled his or her share of taxes. Put another way, individuals could be asked to pay for their consumption of the public good. To accomplish this, individuals could be asked to state their valuation of the public good for the purpose of determining production and tax incidence. If individuals report this information truthfully, the optimal size of the public good could be determined and taxes set appropriately, resulting in what is known as a Lindahl equilibrium.

Once strategic behavior enters into the mix, individuals typically have an incentive to misrepresent their preferences. Suppose Jones is asked to provide his demand schedule, which states how much of the public good he would consume for a given price. He will pay taxes to fund the public good based on those stated preferences. Specifically, his tax share will equal the stated marginal benefit he receives from the public good output selected by government. Jones will clearly have an incentive to understate his valuation because this will guarantee him a much lower tax bill but reduce the public good by only a tiny bit.[4]

Many mechanisms offer the requisite incentives for truthful revelation, thereby eliminating the incentive to misrepresent.[5] One procedure, known as Vickrey-Clarke-Groves, requires individuals to provide their demand schedule for the public good (Vickrey 1961; Clarke 1971; Groves 1973). The tax each person pays is based on the valuations of all other individuals. Even if Jones indicates that he places no value on the public good, he will still pay some taxes. Specifically, Jones's taxes are equal to the cost of providing the public good less the sum of the marginal benefit of all other individuals at a given level of public good provision.

This procedure induces Jones to report his schedule truthfully, no matter what others do. To see this, suppose that Jones, acting as *homo economicus,* wanted to identify his preferred size of the public good, $\bar{x}$, given the above rules. He would do so by setting his marginal benefit, $MB_j(x)$, equal to his marginal cost, which will be the additional taxes he pays from an additional unit of the public good. Assuming for simplicity that the other

$(n - 1)$ individuals reported identical demand schedules and that the cost of each unit is 1, his marginal cost is $1 - (n - 1)MB_{i \neq j}(x)$. Therefore, $MB_j(\bar{x}) = 1 - (n - 1)MB_{i \neq j}(\bar{x})$. This formula can be rearranged so that the sum of the marginal benefits at $\bar{x}$ is equal to the marginal cost of provision, which is 1 in this case. This is exactly the Samuelsonian condition for the optimal public good (Samuelson 1954). In other words, Jones's optimal action is to truthfully report his demand schedule, demonstrating that Jones no longer has a reason to misrepresent preferences. Such an outcome, of course, is precisely the intent of the procedure. This procedure highlights a main insight of mechanism design — that rules influence behavior.

In some cases, asymmetric information creates the need for market-based solutions, as in George Akerlof's market for lemons (Akerlof 1970). Akerlof tackles a seemingly simple matter: buying a used car. Imagine that the quality of a used car is represented by a parameter q that is distributed uniformly from $[0, 1]$, where 1 represents a car in mint condition and 0 represents a clunker. Suppose that the individual selling the car knows q with certainty. She knows whether the car has received regular oil changes, been in twenty accidents, and so on. The buyer, in contrast, knows only how quality varies but has no information about the specific vehicle. Assuming that the price of the car is directly related to q, cars with $q > 0.5$ ("high-quality" vehicles) will cost more than cars with $q < 0.5$ ("low-quality" vehicles).

This seemingly typical market is prone to collapse in the following way. The sellers of high-quality vehicles will not be able to receive their valuation of the vehicle, since buyers will only be willing to pay for a car priced as if it were at $q = 0.5$ or less because, on average, car quality will not be higher than 0.5.[6] This logic in turn implies that only cars in the range $[0, 0.5]$ will ever be on the market. Knowing this, buyers update their beliefs and surmise that the mean car quality is now 0.25, again altering willingness-to-pay. In effect, half the market is again eliminated. The process will iterate until the market for used cars collapses. Even though there may be willing buyers and sellers at market-clearing prices, no transactions will occur.

In practice, of course, there is a market for used cars, in part because these informational problems are resolved to some degree. Car dealers offer "certified pre-owned" vehicles as a way to protect consumers from receiving a lemon. Companies such as CARFAX provide reports on individual vehicles, so that interested buyers can learn whether specific cars have been in several accidents. Prior to these innovations, one could take a vehicle to a mechanic for an inspection, and so on. These market solutions serve to ameliorate informational concerns. In this case, self-interest (i.e., the profit motive) leads to the creation of a market for information, thereby solving a problem created by the incentive to misrepresent.

Related to the market for lemons, principal-agent problems take the form of information asymmetries in the context of one party providing a service to another party. For example, a car mechanic has specialized information about your vehicle. If she tells you that you need a new catalytic converter, you have few options, short of taking the car elsewhere for a second opinion.[7] In the marketplace, institutions or firms may arise to vouch for the credibility of mechanics (e.g., the American Automobile Association's Approved Auto Repair Program) or firms more generally (e.g., the Better Business Bureau). A mechanic who knows that the customer can complain to AAA, threatening the mechanic's "seal of approval," will provide more honest repair service.

Enforcement

Even if these informational problems are resolved, the third issue, rule enforcement, remains. An outside enforcer must have an incentive to implement punishments for violations. In scores of situations this is not the case. The simplest example is a bribe or side payment to "look the other way" as a rule is violated. But even an enforcer who wants to discharge his duties honorably may face a dilemma if the punishments for rule violations are too harsh. For example, suppose that a law was passed requiring that all individuals convicted of theft, no matter how minor, be executed. Police officers who view such punishments as excessive might ignore the crime or deal informally with violators. Likewise, judges might throw out more cases on technicalities or encourage juries to find violators innocent. In this way, harsher penalties could paradoxically have the effect of increasing theft and reducing enforcement.

If rules are to be enforced successfully within an organization, there must be an incentive to adhere to the rules at each decision point.[8] Such incentives exist in cases where deviations from the rules are so costly that the advantages in the short run are not worth the costs in the long run or where the rules do not conflict with preferences. For example, a political party may impose term limits on its legislative leaders to ensure more turnover at the top. What happens, though, when rank-and-file legislators love their leaders and want to waive the term limits rule? Here a viable alternative is to break the rule, perhaps reinstituting it later. This action, of course, renders the rule meaningless. In this scenario, the leaders will only be thrown out if legislators believe that the long-run goal, preventing the consolidation of power, is worth the short-run pain of losing valuable leaders.

Institutional Design: Rules and Enforcement

Institutions are in part designed to address the problems raised in this chapter. Rational choice theory treats the individual as the unit of analysis and seeks to understand how institutions affect behavior given preferences, beliefs, and information.[9] A vast literature, termed the "new economics of organization," focuses on the role that organizational forms play in transactions outside of the marketplace (Moe 1984). Principal-agent problems, for instance, occur inside organizations as well as in the marketplace. A board of directors representing shareholders delegates the day-to-day operations of a corporation to management. To the extent that the interests of management and shareholders are not aligned, management can use its informational advantage to exploit shareholders and the board. This focus on the internal workings of the firm is a sharp departure from the neoclassical economic model, which treats the firm as a black box production function. A central insight of the new economics, then, is that the internal workings of the firm, or any organization for that matter, shape outcomes.

For good reason, leadership credibility is also the focus of much research in the new economics of organization. Can those who make the decisions and enforce the rules be trusted to carry out their duties properly? Kydland and Prescott (1977) show that giving leaders discretion in setting economic policy leads to perverse outcomes compared with rules that prefix decisions; this is the time inconsistency problem introduced in chapter 1. A leader who cannot somehow credibly commit to certain policies in advance will not be able to implement the most effective policy. Shepsle (1991, 246) writes, "Discretion is the enemy of optimality, commitment its ally." North and Weingast (1989) illustrate this principle in the context of England's Glorious Revolution. Concerns that the Crown was confiscating wealth were ameliorated when the Parliament was empowered to vet all changes in the terms of loans or taxes made by the Crown. The Parliament represented those individuals who loaned money to the government and paid taxes, so this new institutional setup lent credibility to the Crown's promises. The idea of leadership credibility has been applied to several areas, including monetary policy (e.g., Keefer and Stasavage 2003), property rights (e.g., Haber, Razo, and Maurer 2003), and international agreements (e.g., Martin 2000).

The new economics literature points to two fundamental and often inseparable issues involved in the design of institutions, though the two are rarely discussed in tandem: the design of rules and the enforcement mechanisms for those rules. Rules influence behavior as well as translate individual preferences into some sort of outcome (e.g., an item is sold, a bill is passed).[10] They are formal or informal. Informal, often unwritten, rules that govern behavior are typically known as norms. Norms need not be less binding on behavior than formal rules. For example, when entering a seminar room, most students will not sit at the head of the class. The implicit, unwritten rule is that the professor will sit at the head of the class. Norms must be internally enforced by an organization, so they are only sustainable if enough actors have an incentive to punish defections, even if such punishment never has to be meted out. The credibility of enforcement is central to a rule's success or failure.

When analyzing the expected impact of a rule, one should first assume that the rule is perfectly and costlessly enforced and establish a baseline for evaluation of enforcement success. If the analysis shows that a perfectly and costlessly enforced rule would not achieve its ends, then weak enforcement cannot be blamed for any lack of rule success. One can analyze several sorts of rules in this way, leading naturally to the question of how one discerns which rule will be chosen as part of a political process. While economists often search for optimal rules that make society best off, the interests of legislators or other designers may lead to the creation of suboptimal rules. This may be due to a desire to short-circuit reform or simply reflect the political compromise necessary to secure most any sort of serious reform. While the process of rule selection is not explicitly modeled in this book, it plays an important role in the analysis of whether effective reforms will emerge in practice.

Rules should not be considered in isolation when analyzing their impact because institutional interactions often come into play. An institutional interaction occurs when the impact of rule *a* is dependent on rule *b*. An analysis of rule *a*'s consequences that does not account for rule *b* may produce incorrect inferences. Suppose that a legislature was considering the impact of conferring gatekeeping power on a committee. Gatekeeping power enables a committee to prevent a bill from reaching the floor of a chamber.[11] Denzau and Mackay (1983) show that when gatekeeping is present, strategic committee leaders will often choose not to report a bill to the floor under an open rule (allowing unlimited amendments to legislation), though under a closed rule (permitting no amendments once a bill reaches the floor from committee) they will do so more often. Denzau and Mackay assume that gatekeeping exists, but instead suppose that a legislature is deciding whether to grant such power to committees. The decision, it turns out, will depend on whether the floor operates under a closed or open rule. Assume that the floor operates under a closed rule. In this case, gatekeeping is equivalent to the committee reporting out a bill at the status quo, and thus gatekeeping will have no impact.[12] If the floor operates under an open rule, then gatekeeping power confers some negative power on the committee. Under certain conditions (Crombez, Groseclose, and Krehbiel 2006), a legislature would never want to implement gatekeeping (i.e., it is a Pareto-dominated institution; cf. Kim and Rothenberg 2005). In a simple, complete information setup, it is clear that the impact of gatekeeping depends on the way in which the floor considers bills that are reported out. In one situation, the impact is nil; in another, it is significant.

Agenda control also plays a role in the budgeting process, and there are institutional interactions between the nature of agenda control and the manner in which the budget is voted on. The models considered in this book primarily feature random proposal power, though we can imagine that these proposers are fixed and have particular interests in securing large spending for their domain (i.e., they are "high-demanders").[13] Further, we can assume that within this domain, there are different ways to expend funds. The impact of offering high-demanders monopoly proposal power depends on the interaction of specific components of the budget process. If a high-demanding bureaucracy gets to state how a pie will be divided, with the public (or a legislature) determining the size of the pie, then spending will be higher than if proposals are competitive over both the division and the size of the pie, under certain reasonable assumptions (Mackay and Weaver 1979, 1983). However, suppose now that agenda control is over a simultaneous proposal for a budget mix and a spending level. Under these conditions, agenda control leads to an even higher level of spending than in the other two cases. In other words, the nature of the proposals that can be offered mediates the effects of agenda control.

In the gatekeeping and agenda control cases, the institutional interactions are straightforward, and legislative leaders may anticipate these interactions when crafting rules, perhaps even designing contingent rules allowing gatekeeping in some circumstances but not in others. In other situations, interactions are not immediately obvious. Consider senatorial courtesy, which gives the home state senators of a presidential judicial appointment the informal ability to kill the nomination of a judge he or she does not want to see on a lower federal court. A senator from New York can halt the appointment of a judge to a federal district court in that state, and a senator from Arizona can do the same for a federal district court located in Arizona. The impact of this "blue slip" depends heavily on whether judicial appointments are subject to a filibuster.[14]

In a filibuster model, bargaining is also affected by the ideological position of certain senators, known as filibuster pivots (Krehbiel 1998), who are decisive in determining whether a filibuster is successful. Regardless of the president's ideology, no change occurs when the existing court's ideological location is between the ideologies of these two senators. Any shift of court ideology makes at least forty-one senators worse off. In contrast to the median voter model, home state senators located between these filibuster pivots will never have an impact on the bargaining process in the filibuster model. In the median voter model, they may have an impact, depending on the location of the president's ideal point. In short, the impact of the blue slip is contingent on whether senators are permitted to filibuster judicial nominations; filibusters mitigate the impact of the blue slip. If filibustering is possible, then outcomes depend on the divergence in preferences between the president and the senators crucial to sustaining a filibuster. In the absence of the filibuster rule, the impact of the blue slip depends on the divergence in preferences between the president and the Senate's median voter relative to the ideological location of the home state senators.[15]

As these examples illustrate, the impact of rules is often dependent on other rules already in place. To understand the impact of a veto, an amendment procedure, or even a supermajority voting rule requires careful attention to the possibility of institutional interactions. The oft-observed failure of rules in politics is in many cases due to a simple lack of accounting for such interactions.[16]

Once a rule's efficacy is established, the next question becomes whether effective enforcement is possible.[17] By enforcement, I mean the ability of an organization to ensure that rules are binding on behavior. Even if optimal rules exist for addressing the problem at hand, successful implementation requires effective policing. Enforcement is either external (exogenous) to the institution or internal (endogenous) to the institution. In the case of a legislature, enforcement may occur within the legislature or be carried out by the courts. Put in a different context, if two individuals have a dispute, they can either resolve it themselves or hire an arbitrator to mediate. Challenges arise with both methods.

Before turning to the different types of enforcement, two issues must first be addressed. First, it is important to assess the effectiveness of enforcement. An enforcer (whether external or internal) with his or her own interests may not be a faithful arbiter, leading enforcement effectiveness to vary. If a constitutional rule constraining legislative behavior is enforced by a court composed of political cronies, it is unlikely to be as effective as one enforced by a court composed of independent judges. Public outrage over legislative behavior may serve as a means to enforce legislative budget rules but will not always be effective. Finally, a member of a congressional ethics committee may hesitate to sanction a colleague for fear of reprisal.

Informational problems also arise in enforcement. Behavior may not always be observable, which leads to imperfect punishment of rule violations. A classic example of this is Green and Porter's (1984) model of cartel behavior in the face of imperfect information about demand. Firms may agree to a certain collective output so as to keep prices artificially high and thereby increase profits. Of course, firms have an incentive to deviate from such an agreement in order to increase profits even more, necessitating punishments for violations of the agreement. Firms observe market prices but do not observe changes in demand or the production of other firms. When a price drop occurs, it could be due to (*a*) cheating on the part of a cartel member or (*b*) a random fluctuation in demand. For the cartel to be successful, firms must engage in a punishment strategy of reducing production whenever the price falls below a trigger level, regardless of the reason for the decline. All members of the cartel would make higher profits if punishments were made only after cheating by a firm. With perfect information about demand, this is possible, since cheating is distinguishable from a random fluctuation in demand. With imperfect information, this outcome is not attainable.

Second, sufficiently low costs are a necessary condition for enforcement. Even if effective enforcement procedures are developed, they may not be implemented if costs are prohibitive. In the discussion that follows, the implicit assumption is that the costs of enforcement are sufficiently low. This focuses attention on the problem of designing effective enforcement procedures but is not meant to imply that costs are not an important issue in the design of institutions.

Let us now turn to the distinction between internal and external enforcement. External enforcement refers to the policing of an interaction by an outside entity, coupled with the inability of the agents involved to change quickly or easily the rules under which they operate. A constitutional rule is (roughly) exogenously enforced, since quickly amending a constitution is difficult if not impossible. Here courts offer the final word on enforcement.

Internal enforcement, conversely, requires that agents have incentives to follow the rules and implement punishments at all points in time. Because endogenously enforced rules can, in essence, be changed on the fly, they will only survive as long as members of the organization want them to. The distinction is important. As Cox (2000) notes, rules that are costly to change or are constitutionally mandated are more stable than those that are easy to alter. I argue in chapter 4 that this insight helps us to understand how potentially unstable rules, enforced endogenously, are rendered stable by tying them to other rules that are changed only at significant cost.

Often the two types of enforcement are confused. For instance, if Congress creates an agency to oversee its behavior, but it can disband the agency at will, this does not represent exogenous enforcement. If, however, Congress, with the assent of three-quarters of the states, institutes a constitutional amendment that has an impact on its internal rules, enforcement of this amendment by the Supreme Court would be exogenous. Importantly, the relevant actors need to be able to "tie their own hands" in order for exogenous enforcement to be credible. Another way to capture the distinction is in terms of the possibility that the organization can change its own rules quickly. Exogenous enforcement procedures cannot be altered by the enforcees in the short run. Endogenous enforcement procedures can. This juxtaposition captures a key difference between an internal legislative rule, which can be changed relatively quickly (though sometimes at significant political cost), and a constitutional provision.

Internal enforcement is sometimes viewed as the very essence of institutions. As Calvert (1995, 78) puts it, "*All* rule enforcement is endogenous, and . . . just as the maintenance of informal agreements is always problematic, so is the enforcement of formal rules." In other words, institutions are equilibrium phenomena that are maintained only when it is in the interests of the players involved to maintain them. Barbera and Jackson (2004) formalize this intuition by introducing the idea of "self-stable" constitutions in which voters would not choose to change the constitution, given the stated voting rule for changes. This perspective also extends to federalism. De Figueiredo and Weingast (2005) frame the bargain between the center government and the states in federal systems in precisely these terms. As Bednar (2006, 36) notes, "In federalism, no external force exists that can disinterestedly settle disagreements. Instead, any enforcement mechanism must come from within; the federal rules must be self-enforcing."

Formal or informal agreements influencing behavior sometimes hinge on repeated play and the ability to punish deviations. A classic example is a "grim trigger" strategy, which produces a cooperative outcome in a Prisoner's Dilemma. This strategy requires that players cooperate until one of them deviates, at which point they defect for the remainder of play. The shadow of permanent punishment looms large and enables cooperation to succeed under a wide variety of circumstances.

Repeated play works well to enforce agreements, but in some respects it works too well. The folk theorem tells us that almost any outcome is sustainable as the equilibrium to a repeated game, provided that actors view the future as sufficiently important. To get around this problem, Schelling (1960) introduced the idea of focal points, suggesting that some equilibria are more likely to be realized than others. This solution has an ad hoc quality to it. A related claim is that theory or specialized knowledge enables one to locate the equilibrium most likely to obtain in a given situation. The problem is that almost any institution can be explained with reference to repetition. Repeated games may tell us why a particular institution is sustained over time, but they are not as helpful for understanding institutional choice. Nor can repeated play be relied on in understanding the creation of institutions; almost any institution can be interpreted as an equilibrium for a given set of interactions. Another problem with this line of reasoning is that most norms, or informal rules, are not objects of choice in the same way that formal rules are.

Repeated play is not central for understanding institutional choice, but it does help us understand institutional maintenance. We often observe institutionally suboptimal states of affairs, such as commons problems like overfishing, maintained over time via repeated interactions. Why would Pareto-dominated institutions, which make everybody worse off than some other institution, ever emerge and be sustained in equilibrium? First, transition costs are incurred when moving from one equilibrium to another. As the number of parties involved increases, these costs may become prohibitive (Eggertsson 2005). Second, informal rules sometimes emerge through a Hayekian spontaneous order rather than through formal selection. If inefficient norms emerge, they may be difficult to change (Eggertsson 2005). Once play proceeds down a particular equilibrium path, it is difficult to move to another equilibrium path without some sort of collective action or shock to the system.

Given the limitations of the repeated play argument, I turn to another possibility: tying budget rules to an existing, stable aspect of an organization. In order to gain tractability in studying new rules or changes to rules, some aspects of an organization must be treated as exogenous. Call these the stable components, or structure, of the organization. Stable components are those that cannot be altered or violated in the short run except at prohibitively high cost. For endogenous enforcement to work, the costs of violating the rules must be made sufficiently great, and those who must incur costs to engage in enforcement must have incentives to be faithful to the rules. One way to make costs sufficiently high is to tie a rule to more general organizational maintenance. For example, coalitions are sustained in parliamentary democracies by tying key votes to dissolution of the government (Diermeier and Feddersen 1998). Because the costs of overturning stable aspects of an organization are so large, they are treated as exogenous. Of course, Riker's concept of inheritability—that the same instability problems plaguing policymaking also plague rule making—must be acknowledged here (Riker 1980). Specifically, the choice of a rule may depend on the voting procedure and agenda for selecting the rule.

This is immaterial for the stability of the rule, though. Once in place, a rule becomes difficult to change as the costs of violating it increase. More generally, the more vital the aspect of the organization to which the new rule is tied, the more stable a new rule for that organization will be.

Tying a rule to another, stable aspect of the organization can increase the costs of violating the provision to a prohibitive level, thereby making that rule equivalent to one that is perfectly (externally) enforced. A typical illustration of this phenomenon is the filibuster rule in the U.S. Senate as it relates to judicial nominations. There is an ongoing debate about whether filibusters on presidential appointments are constitutional. The courts have typically not intervened in internal legislative affairs, and they are unlikely to do so in this case. Still, the controversy could be used as a pretext to challenge and potentially eradicate a rule during normal Senate business. Consider a Republican-controlled Senate with a Republican president facing a filibuster threat from Democrats. During a filibuster of a judicial nominee, a senator who acquires the floor could raise a point of order that a filibuster is out of order when considering presidential nominations. The point of order would presumably be sustained by the presiding officer, who in some cases would be the vice president. The Democrats would almost surely appeal the ruling. If fifty Republicans voted to table that appeal, the filibuster as an institution would effectively be killed.[18]

In the early 2000s, Senate Republicans, frustrated with Democratic threats to filibuster judicial nominations, gave serious consideration to using this "nuclear" or "constitutional" option. It was termed the "nuclear" option by some because unlimited debate is a prerogative that senators value greatly. In many ways the filibuster is the embodiment of the Senate. If the rule were killed in this manner, it would send shock waves through the chamber and Senate business would, at least temporarily, grind to a halt because angry senators could easily gum up the works. A significant portion of legislation is considered under unanimous consent agreements, and a group of senators could easily transform the chamber's functioning by refusing to sign on to any such agreements. Not surprisingly, both sides reached an agreement under which the filibuster would not be used on judicial nominations.[19]

Examples

In some cases rules and their enforcement are distinct; in other cases the lines are blurred. In all cases, my approach — thinking about design and enforcement in tandem — is helpful in analyzing the impact of rules. This general procedure works regardless of the subject matter, as the following examples will demonstrate.

THE FREE RIDER PROBLEM. In simple cases like the Prisoner's Dilemma, where individually rational behavior leads to collectively suboptimal outcomes, matters are improved by delegating enforcement of agreements to an external agent. A famous tale, attributed by McManus (1975) to economist Steve Cheung, describes a group of boatmen on the Yangtze River being whipped as they pull a boat upstream. A horrified American onlooker is reassured that the overseer works for the boatmen to prevent them from shirking, thereby solving a multiperson free rider problem. Incentives are aligned properly here. The "whipper," an external enforcer, wants to get paid, so he has an incentive to enforce the rules. The boatmen know this and therefore do not attempt to free ride.

More generally, cases like this amount to a brute force approach to solving an existing problem: prohibit the behavior that causes it through enforcement. The issue in cases like this is the effectiveness of enforcement. In the case of the boatmen, will the overseer be reluctant to injure his clients? Will he accept side payments from a boatman to look the other way when one of them is shirking? When a rule prohibits the problematic behavior, its impact depends solely on enforcement.

Sometimes defections are punished in unique ways. One of the more interesting solutions to a collective action problem is a voluntary fund that was created in Manchester, Vermont, to pay for schools.[20] In 1997, the Vermont legislature passed Act 60 in response to a Vermont Supreme Court decision regarding school funding for poor communities. Under Act 60, every town received a block grant from the state of about $5,500 per child. If a town wanted to spend more through local taxes, it would have to match every dollar of additional spending with a dollar for the state sharing pool, which was allocated to poor districts. This amounted to a 100 percent tax on local school spending above a certain threshold.

Town leaders were understandably upset about this and came up with a solution. They created a voluntary fund and asked for contributions. The fund was voluntary (i.e., not a tax), so there would be no need to pay into the central fund, thereby offering taxpayers considerable savings. However, the fund posed a classic free rider problem for taxpayers. If everybody contributed, then the town would be able to minimize its outlays for a given "quantity" of education. The town was trying to raise a large sum, $2.4 million, making the impact of any one individual's contribution minimal. Therefore, the system created a temptation to free ride, as one's lack of a contribution had little noticeable effect on the total budget. Yet in

Manchester, there was an 85 percent participation rate in 2002, brought about through a particularly effective enforcement mechanism: embarrassment. The voluntary fund organizers listed the names of those who contributed on the fund's website and in newspaper ads. In the small town of four thousand, this had repercussions. To avoid being tagged as noncontributors, residents were motivated to pay into the voluntary fund.

MECHANISM DESIGN. The mechanism design literature in economics discusses what are called incentive compatible procedures whereby agents are induced to reveal their preferences truthfully. This idea was introduced earlier in the context of public goods provision. Here again, the rule and the enforcement are difficult to separate. If the rule is designed properly, individuals have no incentive to misrepresent preferences. Therefore, there will be no need to worry about rule enforcement. The procedure itself incorporates enforcement. One problem is that most mechanisms are better viewed as thought experiments rather than feasible rules. Asking every citizen to state his valuation for every public good is not feasible except in the smallest of organizations. Rarely will it be the case, then, that mechanisms of this sort are implementable in practice.

LEGISLATIVE RULES. The U.S. Congress and state legislatures illustrate the tension between exogenously and endogenously enforced rules, while at the same time demonstrating how rules and enforcement are distinct. Article 1, section 5, of the U.S. Constitution states that "each House may determine the Rules of its Proceedings, punish its Members for disorderly Behaviour, and, with the Concurrence of two thirds, expel a Member." All state constitutions, except for North Carolina's, have similar provisions. North Carolina's legislature need not worry, though. State constitutions act to limit rather than grant legislatures authority over their internal workings, so legislative self-determination on internal matters is assumed to exist unless explicit provisions in a constitution specify otherwise (National Conference of State Legislatures 2000).

Mason's Manual of Legislative Procedure states, "Unless restricted by the Constitution, statutes, or other superior authority, an organization can adopt its own rules of parliamentary procedure by a majority vote. Also by a majority vote, it can change, suspend or repeal the rules at any time it chooses. Failure to comply with its own adopted rules does not invalidate actions of the organization. . . . The house and senate may each pass an internal operating rule for its own procedure that is in conflict with a statute formerly adopted" (National Conference of State Legislatures 2000, 1, 13). The upshot is that statutes are not binding on legislatures. Moreover, legislatures can change the rules imposed on them by statute. Even more shockingly, state legislatures can violate internal rules with impunity and without jeopardizing any legislation passed when the rules were violated. Still, chaos does not (always) reign in state legislatures, as many restrictions are imposed on them by state constitutions.[21] State constitutions, therefore, constrain legislatures, so much so that state scholar Alan Rosenthal has lamented the "wresting away" of legislative control over internal organization (1996, 195).

When legislatures are not so constrained, there is sometimes a tension between immediate and long-term gain. Consider minority party rights. Rules created by legislatures to establish such rights are subject to change (or to being ignored) by the legislature that creates them. Furthermore, they have indeed changed over time, often for partisan reasons (Binder 1997). Still, even if the majority party has an incentive to change or not enforce a rule that protects the minority party, fear of the future and institutional costs potentially incurred by ignoring a rule will prevent this from happening regularly or without warning.

Implications for the Budget Process

This chapter has demonstrated how institutions facilitate interactions. When thinking about institutional design, two main issues must be considered: What rules will constrain behavior if applied faithfully, and how will those rules be enforced? Sometimes the two questions cannot be easily separated. In other cases they are quite distinct. In terms of enforcement, there are two types, with exogenous enforcement being more likely to offer stable rules than endogenous enforcement. In the next two chapters, I demonstrate that, if properly designed, externally enforced rules can have a desired impact on behavior but that rules that do not take into account the strategic environment are prone to failure. If exogenous enforcement is not possible, an institutional designer should rely on the stable aspects of an organization when designing new rules, as this increases the costs of ignoring those rules.

This chapter has also laid the groundwork for the study of budgeting that follows. Budgeting is multidimensional, with many competing domains: the allocation of spending, the size of spending, the efficiency of spending, and the balancing of budgets. Distributive politics, which focuses on district-specific projects, allows us to consider all of these features of budgeting at once. For this reason, distributive politics bargaining will be the foundation for many of the models that follow. Budget rules are different from other legislative procedures in that the targets of the rules are clear. For example, while the substantive, long-term policy implications of changing the number of votes necessary to end a filibuster from two-thirds to sixty senators is not immediately clear, legislators determining whether to implement a particular budget rule have a better sense of how the rule will affect their constituents or their pet programs. Put another way, interests are entrenched in the budget rule design process. This creates problems for all aspects of rule design. Rules may be designed to be either ineffectual or unenforceable. Either approach serves the purpose of short-circuiting rules' effects. Of course, the rule may not be implemented at all.

To see why incentives are so important, note that constitutional budget rules at the federal level could solve current fiscal problems. The Supreme Court could be expected to be a faithful arbiter of a clear-cut budget rule, and a simple rule could be written to, say, require a balanced budget. Yet, as we will see in chapter 6, proposed constitutional balanced budget rules are almost certain to fail, even if perfectly enforced. The reason is that they are full of loopholes that are the natural result of the political compromise necessary to appease legislators. The easy answer to the question of rule design — pick the optimal rule and then externally enforce it — does not often hold up when political incentives enter the mix.

That is where the U.S. states offer us some solace. I show in chapter 3 that externally enforced spending limits have a dampening effect on spending, and then I establish in chapter 5 that such rules at the state level do in fact lower spending. A major reason is that these rules were typically enacted decades ago, when commitments were fewer and the distributive impact of the rule was not clear. By contrast, a popular (and relatively recent) reform, constitutional tax and expenditure limits in the states, has been shown to be largely ineffective (e.g., Abrams and Dougan 1986; Bails 1990; Cox and Lowery 1990, but see Rueben 1995).[22]

This chapter has offered up conditions under which rules could, in theory, be effective. In chapter 3, I demonstrate how, with external enforcement, certain budget rules are effective. Chapter 4 shows that internal enforcement is feasible but only if it is in legislators' interests to carry it out. The model I present shows that in many cases, the temptation to engage in inefficient distributive (i.e., pork-barrel) spending will trump preferences for reduced spending. Chapter 3 is then connected back up with chapter 5, and in chapter 6 the lessons of chapters 3 and 4 are used to show why federal budget reform has largely failed. Chapter 7 offers up some radical suggestions for effective budgetary reform. The simplest place to begin is with a model in which enforcement is perfect and exogenous, and that is where we now turn.

CHAPTER 3

External Enforcement

One man's pork is another man's sustenance.

REPRESENTATIVE ROBERT CLEMENT (D-TN)

External restraints on behavior define the U.S. checks-and-balances system. The president's appointment power is subject to the advice and consent of the Senate, while Congress's legislative prerogatives are checked by the president's veto authority. The U.S. Constitution acts as a restraint on all sectors of the government, albeit one that is enforced by the Supreme Court.[1] This enforcement may be perfect or imperfect. This chapter considers both perfect and imperfect enforcement since each type sheds light on the design of budget rules.

I begin by assuming that external enforcement is perfect, meaning that a rule is enforced by a costless and error-free process. This admittedly unrealistic assumption serves two purposes. First, it allows us to isolate the impact of the rule apart from the enforcement mechanism. If one knows that a rule is ineffective even when perfectly enforced, then from a normative perspective, it should not be implemented. Second, if enforcement occurs with some error or cost, the baseline of error-free and costless enforcement allows us to analyze the consequences of deviations from this ideal.

At first glance, it may appear that such an analysis is really not about enforcement at all but is merely about design. However, because all rules must have an associated enforcement mechanism, whether explicit or implicit, the study of a rule, where the analyst assumes that the rule is applied as written, implicitly assumes perfect (external) enforcement of that rule. Most game theoretic models implicitly make this assumption. The first part of this chapter, therefore, features an examination of the impact of three budget rules—spending limits, supermajority voting requirements, and executive veto power—and demonstrates their impact under perfect enforcement. I show that under this condition, all of these rules improve collective legislative welfare. Further, spending limits always have a dampening effect on spending, while the impact of supermajority voting rules and executive veto authority on spending are contingent on the presence of a spending limit.

Of course, in most cases rules are enforced imperfectly. I illustrate the imperfect enforcement of legislative budget rules by considering the effects of delegation to an agency or court for enforcement. Decision makers within these organizations have their own preferences and often will not act as faithful agents of the legislature. Next, I consider a different sort of enforcement—public opprobrium—and probe the conditions under which the public's desire for fiscal responsibility will induce the legislature to be responsible. The answers, as we will see, are counterintuitive. These analyses rely on game theoretic models that focus on the allocation of district-specific projects. This process is known as distributive politics.

Distributive Politics and Government Budgeting

Rules are designed to address many budgetary issues, including the allocation of a pot of funds, the size of spending, and the efficiency of spending. This chapter uses the framework of distributive politics to study all of the above.[2] Distributive goods benefit individuals within a district, but nobody outside of that district. Examples include a public park or building to which access is granted only to residents of the district. If these goods were paid for by the districts that benefit from them, a legislator representing the district would choose the economically optimal project because the full costs of the project would be internalized. In the language of economics, a district representative equates the marginal benefits of an additional acre of a park or floor of a building with the marginal cost of this addition.

In situations where no positive externalities are present (i.e., the benefits of the projects stay strictly within the district), it is easy to see that decentralized spending is optimal. Oates (1972) demonstrates this point via a model with a central planner interested in maximizing aggregate welfare, and Besley and Coate (2003) demonstrate this in a legislative context. Some mix of centralized and decentralized spending is optimal if projects in one district benefit other districts (a phenomenon referred to as a spillover).

The models introduced in this chapter will examine a situation in which outcomes are suboptimal and the ways in which institutions improve outcomes. Despite the advantages of decentralization in many cases, projects or programs are often paid for out of a common tax pool.

The federal government often funds local public works projects, and state governments often fund projects in particular cities. More generally, consider a legislature that is tasked with determining the size of district-specific projects. For simplicity, assume that all districts have the same population and are of the same size. Further assume that the costs of projects are paid for out of a common tax pool. This centralization of project spending will change preferences because costs are no longer incurred totally within the district. Each legislator will want to procure a project that is larger than optimal because he or she no longer internalizes the full marginal cost of the project. An example from everyday life is the tendency of restaurant bills that are split equally among diners (by previous agreement or norm) to be larger in total than separate checks would have been. In a group of five individuals, the cost to any individual of an additional dollar of spending is only twenty cents when costs are split equally. When every member of the group thinks this way, larger meals and more drinks will be ordered. Applying this same principle to the lawmaking process, then, all legislators will seek large projects for their own districts while simultaneously seeking to keep the costs of other districts' projects down.

Distributive spending is a small part of government budgets, but as Evans (2004) has established, it is nonetheless an important component of the lawmaking process because it facilitates the passage of legislation. Despite this important function, distributive politics is typically viewed as an unseemly aspect of lawmaking. The term "pork-barrel projects" is used to indicate a belief that the fruits of such politics are wasteful and inefficient. The term, which is thought to be derived from the distribution of salt pork in barrels to slaves, became part of the American political lexicon in the twentieth century (Safire 1993; Wolfensberger 2001).[3] Perhaps its most inventive use was by a political neophyte from Rhode Island, Ron Machtley. He unseated fourteen-term, scandal-ridden congressman Fernand St. Germain, then chairman of the House Banking Committee, with some help from Lester H. Pork, known to his friends as Les Pork. Machtley campaigned with this (actual) pig to point out the "fat" in federal spending, and he won the race.[4]

Machtley was not the first or last politician or activist to rally against pork. The nonpartisan Citizens Against Government Waste publishes the *Congressional Pig Book,* which details the recipients of federal largesse. From 1975 to 1988, Senator William Proxmire awarded a monthly Golden Fleece Award for "wasteful, ridiculous or ironic use of the taxpayers' money" (Proxmire 1988). Senator John McCain (R-AZ) has taken to compiling a list of projects that he considers wasteful according to the following criteria (taken verbatim from McCain's website):

- An appropriation that is not properly authorized by the Senate and not requested by the Administration.
- An unauthorized and unrequested, locality-specific or facility-specific earmark (including those funds that are above the Admin. request).
- A budget add-on that would be subject to a budget point of order.
- The transfer or disposal of federal property or items under terms that circumvent existing law.
- New items added in conference that were never considered in either bill in either House (McCain 2005).

McCain's criteria are primarily procedural, but the typical evaluation of pork in political science and economics is efficiency-based and therefore focused on whether the benefits of the projects exceed the costs. The manner by which projects enter into a piece of legislation may be indicative of their merits but is certainly not the only factor to consider. One of McCain's examples is a $200,000 grant for the construction and renovation of a shopping center in Guadalupe, Arizona (McCain 2004). In the absence of more detailed information, one could imagine many scenarios under which this spending would be economically sensible, as well as many scenarios under which it would be a wasteful use of resources. Despite being a target for those wishing to point out government excess, distributive projects need not be wasteful or inefficient.

The question addressed in this chapter is how rules serve to shape the types of projects agreed to during legislative bargaining. One problem discussed above is the desire to fund projects that are inefficient. The second relates to proposal power. While all legislators may be created equal in their seemingly insatiable appetite for pork, some are better than others in obtaining it. Legislative leaders and committee chairs are especially well-positioned to secure these goodies. They are the proposers in the legislative process, and there is ample evidence (e.g., Romer and Rosenthal 1978; Baron and Ferejohn 1989) that such individuals have an advantage in bargaining.

Two such legislative leaders are exemplars in this regard. From 1997 to 2004, Senator Ted Stevens (R-AK) was the chair of the Senate Appropriations Committee and an unabashed pork barreler. He was so adept at obtaining pork for his state that federal funds for local projects were referred to by Alaskans as "Stevens money" (Alvarez 1999). In 2004, Stevens and Don Young, his colleague in the House, fought for over $400 million in federal funding for two "Bridges to Nowhere," one of which would rival the Golden Gate in size and connect a town of eight thousand with an island of population fifty and a tiny airport. Stevens defended the projects by noting that when the Golden Gate Bridge was built, Marin County was not heavily populated either (Joling 2005). Funding was approved in 2005 and the bridges became symbols of waste. In response to widespread criticism, Congress later reclassified the funds for use toward any transportation project in Alaska, not just the bridges.

In spite of this, Stevens cannot hold a candle to Senator Robert Byrd (D-WV), who is unparalleled in his ability to secure pork for his state, whether as the chair, ranking minority member, or plain-vanilla member of the Appropriations Committee. Byrd has directed billions of dollars in federal aid to West Virginia, leading the Citizens Against Government Waste to dub him the King of Pork. In what is perhaps a nod to the advantages that proposal power confers, many have noted that Byrd merely does what any faithful public servant in his position would do. Former Senator Dale Bumpers (D-AR) told one journalist, "If you are on the Appropriations Committee, which I was for 22 years, and you don't take advantage of it, quite frankly you don't deserve to be re-elected. If I were in Robert Byrd's position, I [would] do exactly what he does. I'd try to take care of my constituents" (Wilson 2001).

Competing Approaches

In the previous section, I established that centralized spending and decentralized projects induce preferences for inefficient pork-barrel projects. The next question is how these preferences will be translated into a collective choice. One possibility, suggested by Weingast (1979) and elaborated on by Shepsle and Weingast (1981) and Weingast, Shepsle, and Johnsen (1981), is that a norm of universalism will develop whereby each legislator picks a project for his or her district. The implicit agreement is that legislators will receive the projects they request. Such a norm eliminates the specter of being left out of a minimum winning coalition (e.g., a bare majority under simple majority rule). Riker (1962) and Buchanan and Tullock (1962) have theorized that minimum winning coalitions are likely under certain conditions, such as zero-sum bargaining.[5] The drawback to a norm of universalism is that it leads to massive overspending in each district, as legislators pick their preferred (larger than efficient) projects.[6]

The successful establishment of a norm typically implies some sort of repeated interaction or institutional memory, with many norms being sustainable in equilibrium due to the folk theorem. One question, then, is why a norm of inefficient universalism would develop, since everybody would be made better off by a norm of efficient universalism that induces each legislator to pick the efficient project for his or her district.[7]

To explain this apparent inconsistency, consider the following example. Suppose that a legislator receives a benefit of $7 for the first $5 of spending, a benefit of $6 for the second $5 of spending, and a benefit of $4 for the third $5 of spending. This embodies a typical assumption that marginal benefits are nonincreasing in the size of spending, so that the first $5 of spending confers at least as many benefits as the last $5. If costs are fully internalized (i.e., a district pays all of its project costs), then $10 is the efficient spending level, producing total net benefits of $13 − $10 = $3. Suppose now that costs are shared across five districts, meaning that each $5 of spending costs the legislator only $1. Her ideal level of spending becomes $15, which produces net benefits for the legislator of $17 − ($15/5) = $14. This may seem like a great deal at first glance, but the calculation does not account for the fact that every legislator will think the same way. Under the norm of inefficient universalism, if every legislator selects her preferred project, a total of $75 is spent. Divided five ways, this means that every legislator receives total net benefits of $17 − ($75/5) = $2. Under the norm of efficient universalism, every legislator selects only $10 of spending, and the net benefits for each district will amount to $3.

Without introducing new elements to the theory, there is no particular reason to believe that inefficient universalism should emerge rather than efficient universalism. To avoid the pitfalls of norm-based institutional analysis, I adopt a game theoretic approach — one that does not rely on repetition — to determine how individual preferences will get translated into group outcomes. As chapter 1 discussed, noncooperative game theory treats players as self-interested actors who cannot contract in advance.

The Model

There are n legislators, where n is odd for convenience, who are tasked with determining the size of district-specific projects. The benefits for each project are localized, meaning that the project will benefit only the district to which the project is awarded. The costs are taken from a common tax pool to which all districts contribute equally. For simplicity, all districts are identical in this model. It is possible for a district to receive no project. This model builds on the work of Baron and Ferejohn (1989) and Baron (1993).

Each legislator receives benefits of bx from a project of size x in his district and pays costs of $(.5/n)cx^2$, where b and c are both greater than zero.[8] Each legislator's ideal project size is therefore nb/c rather than the efficient size of *b/c*. This is the distributive politics problem at work. The game proceeds as a sequence of moves by the legislators and, in some cases, an executive who acts as a veto player. The member of the legislature selected to make a proposal is referred to as the agenda setter, or proposer. The model focuses on two features of the legislative process: (1) the proposer's advantage in allocating projects and (2) legislator preferences for inefficient projects due to cost sharing. The budget rules discussed in the next section attempt to mitigate these problems.

Before discussing the way the game is played, several assumptions operating in the background will be addressed.

1. *Legislation is proposed under a closed rule, with no amendments allowed.* In practice, at least some amendments are allowed on most pieces of legislation, but a closed rule simplifies the game. A model allowing for unlimited amendments (an open rule) is considered in the next chapter.

2. *In principle, bargaining can continue forever.* This assumption prevents what are known as end-of-game effects, where the knowledge that bargaining will end with certainty at a predetermined point changes strategic behavior in ways that are not relevant to the question at hand.

3. *Legislators may view delay as costly.* Just as a dollar today is worth more than a dollar tomorrow, legislators discount the value of future agreements relative to agreements today. Patience is captured by a discount factor, which takes on a value greater than 0 and less than or equal to 1, inclusive. A discount factor of 0 implies that future agreements have no value, while a discount factor of 1 implies that a legislator is perfectly patient and weighs the future identically to the present.

4. *The agenda setter is selected randomly each time a new round of bargaining begins, and legislators are chosen to receive projects at random.* This assumption is not intended to represent a real-world situation — legislators are not chosen randomly in practice — but rather to account for the fact that different legislators make proposals at different points in time. Since proposals can in theory be made indefinitely in this model, this is a convenient assumption. In addition, by treating all legislators as identical in their ability to propose and receive projects, I am able to isolate the impact of rules.

5. *Legislator and district preferences do not vary across districts.* Heterogeneity can always be added to a model but usually at the expense of analytical tractability.

6. *Social welfare is defined as the sum of net benefits for all legislators, and efficiency is defined as maximizing social welfare.* The functional form used in this model has the property that maximizing social welfare is

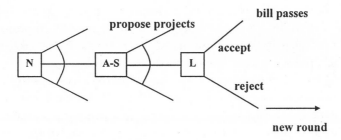

Figure 3.1 Extensive form, baseline model. N = nature; A-S = agenda setter; L = legislature voting.

efficient in the standard economic sense of being Pareto optimal.[9] I will use the terms "less efficient" (or "more efficient") to mean farther away from (or closer to) this social optimum. The efficient allocation in this model is for every district to receive a project of size b/c.

The game, depicted in figure 3.1, proceeds as follows:

1. An agenda setter is selected randomly from among all legislators to make a proposal to the legislature. This proposal consists of project sizes for every district, with zero being a possible project size.
2. The legislature votes on this proposal by majority rule.
   a. If the bill passes, the game ends and the projects are awarded.
   b. If the bill does not pass, then the game returns to step 1.
3. This process continues until a proposal is successful.

Given that infinitely many equilibria to this model exist, I focus on a "simple" and reasonable equilibrium concept whereby individuals act in similar ways when faced with similar situations.[10] This "stationarity" means that a legislator, when deciding whether to vote for a piece of legislation, acts under the belief that the agenda setter in the next period will behave in the same way as the current agenda setter.

When offered a bill containing a project of size y for his district, a legislator compares the benefits of y, or by, along with the total costs of the bill, I, to his continuation value. Continuation value refers to what the legislator could expect to receive if he rejected the offer and the bill failed, leading to a new round of bargaining. Under simple majority rule and minimum winning coalitions, this continuation value will be the discounted value of $(1/n)bx + [(n-1)/(2n)]by - I/n$. This value is derived as follows. In the next period, there is a probability of $1/n$ that the legislator will be selected as the agenda setter and receive a project x. With probability $(n - 1)/(2n)$ he will again be selected to receive y.[11] With probability $(n - 1)/(2n)$, he will be left out of the coalition and receive no project. Regardless, he is sure to pay I/n of the costs of projects because the stationarity of behavior guarantees that spending will be the same in both periods. This constraint tells us that in equilibrium, y will be a small fraction of x. For instance, if legislators are perfectly patient, then the agenda setter must ensure that $by = (1/n)bx + [(n - 1)/(2n)]by$, or $x = [(n + 1)/2]y$. The precise values will be determined by the agenda setter, who maximizes his net benefits subject to the constraint that a majority of legislators receive enough benefits from the bill that they prefer it to moving to the next period.

The Baseline Outcome

I now characterize five significant features of equilibrium behavior in this baseline model.[12]

Minimum winning coalitions. The agenda setter offers projects to as few legislators as possible. He has no incentive to do otherwise. It is costly to add additional members to his coalition, and properly selected project sizes will guarantee that his proposal will pass with a bare majority of legislators receiving projects.

Agenda setter power. The agenda setter's project is significantly larger than the projects all other legislators receive. This advantage emerges because legislators receiving a project compare the bill they are offered today to what a future agenda setter is expected to offer. The future includes the possibility of getting no project at all, since a new agenda setter may not select them to be part of the minimum winning coalition. Therefore, legislators are willing to vote for a bill that provides a large project to the agenda setter and relatively small projects to the remainder of the minimum winning coalition.

Negative net benefits for all other legislators. All legislators bear the burden of paying for a portion of the proposer's project. In addition, half of them receive no project but still must pay some taxes. Because of this, all legislators in this model except the agenda setter have negative net benefits (i.e., the benefits from their projects are less than their share of the cost of all projects).

Higher-than-efficient spending. Even though only a minimum winning coalition receives projects, the agenda setter's project is so inefficient that spending levels are higher than what a set of efficient projects for all legislators would cost.

Inefficient projects for all legislators in the minimum winning coalition. With one exception — the case in which legislators are perfectly patient — the projects of all legislators receiving them are inefficient, with the agenda setter's project being significantly more inefficient than others. (If legislators are perfectly patient, then the agenda setter awards efficient projects to the members of his coalition.) The intuition here is that legislators exploit those districts receiving no projects by taxing them to pay for projects in other districts.

A Numerical Example

The U.S. House of Representatives will be used to illustrate the equilibrium described above. There are 435 legislators in the House, with 218 needed for most legislation to pass if all legislators are present and voting. Assume that each legislator's discount factor is a relatively patient 0.8.[13] Let the terms b and c both equal 1, which means that the efficient outcome is for each legislator to receive a project of size b/c, or 1. The cost of a project of size 1 is $0.50, so the efficient level of spending is 435×0.50, or $217.50. The equilibrium outcomes are vastly different: The agenda setter receives a project of size 58.4, while 217 other legislators each receive a project of size 1.7. The remaining 217 legislators receive no projects. Spending is over $2,000, as costs are one-half the sum of the squares of each project size. From these figures, it is easy to see why the agenda setter does so well in this model and why other legislators do so poorly.

Which Rule to Choose?

The preceding analysis demonstrated that in a majority-rule distributive politics setting, the agenda setter exploits the legislature and secures a large, inefficient project for his district. In most cases, the projects for other legislators are also inefficient, though not to the same degree. The results are inefficiently high levels of spending and negative net benefits for all legislators except the agenda setter. From an institutional design perspective, then, the question is whether an innovation will improve the situation. One simple solution is the imposition of unanimity rule, in combination with the assumption of perfect patience, which guarantees that an efficient outcome will occur.[14] Under unanimity rule, all legislators have what amounts to a veto over legislation, meaning that the agenda setter must make them as well off as he is in order for the bill to pass. In this scenario, the agenda setter no longer has the ability to exploit others for his own gain, so he acts like a benevolent central planner. I am not aware of any legislature that uses such a rule to enact spending bills. Three real-world institutional rules are considered here instead: a spending limit, supermajority voting requirements for budget passage, and executive veto authority. These rules are assumed, for now, to be perfectly enforced via an unspecified mechanism. Operationally this is done by making these rules part of the game structure.

Rule 1: Spending Limit

A spending limit is put into practice in the model by requiring the legislature to set the size of spending in advance of the bargaining process. The spending limit adds a constraint to the bargaining process. The effect of the rule, therefore, will depend on the impact of this constraint on the behavior of the legislators. Further, the size of spending will be chosen strategically, with the limit acting as a ceiling. Figure 3.2 depicts the location of the spending limit in the legislative process. A spending limit will lead to lower spending only if the preferences of the legislature as a whole differ from the preferences of the agenda setter when allocating projects. In this case, they do. As with all the rules considered in this section, perfect enforcement of the spending limit is assumed.

Because the agenda setter is chosen at random in this model, legislators view the future identically when selecting a spending limit, leading to unanimous agreement about the proper size of spending.[15] In setting the spending limit, the legislature has to anticipate rationally how the agenda setter will respond to such a restraint. The agenda setter can reduce the

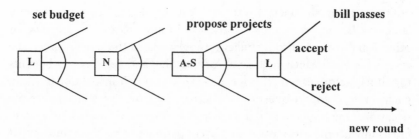

Figure 3.2 Extensive form, model with spending limit. N = nature; A-S = agenda setter; L = legislature voting.

size of his project, keeping all others the same size, keep his project the same size and reduce the size of all other projects, or reduce the size of all projects. Some simple math (again assuming that legislators are perfectly patient) will show that the last of these is the optimal choice.

Let x be the agenda setter's project and y be the project for other legislators receiving a project. A legislator receiving y compares that offer (and associated spending for all other projects) to what he could expect to receive if the game moved to the next round. He has a $1/n$ chance of being selected as the agenda setter and receiving x, an $(n-1)/(2n)$ chance of being selected to receive a project of size y, and an $(n-1)/(2n)$ chance of receiving nothing. In both rounds total spending will be equal to the spending limit, so total spending is not relevant for this comparison. This means that y must be set so that the benefits, by, from receiving y are at least as large as the expected benefit of continuing to the next round, which will be $(1/n)bx + [(n-1)/(2n)]by$, implying $x = [(n+1)/2]y$. Therefore, a reduction in y must be associated with an even greater reduction in x. The ratio will need to be adjusted and more complicated calculations made if legislators are at all impatient.

Knowing the above, the legislature will reduce spending to a level below what obtains in the baseline model since the reduction in the agenda setter's inefficient project improves its overall welfare. It will stop at the point where the additional reduction in x is not worth the loss in utility associated with a smaller y. *The spending limit thus reduces spending, mitigates the model's inefficiencies, and improves the overall welfare of the legislature.*

Let us now return to the numerical example using the House of Representatives. When a spending limit is in place the agenda setter's project shrinks to about 2, compared with 58.4 when unconstrained, while the projects other legislators receive shrink to a miniscule 0.01 from 1.7. Spending is reduced to about $2 from well over $2,000. In short, the spending limit shrinks spending, as well as most projects, to smaller-than-efficient levels. The legislature as a whole is still better off with a spending limit, though, largely because the agenda setter's project has been so severely constrained.

Rule 2: Supermajority Voting

Another real-world institution is supermajority voting for the passage of a budget. This is incorporated into the basic model by requiring that more than a simple majority of legislators approve budget bills. The agenda setter must determine how to respond to this requirement. He clearly needs to offer projects to more legislators, but he has a choice regarding the size of projects to offer relative to the baseline case. His optimal choice is to reduce the size of all projects (except in the case of perfectly patient legislators, in which case the projects of coalition members are left unchanged), for the following reason. The distributive politics problem is ameliorated by having larger coalitions, since the supermajority requirement means that fewer legislators are subject to exploitation by having to incur taxes for other districts' projects while receiving none for theirs. (Recall that unanimity rule essentially eliminates the distributive politics problem by preventing exploitation completely.) Inefficient projects become more costly to the winning coalition, thereby constraining the size of projects and spending. *Therefore, a supermajority voting rule reduces spending, mitigates the model's inefficiencies, and improves the overall welfare of the legislature.*

Returning again to the numerical example, a supermajority two-thirds voting rule reduces the agenda setter's project to 43 and other legislators' projects to 1.4, compared to the baseline model. Spending drops to $1,207. While projects and spending are still grossly inefficient, this rule produces a significant welfare improvement over simple majority rule.

Rule 3: Executive Veto Authority

Supermajority voting can be reinterpreted as a reply to an executive who credibly threatens to veto all distributive politics legislation. Call this type of executive a conservative, and contrast this behavior with that of a liberal executive, who vetoes no distributive politics legislation.[16] The latter has no effect on bargaining and, therefore, leads to the same result as the baseline model. The former leads to the building of a supermajority coalition with effects equivalent to those of rule 2. *This implies that a conservative executive with veto power reduces spending, mitigates the model's inefficiencies, and improves the overall welfare of the legislature, relative to an executive with no veto power or a liberal executive with veto power.*

The Importance of Interactions

Thus far I have considered the impact of just one institutional change at a time. In reality, though, legislative rules are implemented in more complex institutional environments. Even combining just two of the above rules has a surprising impact on outcomes. The effect of supermajority coalitions, whether through executive veto authority or a supermajority passage requirement, depends on whether a spending limit is in effect. *Specifically, spending is increasing in the supermajority voting requirement either for bill passage or veto override (if the executive is conservative) when a spending limit is in effect, but it is declining when a spending limit is not in effect.*

The legislature, when selecting the size of spending under a limit, observes that as the size of the supermajority required for enactment — call this q — increases for a given level of spending, the agenda setter's power is mitigated and he must "share the wealth" with coalition members. Therefore, a greater proportion of each additional dollar of spending is allocated to relatively more efficient spending (i.e., projects for coalition members instead of the agenda setter). This makes an increase in spending attractive. Notice that there are two effects here. The first is the effect of q on the agenda setter's behavior. The second is the effect of q on the legislature's behavior in choosing a limit on spending, rationally anticipating what the agenda setter will do. These combined effects increase spending.

When no spending limit is in place, only the agenda setter's behavior changes. He decreases the size of all projects to "pay" for new legislators in the coalition. Because costs are related to the squares of project sizes, this has the effect of decreasing spending. Though spending moves in opposite directions in these two cases, overall legislative welfare is improved in both cases by supermajority voting rules, as they ameliorate the distributive politics problem.

This example demonstrates the importance of considering the interaction of institutions when analyzing the impact of budget rules. An important principle, then, is that the effect of rules is contingent on other rules already in place. When using game theoretic techniques to assess the expected effect of new rules, careful attention must be paid to the institutional environment in which the rules are considered.

Another important implication is that changes in efficiency cannot in general be measured by changes in spending. In the above models, both positive and negative changes in spending were associated with increased efficiency. Absent knowledge of the starting point — whether existing spending levels are efficient, inefficiently high, or inefficiently low — one cannot know whether an increase in spending is beneficial. Also, holding spending constant, allocations influence efficiency if funding is taken from an inefficiently large project and reallocated to an inefficiently small project.

The (Sometimes Surprising) Effects of Imperfect Enforcement

The analysis thus far assumes that rules are perfectly enforced; the structure of the game is, in essence, the enforcer. This is not always a reasonable assumption, and several factors come into play. For example, who enforces the enforcer? Is it reasonable to think that state courts are going to enforce faithfully a state balanced budget requirement? The enforcer may interpret the rules or utilize private information in ways contrary to the interests of the enforcees.

Perfectly enforced rules are represented by a game form that restricts the actions of the players. In the spending limit example, the agenda setter cannot propose a budget that breaks the bank. What if, instead of formally restricting strategies, enforcement came in the form of an individual or group of individuals, with their own incentives, who determined whether a rule was violated? This situation alters the strategy of decision makers, as they now must consider the preferences of the enforcers.

External rule enforcement, then, will only be successful if the enforcers have incentives to see that rules are followed. One argument is that elected members of state courts are less likely to be beholden to the legislature and governor of a state than are appointed judges and, therefore, are more likely to enforce balanced budget rules (Bohn and Inman 1996). This possibility is examined further in chapter 5. It is also possible to model the preferences of the enforcer explicitly and incorporate him as a player in the game. An example of this second approach is Milgrom, North, and Weingast's (1990) study of the medieval institution of the law merchant. The authors consider the possibility that a judge monitoring behavior in economic transactions may try to extort money from honest traders in return for relaying truthful information about their past trading behavior.

In what follows, I consider two ways in which enforcement occurs, one formal and one informal. First, elected officials may delegate the authority to enforce rules to an outside organization, such as a court or a bureaucracy. Second, the public, by punishing legislators who deviate from the path of fiscal responsibility, may induce changes in spending practices. Both methods are prone to failure, but they represent ways in which external restraints on behavior might be effective, even in the absence of a perfect enforcement mechanism.

Example 1—Delegation: The Courts or Agencies as Enforcers

In political science, delegation typically is discussed in the context of agencies exercising discretion in carrying out a regulation or administering a decision made by a legislature. In the cases I will be discussing here, delegation means something more specific. It refers to the assignment of some type of enforcement authority to an agency.

Suppose a court is composed of judges interested in implementing their own spending preferences.[17] The legislature, when passing a budget, has to take into account the response of judges if its actions are challenged in court. To date, there have been few cases related to budget rules decided by the courts, but still, rational anticipation of a judicial response may be sufficient to induce a change in behavior.

Consider an agenda setter who is required, constitutionally, to abide by a spending limit set by the legislature. Violations are subject to court enforcement. In other words, the rule is adherence to the spending limit, and the enforcement mechanism is the court. Imagine two types of judges: those who have preferences for spending greater than what the legislature wishes to implement, and those who have preferences for less spending than what the legislature wishes to implement. Suppose that a legislature sets a spending limit. In the next stage the agenda setter either abides by this limit or ignores it. If he abides by it, the game proceeds as normal and the courts have no influence. If he ignores it, then the courts may step in. However, only those courts whose median judges prefer lower spending than what the agenda setter has selected have the incentive to step in and rule that the spending limit has been violated. The court will not intervene when spending limits are violated if it is favorably disposed to the legislature's spending decision. Spending limits will be effective, therefore, only when judges are credible enforcers of those limits.[18] The identical argument applies when substituting bureaucrats for judges because the same type of problem exists when delegating to an agency (e.g., Ferejohn and Shipan 1990; Epstein and O'Halloran 1999; Huber and Shipan 2002).

Implication: To the extent that courts or agencies attempt to impose their own preferences on policy outcomes, rules will tend to be less effective than if perfectly enforced.

Example 2 — Constituency Costs: The Public as an Unwitting Enforcer

Just as Americans hate Congress but love their member of Congress (Fenno 1978), the public tends to like localized spending but dislike "excessive" levels of total spending.[19] As Wildavsky and Caiden (2004, 23) put it, "Each of us has particular programs that benefit us or aid someone we know, or we may view particular governmental activities as essential to the community or the nation. . . . What we desire in particular (more programs) turns out not to be what we desire in general — less total spending and lower taxes."

Suppose that a spending limit is not enforceable internally or through delegation. In such cases the public may act as an enforcer by imposing costs on legislators who overspend. Assume that members of a legislature pay a constituency cost if they vote for a budget that exceeds some threshold, V, which reflects voters' upper bound on acceptable spending levels.[20] Voters are primed by the media to view distributive politics projects as wasteful and inefficient; each year the news media write stories about Congress's profligacy and wasteful spending, with local reporters tackling state legislative and gubernatorial decisions. Voters, therefore, will punish legislators who vote for distributive politics bills that are perceived as wasteful, even if the legislation includes projects for their own districts. Whether this punishment is sufficient to alter legislative behavior depends on the size of constituency costs relative to the benefits of the projects. Legislators will vote for a budget-breaking spending bill if it means goodies for their districts, so long as the project benefits outweigh the constituency costs from breaking the budget.

This is formalized as follows. Assume that a legislator whose district receives a project pays a cost z if spending exceeds V. Assume that V is always lower than the level of spending enacted when the agenda setter is unconstrained; otherwise these costs are irrelevant. A legislator receiving a project obtains the utility from that project but also pays a cost z.[21] The public, in other words, has implicitly created a budget rule for the legislature: abide by the spending limit V. The public enforces this rule via constituency costs. Therefore, the agenda setter must factor z into his calculations and compare two options: passing a bill that adheres to the spending limit V or passing a bill that violates it. The former does not require accounting for z; the latter does. To counteract constituency costs, the agenda setter will have to sweeten the offers he makes to coalition members, in a sense offering them partial "reimbursement" of these costs. The agenda setter then selects the action that makes him best off—abiding by V and not having to worry about constituency costs, or violating V and compensating coalition members for the constituency costs they will pay to enact a budget. The proofs in the appendix establish the effects of V and z on budget rule enforcement.[22]

The more fiscally conservative the public (the lower V is), the less effective are constituency costs. This result is surprising, but some simple analysis will clarify the reasons for the outcome. As V decreases, the agenda setter must constrain spending to a greater degree in order to avoid constituency costs. Abiding by the public's constraint is therefore often less beneficial for the agenda setter than compensating legislators for incurring constituency costs. The public's fiscal conservatism makes paying the constituency costs z relatively more attractive, meaning that there will be fewer values of z for which abiding by the spending limit is preferred. This result is similar to Romer and Rosenthal's (1978) finding that the lower the level of spending that would be imposed if bargaining between two parties broke down, the more spending that tends to occur. As V decreases, the "cost" of adhering to the constraint increases, meaning that paying z looks relatively more attractive.

For a given V, *the more outraged the public becomes for violations of spending thresholds (i.e., the higher is* z), *the more likely is the agenda setter to adhere to* V. *In cases where the agenda setter does not adhere to* V, *spending declines as the public becomes more outraged.* For a given V, the agenda setter compares the benefits of adhering to the limit or ignoring it and accounting for z. Regardless of the value z takes, it has an impact on spending. Even in cases where the agenda setter does not adhere to V, the increase in z makes projects less inefficient and lowers spending because the agenda setter has to take from her own pocket to "pay" other legislators for the imposition of constituency costs. For a given level of V, then, below a certain threshold, call it z^*, spending is declining in z. Above z^*, the agenda setter wants to adhere to the limit, so spending will stay at V.

Because constituency costs either reduce spending to V or force the agenda setter to give larger projects to his coalition members and a smaller project to himself, the effect of constituency costs on legislative welfare is positive, even though enforcement, in the sense of having some limit on spending enforced externally, succeeds only in some cases. We see a similar pattern when studying the impact of vetoes; they have an impact on behavior and outcomes even if they are never used. If a president credibly threatens to veto legislation, that threat may be sufficient to change the outcome of interbranch bargaining, making a simple count of vetoes a poor measure of executive power or ability.[23] Similarly, though we may observe that public demands for more efficient spending or budgetary reform are not heeded by legislators, it is equally important to think about what we do not see. Specifically, we do not see what would have occurred without the threat to impose constituency costs.

This model also applies to legislation on a single dimension, such as the stringency of a budget procedure. In chapter 5, which examines state budgets, I show that z will have no effect on budgetary reform until it reaches some threshold level. As this discussion makes clear, constituency costs will be an imperfect enforcer of budgetary discipline.

Implication: As the public becomes more fiscally conservative, constituency costs will be less effective at constraining spending. As the public imposes higher constituency costs for excessive spending, the more effective are those constituency costs.

Lessons

This chapter demonstrated that externally enforceable rules can theoretically be effective at limiting spending. Spending limits and supermajority coalitions, whether due to a voting rule or a veto threat, have the effect of lowering spending and improving legislative welfare. When combined, these institutions improve legislative welfare, but the impact of supermajority coalitions on spending is contingent on the presence of a spending limit. These budget rules are appropriate for the bargaining environment and the distributive politics problem. One size does not fit all in the design of budget rules, though, so the results here should not be taken to mean that supermajority rules, executive veto authority, and spending limits should always be implemented. Rather, the first model in the chapter demonstrated one way in which these rules could be effective. And of course, in that case legislators were operating in a world without existing constituencies for specific programs. Entrenched interests could alter the calculus of legislators.

The section on imperfect enforcement offered examples of conditions where delegation to a court or agency may lead rules to be less effective than in the perfect enforcement ideal. I also considered how the public, via constituency costs, could enforce fiscal discipline. As constituency costs for fiscal irresponsibility increase, legislators are more likely to hew to the public's preferences. A counterintuitive result emerged, as well. The more conservative the public is on spending, the less successful it will be in constraining spending. The reason is that as legislators must cut spending more and more, absorbing the constituency costs becomes a more attractive option.

Given these theoretical results, why are some externally enforced rules ineffective or not implemented at all in practice? One reason is a lack of information about the institutional environment in which the rules would be implemented. Models tell us about idealized worlds — to the extent that the real world deviates in some important way, unanticipated consequences may result. A second reason is that rules are designed as part of political processes, not by a benevolent central planner. To the extent that there is disagreement about the rules in practice, the resulting requirements may be ineffective due to compromise or intentional sabotage of the rules. In the concluding chapter, I discuss the reasons why we should not expect effective budget rules to emerge from legislatures and suggest ways in which reformers could adopt theoretically effective rules, like the ones discussed in this chapter. Finally, it may be the case that an external enforcement mechanism is not feasible or desired by designers, necessitating internal enforcement, which takes us to the next chapter.

CHAPTER 4

Internal Enforcement

*Mr. President, if this Senate is going to operate
and function, it has to follow its own rules.*

SENATOR BARBARA BOXER (D-CA), RAISING
CONCERNS ABOUT PARLIAMENTARY PROCEDURES
DESIGNED TO CIRCUMVENT SENATE RULES

In the previous chapter, I demonstrated that budget rules, if properly designed and externally enforced, could reduce spending and improve project efficiency in a distributive politics framework. Of course, in several instances external enforcement will not be possible. First, for a variety of reasons, the legislature may choose not to delegate enforcement authority to courts or agencies, for fear that the benefits of outside enforcement do not outweigh the costs of losing control over the rules. Second, external enforcement in the form of constituency costs will be ineffective in many situations, as I noted in the previous chapter. The public may be too conservative on fiscal matters — viewing government spending as nearly always excessive — thereby giving elected officials an incentive to absorb the constituency costs and go about their business. This chapter is concerned with how legislatures, like the U.S. Congress, address rule design when external enforcement is not a viable option.

When exogenous enforcement is not possible, rules must be enforced from within an organization. There are at least two ways that budget rules are enforceable within a legislature. First, in repeated games, the specter of future punishment may induce cooperation and adherence to rules. The second means of enforcement, and the focus of this chapter, is to tie rules to stable aspects of the organization (which may be stable due to repetition or some other factor).

In this chapter, I construct a framework for understanding how budget rules are made enforceable within a legislature by upping the ante for violating the rules. Specifically, suppose that there is an additional cost to violating a budget rule, one incurred because a violation of a budget rule would simultaneously do damage to an otherwise stable, vital aspect of an existing organization, such as amendment procedures, blocking rights, or the structure of voting. Think of this as akin to tying a vote of confidence to the passage of legislation in a parliamentary system — doing so increases the stakes of the vote (Diermeier and Feddersen 1998).

While of course all institutions are subject to change, a stable aspect of an organization is one that is unlikely to change suddenly or without warning. For example, the nuclear option to eliminate the filibuster on judicial nominations, discussed in chapter 2, was the subject of much debate and was a last resort for Senate Republicans frustrated by their inability to overcome Democratic objections to judicial nominations. When it comes to the fundamental rules of an organization, surprises are rare. The reason is that the stability of these facets of an organization stems from the long-term benefits to seeing these features remain in place. A violation of a budget rule tied to such a feature would impose additional costs on the organization. By assuming that these costs are high enough, this stable aspect of the organization is treated as exogenous. Internal enforcement of budget rules is feasible, therefore, by tying the rules to an amendment procedure or other well-established, stable component of the organization.

This approach reflects an alternative to the models posited in the previous literature, which have focused primarily on repetition as the means to attain endogenous enforcement. To be sure, a designer may take advantage of the aspects of the organization that have been made stable by repeated interactions, but that is where reliance on norms and repetition ends. Put another way, the institutional designer need not attempt to create a norm, though she may use an existing norm to enforce a new budget rule.

While the last chapter established that, in theory, spending limits are effective when exogenously enforced, this naturally leads to a new question: when exogenous enforcement is not feasible, is endogenous enforcement of spending limits possible in a distributive politics framework? Specifically, is endogenous enforcement of a spending limit feasible in the context of a distributive politics model where spending is not prefixed?

To examine these questions, I present a bargaining model that demonstrates how amendments could be used to enforce budget rules. The model suggests that if the bill passage requirement is low enough, then it is possible for amendment procedures to be structured such that an agenda setter has an incentive to keep spending down and thus improve the overall welfare of the legislature. The success of the rule hinges on the alignment of the legislature's prebargaining incentives with the agenda setter's incentives at the time he makes a proposal. The rule in this model is a spending limit. The entire legislature engages in enforcement via the selection of a binding amendment procedure that is tied to adherence to the rule. Two conditions are necessary for the rule to be effective. First, the legislature must want to require amendment procedures that provide the agenda setter with the "right" incentives. Second, these amendment procedures must alter the behavior of the agenda setter. Otherwise the threat of enforcement will not be sufficient to induce adherence to the spending limit.

A note on terminology: for clarity, in this chapter I will refer to amendment procedures rather than amendment rules to clarify the distinction between the budget rules and the enforcement mechanism. I assume here that the legislature will use well-established protocols regarding amendments to create an enforcement mechanism that encourages agenda setter adherence to a specific budget rule — a spending limit. While amendment procedures are technically rules, using this terminology would confuse matters about what the rule under study is and what the enforcement mechanism is. There is one exception: I will refer to open and closed rules, since that is the standard terminology in the literature.

I demonstrate that under certain limited conditions (including simple majority voting requirements), the legislature will induce the agenda setter to abide by a spending limit. I also demonstrate that in many cases, the legislature will not have the incentive to impose a spending limit, even though the agenda setter would abide by the limit if it was created. As I show in this chapter, legislative preferences for an open rule are so powerful that in most cases the legislature is not willing to create an enforcement procedure that induces the agenda setter to reduce spending. The ultimate lesson is that endogenous enforcement is difficult but possible to achieve by tying budget rules to stable aspects of an organization.

Stability and Rule Enforcement

The special challenge of internal enforcement is that legislatures can alter rules with impunity. Therefore, to be effective a rule must be constructed so that legislators have incentives to adhere to its provisions. This problem is not lost on congressional scholars. Allan Schick, discussing legislation passed by Congress in the 1980s to stem growing deficits, writes, "The premise of [Gramm-Rudman-Hollings] was that politicians require prefixed rules barring them from making certain budget choices because they cannot be trusted to do the right thing on their own and they certainly cannot make the hard decisions needed to discipline federal revenue and spending" (2000, 22). Certainly deficit spending may give rise to strict rules for spending increases. But if political demands for spending increases in a popular program emerge, it is unlikely that internal enforcement of the rules will be successful. Gilmour (1990, 6) writes, "Members can and do change the procedure of Congress when they perceive that it obstructs their will or otherwise produces undesirable consequences." Kiewiet and McCubbins (1991, 80) note that "the belief that Congress could use the budget process to hold down deficits is based on the faulty premise that members of Congress can commit either themselves or future Congresses to binding levels of revenues, spending, or deficits. In a majority-rule institution like Congress, any spending proposal can be amended upward, and any limitation on expenditures that is adopted one day can be overturned the next." In discussing "framework laws" that guide the formation of particular policies such as base closings or budgeting, Garrett (2004) argues that such laws are not self-binding because a majority may undo its own rules at any time.

If key features of a legislature (the committee system, floor procedures, and the structure of amendment procedures) are taken as exogenous and fixed for the purposes of analysis, then they can be utilized to design effective enforcement techniques for budget rules. Endogenous enforcement of budget rules occurs if the existing (equilibrium) institutional framework is successfully used for enforcement. Specifically, endogenous rule enforcement is possible if the budget rule is tied to a stable part of the organization that is changed only at prohibitive cost. While all features of legislative organization are subject to change, some are more inviolate than others.

To understand whether spending limits are enforceable by taking advantage of existing legislative organization, I assume that the procedure for amending a bill, once selected, will not be violated by the floor. The amendment procedure is then used as an enforcement mechanism for the spending limit in the following way. As I establish later in this chapter, the agenda setter prefers that no amendments be allowed on distributive politics legislation, while the legislature as a whole prefers that amendments not be limited. In addition, the agenda setter prefers that legislation not be subjected to a spending limit. Because the agenda setter's preference for a closed rule outweighs his preference for no restraint on spending, the legislature can, at the outset of the game, establish the following amendment procedure tied to a specific limit on spending. If the agenda setter adheres to a limit on spending, then his proposal will be considered without amendment (a closed rule). If the agenda setter violates the limit, then unlimited amendments will be allowed on his proposal (an open rule). I show that it is possible to implement this mechanism under simple majority rule, though not for most supermajority rules.

The analytical technique presented here is applicable to the enforcement of budget rules more generally. In what follows, the rule is considered to be implemented if (*a*) the legislature has an incentive to set a spending limit greater than 0, (*b*) the agenda setter abides by the spending limit, and (*c*) the amendment procedure laid out by the legislature is faithfully followed. By assuming *c*, the model is designed so that enforcement failure does not occur in the sense of the legislature not following through with enforcement, since I assume that the costs of violating the amendment procedure are sufficiently high for legislators. This, in other words, is the best-case scenario for internal enforcement. Even here, though, implementation of the rule is far from guaranteed.

Amendments and the Budget Process

The rules that apply to the consideration of distributive politics bills will affect the size and allocation of spending. While there are endless ways to structure consideration of a bill, it is useful to apply a simple distinction between open and closed rules. Closed rules permit a straight up-or-down vote on a piece of legislation, whereas open rules allow for potentially unlimited amendments to the legislation.[1]

If only one policy dimension is under consideration and legislators' preferences are well-behaved, then an open rule will be optimal from the perspective of the median voter. Since his ideal point beats all other policies in head-to-head competition (i.e., it is a Condorcet winner), it will be the policy outcome of a bargaining process so long as amendments are not restricted. A closed rule, in contrast, may permit a proposer to prevent policy from being set at the median's ideal point, even in infinite-horizon bargaining (Romer and Rosenthal 1978; Primo 2002).[2]

Despite the apparent advantage of open rules for the median voter in legislative settings, restrictive rules have become more common in recent years (Sinclair 2000; Oleszek 2004). Gilligan and Krehbiel (1987) posit that restrictive (closed) rules, which ostensibly give committees greater power, may induce a committee to gather information, thus reducing the uncertainty inherent in policymaking: "Acting in its self-interest, the parent body often restricts its ability to amend committee proposals" (288).

In many cases, however, spending bills are multidimensional, so the single-dimensional results may not apply. For instance, a piece of legislation allocating district-specific projects becomes multidimensional when a legislator cares about how that allocation takes place rather than just the total size of spending. One of the most-cited distributive politics bargaining papers shows that closed rules will be preferred by the chamber to open rules when the size of spending is fixed exogenously (Baron and Fere-john 1989). In the Baron and Ferejohn model, a randomly selected agenda setter proposes the division of a dollar. Bargaining continues, and a new agenda setter is chosen, until a proposal is voted on favorably by a majority. Delay reduces the size of the dollar. Under a closed rule, agreement is reached immediately. Under an open rule, delay is possible. Because the full dollar is always allocated in the model, only delay affects the game's expected value. Thus, the sole advantage of the closed rule in terms of the game's expected value is the elimination of delay.

Baron (1991) finds that when a different type of inefficiency is intro-duced—project inefficiency—then open rules will tend to be preferred. In this model, one large project is given exogenously to the legislature for division, and therefore a key aspect of the legislative process (i.e., deter-mining the size of spending and allowing for the possibility that project efficiency may differ from district to district) is outside of the model. In this chapter, the size of spending is determined within the model and the efficiency of projects varies across districts. I demonstrate that Baron's findings regarding the open rule apply to a wider domain than he consid-ered. As the model below will show, inefficient projects will still result un-der an open rule and total spending will be greater than what would result if every district received an efficient project. (As in earlier chapters, efficiency is defined here as social-welfare maximizing.) More important, however, the new model allows for the consideration of questions that cannot be addressed within existing frameworks. Specifically, can the structure of the legislative process be utilized to entice an agenda setter to limit spending even when exogenous enforcement is not possible?

The Model

The baseline model is identical to the one presented in chapter 3, with the exceptions that any supermajority threshold for bill passage is allowed and two types of amendment procedures are considered: a closed rule and an open rule. A closed rule permits no amendments to an agenda setter's bill, while an open rule permits unlimited amendments to the legislation until a randomly chosen amender wishes to bring the bill to the floor for a vote. The solutions to these two versions of the model provide interesting in-sights in their own right and provide a foundation for further study of rule enforcement. The procedures considered, and the different logic operating in the two models, are as follows.

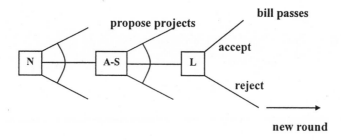

Figure 4.1 Extensive form, closed rule model. N = nature; A-S = agenda setter; L = legislature voting.

CLOSED RULE. At the beginning of every period, nature selects a legislator at random to serve as an agenda setter. Each legislator's probability of being selected is $1/n$. The agenda setter makes a proposal that consists of a project for each district, with a possible project size being zero. The legislature, operating under a closed rule (i.e., no amendments allowed), then votes on the proposal. If the proposal receives at least q votes, with $(n + 1)/2 \leq q \leq n$, it is accepted, and the game ends. If the proposal is rejected, nature selects a new agenda setter at random, and she offers a new proposal. The game continues indefinitely until an agreement is reached. A representation of the game's extensive form appeared in the previous chapter and is reproduced here as figure 4.1.

OPEN RULE. At the beginning of every period, nature selects a legislator at random to serve as an agenda setter. Each legislator's probability of being selected is $1/n$. After the agenda setter proposes legislation, a legislator is selected randomly to either propose an amendment to the legislation or to ask that the bill be voted on. I will term the latter option (in a slight abuse of terminology) "moving the previous question" (MPQ).[3] If she moves the previous question, then the previous question (PQ) comes up for a vote. If it receives at least q votes, it is accepted, and the game ends. If it is rejected, a new agenda setter is chosen, and play proceeds as above. If she offers an amendment, then the proposal and the amendment are pitted against each other in a vote. The proposal receiving the most votes is then subject to amendment by another randomly chosen agenda setter, as before. The game continues indefinitely until the previous question is moved and receives q votes. Let $k \geq q$ be the number of members that receive projects in equilibrium. Unlike under a closed rule, k may be larger than a minimum winning coalition, since the agenda setter may want to insure against

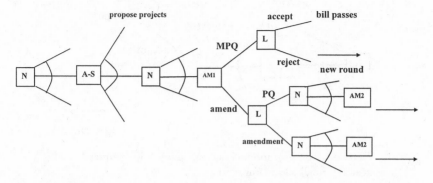

Figure 4.2 Extensive form, open rule model. N = nature; A-S = agenda setter; L = legislature voting; AM1 = first legislator selected to make an amendment; AM2 = second legislator selected to make an amendment.

amendments being made to his proposal by adding to his coalition. A representation of the open rule game's extensive form appears in figure 4.2.

The Bargaining Logic under Closed and Open Rules

The bargaining logic in the two models differs significantly, as the following example will demonstrate. The example features a five-member simple-majority-rule legislature. Recall from chapter 3 that a legislator's net benefit function for a project of size x, paid for equally by n districts, is $bx - [c/(2n)]x^2$. Letting $b = 1$ and $c = 2$ and assuming perfectly patient legislators, I write each legislator i's net benefit function as $x_i - (1/5)\sum_{j=1}^{5}x_j^2$. This function includes the benefit that legislator i receives from project x_i as well as the legislator's share of all project costs. Suppose that legislator 1 is selected to make a proposal to the legislature. In a closed rule equilibrium, he offers projects to two randomly selected legislators, thereby forming a minimum winning coalition. In a stationary equilibrium, the legislators know that the agenda setter in the next period will follow the same strategy and, therefore, are willing to accept y that gives them the same utility as the expected value of moving to the next period of play. In the next period, a legislator is selected as the agenda setter and receives a project of size x with probability $1/n$, or $1/5$. A legislator is not selected as the agenda setter but is offered a project of size y with probability $(n - 1)/(2n)$, or $2/5$. With the same probability, a legislator receives nothing. A legislator pays one-fifth of the total project costs regardless of whether he receives an offer. Using these values, I calculate the expected value of the next period of play as $(1/5)x + (2/5)y - (1/5)(x^2 + 2y^2)$. Since the costs will be the same in all periods (as every legislator pays the same tax share, regardless of whether he receives a project), the values of x and y that solve the agenda setter's problem will satisfy $y = (1/5)x + (2/5)y$, or $x = 3y$.

Under an open rule, after the agenda setter makes a proposal, another legislator will be selected at random to propose an amendment or move the bill for a vote. That legislator, once selected, decides whether to take the proposal in the bill and move the previous question or, alternatively, to place herself in the shoes of the agenda setter and offer an amended bill. Therefore, the original agenda setter's offer must be larger than the closed rule offer described above to forestall an amendment. In addition, the agenda setter must decide whether to give projects to two, three, or four other legislators. This decision is important because those legislators not receiving offers will be sure to propose an amendment. For the parameter values used in this example, the agenda setter will choose to build a minimum winning coalition, offering the two members of his coalition a substantially larger project than offered under a closed rule in exchange for not proposing an amendment.[4] In short, the threat of amendments changes the nature of the bargaining process.[5] This example illustrates how outcomes differ under open and closed rules.

Under a closed rule, the agenda setter must make those legislators receiving projects as well off as they would be if they rejected the offer and moved the game to the next period, when a new agenda setter would be chosen. All legislators are therefore comparing their current offer to the (discounted) value of a lottery in which they have a $1/n$ chance of being the next agenda setter, an $(n-1)/(2n)$ chance of receiving an offer in the next period, and an $(n-1)/(2n)$ chance of receiving nothing.

When an open rule is in effect, the agenda setter must construct an offer that does not encourage those who receive a project to propose an amendment if given the opportunity. In other words, members of his coalition must be indifferent between offering their own proposal and bringing the agenda setter's proposal up for a vote. Under an open rule, the agenda setter has to offer members of his coalition a premium since any of them may soon be in the position to "unseat" him by offering an amendment. The power to overtake an agenda setter is valuable and makes all potential amenders (i.e., the entire legislature excluding the agenda setter) more costly to "buy" than under a closed rule. In addition, those who do not receive an offer are sure to propose an amendment. This risk is reduced by building a larger than minimum winning coalition. Assuming that project sizes are set appropriately, the probability of avoiding an amendment increases with coalition size. In the extreme, every legislator would be offered a sufficiently large project, and the agenda setter's offer would never be amended. Increasing the coalition size is costly, though, so minimum winning coalitions are typically optimal.

In sum, the difference between open and closed rules lies in the sequence of play and what has been observed at each step in the process. Under a closed rule, a vote immediately follows the agenda setter's proposal. In this vote, all legislators compare their offers to the expected value of allowing negotiations to proceed into another round of bargaining. Under an open rule, an amender is selected after the initial proposal. This amender can observe her current offer and compare the value of that offer with the value of making her own proposal.

This bargaining logic shapes equilibrium outcomes. Under a closed rule, the agenda setter secures an extremely inefficient project for himself, while giving other players efficient or slightly inefficient projects (depending on their patience). The agenda setter can exploit other legislators because they have no power to amend his proposal and must either accept it or reject it. If they choose to reject it and move to the next period, they may face an even worse outcome: receiving no project at all. The agenda setter's bargaining advantage leads to a collectively inefficient outcome.

The agenda setter's power is constrained under an open rule because the amender is sure to offer a counterproposal if she dislikes the initial bill. The agenda setter deals with this by sweetening the pot for members of his coalition while cutting the size of his own project, relative to a closed rule, leading to significant efficiency gains. The cut occurs because the coalition members' projects must be large enough so that they are not motivated to propose an amendment, implying that their project sizes must be comparable to that of the agenda setter. Because these projects get expensive quickly, an extremely inefficient agenda setter project is suboptimal in this case.

As in the Baron-Ferejohn model, a closed rule equilibrium is a no-delay equilibrium, while delay sometimes occurs in the open rule equilibrium. The tradeoff between open and closed rules, then, is between the more efficient projects that result under open rules and the no-delay equilibrium that results under closed rules. As the next section demonstrates, the increased efficiency of projects under open rules outweighs the efficiency loss from delay.

Comparative Statics

The open and closed rule models will be compared on four dimensions: (*a*) the size and efficiency of projects received by the agenda setter and by coalition members; (*b*) the expected benefit before play begins, or the expected value of the game; (*c*) net benefits for players in the model; and (*d*) total spending.[6] To derive comparative statics from the models, I vary key parameters of the model—the voting rule *q* and the patience parameter δ—for particular values of *b*, *c*, and *n*. Consider the case of *b* = *c* = 1 for *n* = 435 and *n* = 101. These values correspond to the size of the U.S. House of Representatives and the U.S. Senate (plus one for convenience). Table 4.1 demonstrates how equilibrium outcomes change as δ, *q*, and *n* are varied. Figures 4.3–4.5 depict equilibrium results for *n* = 101, δ = 0.8, and *q* varying from 51 to 101. Note that the efficient outcome is achieved for both open and closed rules when δ = 1 and the voting rule is unanimity; the results of this simulation are compared to this efficiency baseline. As noted earlier, efficiency is defined here as social-welfare maximizing.

The following relationships hold, setting aside the special case where δ = 1 and the voting rule is unanimity:

1. The agenda setter's project size and net benefits are larger under a closed rule than under an open rule.
2. All other legislators have smaller net benefits and, in the case of coalition members, smaller projects under a closed rule than under an open rule.
3. For all legislators, the ex ante expected value of the closed rule is lower than that of an open rule.
4. Spending is higher under a closed rule than under an open rule.
5. Project sizes are inefficient under both closed and open rules. That inefficiency is more pronounced for the agenda setter's project under a closed rule, but for coalition members' projects, it is larger under an open rule.

The first two results are consistent with the intuitions presented in the previous section. The agenda setter's power is constrained by the open rule, which benefits the other legislators but limits the agenda setter. The ex ante expected value of the game is greater and spending is lower under an open rule because of the dramatic reduction in the agenda setter's project size. Because the agenda setter's project is so inefficient under a closed rule, the switch to an open rule increases expected net benefits and decreases spending. While other coalition members receive larger (and more inefficient) projects under an open rule, these increases are more than compensated for by the corresponding reduction in the agenda setter's project.

While delay is possible under an open rule in equilibrium, the potential welfare losses from delay are outweighed by the efficiency gains due to changes in the agenda setter's project. Put differently, the expected value of the game is lower under a closed rule because the benefit gained by

Table 4.1 Comparison of open and closed rule results

			Closed Rule Model							Open Rule Model						
δ	q	n	x^*	y^*	$E(NB)$	NB_{x^*}	NB_{y^*}	NB_0	Spending	x^*	y^*	$E(NB)$	NB_{x^*}	NB_{y^*}	NB_0	Spending
.4	51	101	17.02	1.68	-1.13	14.89	-.45	-2.13	215.39	5.52	1.91	-.03	2.14	.34	-.45	106.38
.4	68	101	13.79	1.30	-.50	12.28	-.20	-1.50	151.79	3.44	1.46	.18	1.74	.47	-.44	76.95
.4	101	101	9.47	.92	.14	8.61	.06	...	86.74	1.73	.99	.50	1.23	.49	...	50.77
.6	51	101	19.65	1.63	-1.57	17.09	-.94	-2.57	259.30	4.31	1.93	-.01	1.53	.34	-.40	102.78
.6	68	101	15.28	1.28	-.70	13.58	-.42	-1.70	171.55	2.65	1.47	.21	1.20	.49	-.40	75.70
.6	101	101	8.81	.92	.20	8.00	.12	...	81.29	1.33	1.00	.50	.83	.50	...	50.55
.8	51	101	24.80	1.52	-2.62	21.18	-2.10	-3.62	365.61	3.65	1.95	.00	1.18	.33	-.36	101.43
.8	68	101	18.33	1.23	-1.17	16.17	-.94	-2.17	219.08	2.25	1.47	.23	.91	.51	-.36	75.30
.8	101	101	7.18	.94	.31	6.49	.25	...	69.79	1.12	1.00	.50	.62	.50	...	50.51
1	51	101	51.00	1.00	-12.12	37.88	-12.12	-13.12	1,325.50	3.25	1.96	.00	.96	.32	-.33	100.83
1	68	101	34.00	1.00	-5.05	27.95	-5.05	-6.05	611.50	2.00	1.48	.26	.73	.53	-.32	75.14
1	101	101	1.00	1.00	.50	.50	.50	...	50.50	1.00	1.00	.50	.50	.50	...	50.50
.4	218	435	36.75	1.84	-1.39	34.35	-.56	-2.39	1,040.57	5.99	1.98	-.01	2.40	.40	-.43	442.02
.4	290	435	29.75	1.40	-.67	28.08	-.27	-1.67	726.63	3.61	1.49	.19	1.84	.50	-.44	328.49
.4	435	435	20.23	.96	.07	19.31	.03	...	402.87	1.75	1.00	.50	1.24	.50	...	217.78
.6	218	435	43.72	1.80	-2.01	40.71	-1.20	-3.01	1,308.42	4.50	1.98	.00	1.63	.37	-.39	437.16
.6	290	435	34.01	1.39	-.97	32.04	-.58	-1.97	856.43	2.73	1.50	.21	1.24	.51	-.40	327.01
.6	435	435	19.48	.96	.11	18.59	.06	...	388.69	1.33	1.00	.50	.83	.50	...	217.56
.8	218	435	58.44	1.74	-3.68	53.76	-2.94	-4.68	2,034.29	3.75	1.99	.00	1.23	.35	-.36	435.56
.8	290	435	43.40	1.36	-1.78	40.63	-1.42	-2.78	1,207.15	2.30	1.50	.23	.93	.52	-.36	326.57
.8	435	435	17.42	.96	.19	16.61	.15	...	352.69	1.12	1.00	.50	.62	.50	...	217.51
1	218	435	218.00	1.00	-53.87	163.13	-53.87	-54.87	23,870.50	3.31	1.99	.00	.99	.33	-.33	434.87
1	290	435	146.00	1.00	-23.83	121.17	-23.83	-24.83	10,802.50	2.03	1.50	.25	.75	.53	-.32	326.39
1	435	435	1.00	1.00	.50	.50	.50	...	217.50	1.00	1.00	.50	.50	.50	...	217.50

NOTE: Equilibrium project sizes, budgets, and net benefits are shown here as a function of coalition size, legislature size, and δ. The expected net benefit term refers to the ex ante expected benefit of the game, while the other net benefit terms refer to the net benefits of the game to a legislator receiving projects of size x^*, y^*, or 0 in the equilibrium.

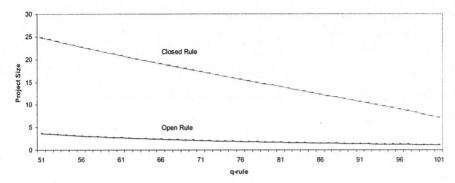

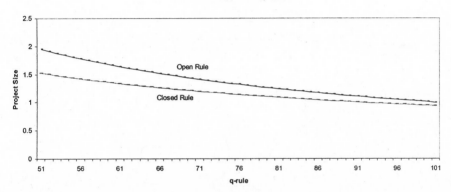

Figure 4.3 Open and closed rule model comparison, part 1. Comparison of open rule model and closed rule model, with $b = c = 1$, $n = 101$, $\delta = 0.8$, based on the q-rule for legislative passage.

eliminating the risk of delay is outweighed by the cost of the oversized project that the agenda setter will receive.

To verify that the above relationships hold more generally, b and c both were fixed at values of 1, and δ was set at values from 0.2 to 1 in increments of 0.08. For each of these values of δ, n was set at values from 25 to 505 in increments of 20. For each of these values of n, all q-rules from $q = (n + 1)/2$ to $q = n$ were considered; 36,575 possible combinations of parameter values for each model result. All of the above relationships held in this simulation, with two exceptions. When $\delta = 0.2$, $n = 25$, and $q = 13$ or $q = 14$, the members of the coalition received slightly smaller projects under an open rule than under a closed rule; even in these cases, though, coalition members still received higher net benefits under the open rule.

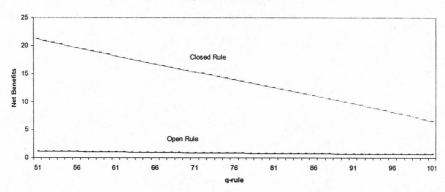

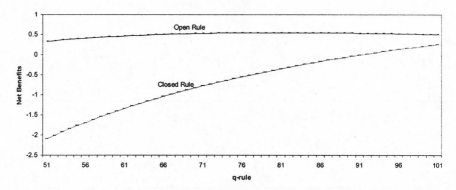

Figure 4.4 Open and closed rule model comparison, part 2. Comparison of open rule model and closed rule model, with $b = c = 1$, $n = 101$, $\delta = 0.8$, based on the q-rule for legislative passage.

Two important implications emerge from this model. First, open rules tend to be preferred by the legislature to closed rules. This result differs from Baron and Ferejohn's (1989) finding that closed rules are preferred but is consistent with the findings in Baron (1991). Second, the agenda setter's preference is for a closed rule, which is consistent with what Baron and Ferejohn (1989) and Baron (1991) find.

Spending Limits and the Enforcement Problem

While the open rule mitigates the inefficiencies of distributive politics bargaining, there is still room for improvement. The legislature may wish

Ex Ante Expected Net Benefits

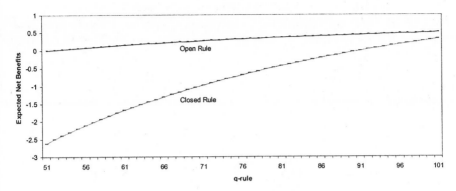

Spending

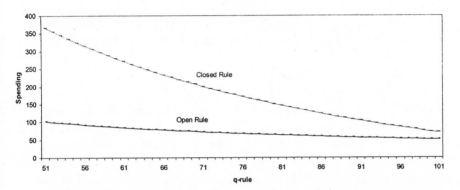

Figure 4.5 Open and closed rule model comparison, part 3. Comparison of open rule model and closed rule model, with $b = c = 1$, $n = 101$, $\delta = 0.8$, based on the q-rule for legislative passage.

to address this issue by imposing spending limits on the agenda setter. Because exogenous enforcement is not possible, the legislature will have to offer the agenda setter an incentive to abide by the limit. Recall from the previous section that the agenda setter prefers a closed rule to an open rule. This result suggests that the agenda setter may abide by a spending limit if the legislature offers him a closed rule on his legislation in return. This provision will only be implemented if the additional benefits to the legislature obtained by limiting spending outweigh the loss from switching from an open to a closed rule. Otherwise, it has no reason to craft such a rule. It must also be the case that the agenda setter views this tradeoff similarly, or he will ignore the spending limit.

I assume that the amendment procedure set out by the legislature will ' be followed because it is a well-established aspect of the legislative process. To tinker with that on any given vote imposes large long-term costs on the organization. Therefore, the procedure is assumed to be fixed at any point in time. Given this, we can ask whether the legislature has an incentive to create a (credible) enforcement procedure that punishes the agenda setter for exceeding the spending limit set by the legislature.

The endogenous enforcement model ties the amendment procedure to the agenda setter's adherence to a spending limit. A representation of the game's extensive form appears in figure 4.6. The sequence of play is as follows:

1. The legislature sets a limit on total spending. An amendment procedure is attached to this limit that states that any legislation satisfying this cap will be considered on the floor under a closed rule. Any legislation violating this cap will be considered on the floor under an open rule. Because all legislators are equally likely to be selected as agenda setters or as members of the winning coalition, the first period decision will be unanimous; thus, the collective choice mechanism for this period does not need to be specified.
2. The agenda setter makes a proposal.
   a. If the total costs of the proposal are within the spending limit proposed by the legislature, then the chamber operates under a closed rule and votes on the proposal by some q-rule, where q is the number of legislators required to enact a piece of legislation, ranging from a simple majority [$q = (n + 1)/2$] to all legislators [$q = n$]. If the proposal is rejected, the legislature reconvenes to select a new spending limit, and the game continues.
   b. If the initial proposal violates the limit set by the legislature, then the chamber operates under an open rule as defined earlier.

This structure makes use of the fact that the agenda setter will be at a disadvantage under the open rule, since he must build a coalition to defend against a new proposer who can choose to amend the legislation. Players face two key choices in this game. First, the agenda setter must decide whether to pursue an open rule or a closed rule strategy, as a function of the spending limit. Second, the legislature, knowing that the agenda setter's equilibrium strategy is a function of budget size, must select the budget size appropriately.

By stationarity, the game can be separated out into closed and open rule versions. The closed rule model is solved as a function of budget size. (This

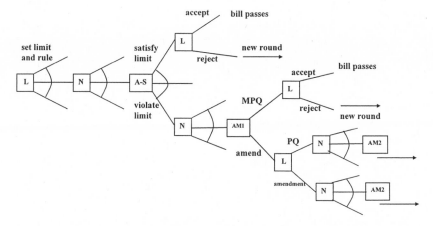

Figure 4.6 Extensive form, enforcement model. N = nature; A-S = agenda setter; L = legislature voting; AM1 = first legislator selected to make an amendment; AM2 = second legislator selected to make an amendment.

is solved as Proposition 2 in the appendix.) For every budget size, the agenda setter will choose to stay within the limit only if the value of the game under a closed rule is higher than it would be with an unlimited budget under an open rule. Then the legislature's choice is simple. It will select the budget size that provides the maximum expected net benefits to the legislature. If the legislature prefers to implement an open rule to a closed rule with a spending limit, it can set the spending limit to zero, thereby inducing the agenda setter to select the open rule.

In a stationary equilibrium of the complete model, if an agenda setter adheres to a closed rule in one period, he must do so in every period. Similarly, the legislature must select the same budget every time it sets a cap. Therefore, to assess what the legislature should do, the expected net benefits of the open rule model are compared with the expected net benefits of the closed rule model with a strategically chosen spending limit. Implementation will occur if the legislature can set the size of the closed rule spending limit such that (*a*) it gives it a higher expected value than the open rule and (*b*) it gives the agenda setter a higher expected payoff than the open rule. In cases where implementation does not occur, the failure to satisfy either *a* or *b* could be the cause.

Again, because of the model's complexity, I utilize simulations to determine the conditions under which implementation occurs. For the House of Representatives and Senate examples discussed earlier, implementation is possible only for simple majority voting or *q*-rules close to it. Implemen-

Comparison of *Ex Ante* Expected Net Benefits

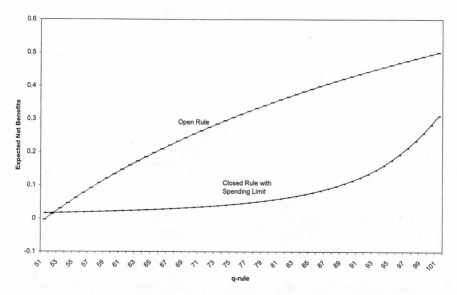

Figure 4.7 Net benefits, open rule vs. closed rule with spending limit. Comparison of the ex ante expected net benefits of the open rule and closed rule with spending limit models, with $b = c = 1$, $n = 101$, $\delta = 0.8$, based on the q-rule for legislative passage.

tation will not be effective for most other voting procedures. Figure 4.7 compares the ex ante expected net benefits of the closed rule with spending limit model and the open rule model for $n = 101$ and $\delta = 0.8$. The budget is set to maximize the legislature's expected net benefits. The agenda setter in all cases would happily take the closed rule with a spending cap, but even at the optimal (positive) budget, the legislature does better under an open rule. Therefore, in all cases except for $q = 51$ or $q = 52$, the legislature would select a spending limit of zero, thereby inducing the agenda setter to avoid the limit and receive an open rule.

The spending limit was implemented in 1,022 of 36,575 scenarios considered.[7] These successes are parsed as follows:

- For simple majority rule, implementation occurred for all n and δ considered, except for $\delta = 0.2$, $n = 25$, and $q = 13$. The simple majority rule cases made up 274 of the 1,022 successful cases. Of the remaining 748 cases, the largest supermajority for which implementation occurred was $q = 62$. Over 95 percent of instances of implementation were for supermajority rules less than or equal to 55.

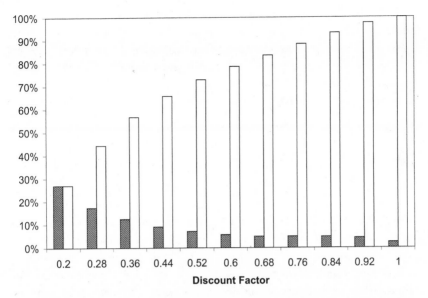

Figure 4.8 Implementation of the spending limit. Graph depicting for which discount factors the spending limit is implemented. Percentages (*cross-hatched bars*) and cumulative percentages (*plain bars*) are presented in the graph. These values refer to the proportion of all successes that occur for each discount factor. For example, about 27 percent of all cases occur when $\delta = 0.20$.

- Implementation occurred more often in cases where legislators were impatient. See figure 4.8.

  I draw the following conclusions from these simulations:

1. The smaller the coalition required for legislation to pass, the more often spending limits, endogenously enforced through amendment procedures, will be implemented. The smaller the coalition, the greater the agenda setter's ability to extract a large project from the legislature, and the greater the legislature's willingness to trade-off the increased efficiency of projects under an open rule for the lower spending under the closed rule tied to a spending limit.[8] As the majority required for passage increases, fewer legislators are left out of the winning coalition, and overspending lessens in severity.[9]

2. For sufficiently large legislatures, as legislators' patience increases, spending limits are less likely to be used. The higher δ gets, the less costly is delay, making the open rule relatively more attractive to the legislature.[10]

In short, then, a legislature's ability to limit spending depends on the tradeoff between reducing spending, thereby curbing the tendency of the agenda setter to propose inefficient projects, and the equalizing effect of the open rule on the projects received by the agenda setter and by other legislators. Under simple majority rule, the first effect dominates. But for larger values of q, the latter effect dominates.

Lessons

This chapter used a distributive politics model to demonstrate that open rules will be preferred ex ante by legislators to closed rules when spending is not prefixed, while proposers will prefer closed rules under these same circumstances. This differs from Baron and Ferejohn's divide-the-dollar finding but is consistent with the U.S. House of Representatives' budget process, in which appropriations bills are typically considered on the House floor without significant limitations on amendments (Kiewiet and McCubbins 1991), and U.S. states' budget processes, in which open rules dominate on state appropriations bills (Grooters and Eckl 1998). The central insight of the model is that the reduction in agenda setter power under an open rule outweighs the reduced probability of bargaining delay under a closed rule, leading to more efficient outcomes and higher expected net benefits.

In terms of enforcement, I showed that an enforcement mechanism that harnesses the agenda setter's preference for a closed rule will be effective for simple majority rule but less so under other q-rules. This finding suggests that endogenous budget rule enforcement is possible but challenging. The key to successful internal enforcement is that the rule matches the institutional environment in which it is to operate and that it is able to account for the incentives of the actors involved.

What are the implications of these findings for institutional design? First, an exogenous enforcer is not needed for successful rule enforcement. Second, the proper design of an endogenously enforced rule will require trial and error, as well as extensive information about preferences and the institutional environment in which it will be operating. This chapter has offered up the possibility of successful enforcement — a possibility that has rarely been realized in practice. The recent history of federal attempts at budget rule enforcement, explored in chapter 6, illustrates why successful enforcement has thus far proven elusive.

The tensions explored in this chapter indicate why rule designers face an uphill battle. Even if internal enforcement procedures are made credible by increasing the costs associated with violating them, there is still the problem of creating rules that are effective. This reinforces the duality of budgetary rule design. Effective internal enforcement is meaningless in the absence of incentives to create rules with bite. Similarly, rules with bite are unhelpful in the absence of effective enforcement. I have shown here that a spending limit tied to an internal enforcement procedure is effective but only when the legislature as a whole has an incentive to promulgate the rule.

Chapters 3 and 4 have outlined a theory of budgetary rule enforcement. In the following chapters I apply this theory to budgeting in the U.S. states and the federal government. Chapter 5 takes advantage of variation in the U.S. states to demonstrate how effective exogenous enforcement of balanced budget rules lowers spending. It also explores the impact of constituency costs and shutdown provisions. Unlike state legislatures, Congress must typically enforce its budget rules internally. Chapter 6 analyzes recent congressional attempts to do so using the theory developed in this book. Analysis of the failures of congressional budget reform will explain why the potentially successful rules outlined here have not materialized.

CHAPTER 5

The U.S. States

The states may still be "laboratories of democracy" but their
big thinkers are starting to look like mad scientists.
DONALD F. KETTL, PUBLIC ADMINISTRATION SCHOLAR

I begin this chapter with a puzzle. All states except for Vermont have a balanced budget requirement on the books, yet states vary dramatically in
deficit spending. Shouldn't all states with balanced budget laws on the books
have zero deficits? Or if they run deficits from time to time, shouldn't they
be tiny? It turns out that balanced budget rules are not created equal with respect to design and enforcement. Therefore, states with different budget
rules and legislative procedures may exhibit vastly different patterns of
spending.

This chapter will study state spending outcomes and budgetary bargaining from three different perspectives in an effort to shed light on how
budget rules shape fiscal practices in the states. The U.S. states are an ideal
arena for examining the design, enforcement, and impact of budget rules.
First of all, there are fifty of them, producing cross-sectional variation.
Furthermore, any individual state can also be observed at several points in
time, providing further variation. In addition, the effects of budget rules
are easily isolated because the states do not differ greatly in electoral or
governmental structure.

The puzzle that introduces this chapter will be examined through a
large-scale data analysis, using thirty-two years of budget data. Then, a
model will be introduced to address the impact of constituency costs on
budgetary reform. Using this very simple setup, I show why states can go
several years without any type of reform and then, without warning, see a
groundswell of support for significant change. A primary example of this
sort of significant change comes from New York, where several proposals
for reform emerged when pressure from the public and interest groups
grew in intensity. Finally, I examine an all-too-common phenomenon in
budgetary politics — the failure to approve a budget by the deadline. The

laws in the states vary in terms of how they handle these delays; some allow government to operate on a shoestring budget, while others require the government to shut down. I show that the effects of stringent shutdown rules are surprising and counterintuitive, demonstrating the importance of careful attention to rule design.

Balanced Budgets: The Design, Enforcement, and Impact of Rules

A balanced budget is a powerful political symbol, reflecting the idea that if average Americans are expected to balance their checkbooks and make ends meet, the government should be expected to do so as well. (Never mind that many Americans fail to balance their household budgets!) A balanced budget rule is typically viewed as a restraint on government profligacy, but this need not be the case. History shows that balanced budget rules can also be used to justify higher spending. A balanced budget requires only that revenues and outlays coincide. It makes no difference whether this occurs at a spending level of a million, billion, or trillion dollars. Both a small town and the federal government might have balanced budgets, but their spending levels would presumably differ greatly.

It is easy to construct scenarios in which balanced budget requirements lead to lower, unchanged, or even higher levels of spending. The model in chapter 3 demonstrates that under some conditions balanced budget rules do limit spending. In this case, a balanced budget rule allows a legislature to cap spending by setting taxes and outlays at a certain level, thereby tying the hands of the agenda setter. Another interpretation is that if budgets must be in balance, then new spending must be paid for with new taxes. Raising taxes is unpopular, so legislators will have reason to put the brakes on spending in this scenario. (See the section titled "Connecting Model and Data" for further discussion of the link between the spending limit in chapter 3 and the balanced budget rules described in this chapter.)

It is also possible to imagine a scenario under which a balanced budget or related rule would have little impact on spending. If legislators are already operating under a balanced budget norm, then the rule would have little impact on behavior. Similarly, if the agenda setter is allowed simultaneously to propose a level of spending along with an allocation of projects, then he merely sets spending to the level that exactly funds the proposed project allocations.

The third case, where a balanced budget rule leads to higher spending, is counterintuitive. After all, how can requiring a balanced budget produce higher spending? One answer lies in legislative preferences for tax instruments. Dennis Ippolito, discussing the early American period, writes, "The balanced-budget rule, with its corollary requirements for debt retirement, was viewed by Jeffersonians as a prescription for limited government. The post-Civil War period, however, demonstrated that this prescription did not work automatically. The Republican party that dominated national politics for much of this latter period embraced the balanced-budget rule, but Republicans were also wedded to the protectionist tariffs that produced surplus revenue levels. To protect high tariffs, Republicans promoted additional spending, first for aggressive debt retirement and later for internal improvements and pensions" (2003, 97). Put another way, legislators had preferences not only for spending but also for how revenues were raised.[1] These preferences aligned such that legislators could easily generate a large amount of revenue that in turn fed a large amount of spending.

The lesson here is that even rules whose effects seem obvious can sometimes produce unexpected consequences. To determine the impact of balanced budget rules in the U.S. states, I consider two questions. First, what form do the rules take? Second, how are the rules enforced?

Types of Rules

State balanced budget rules constrain legislatures either prospectively or retrospectively.[2] A prospective rule requires that the budget being proposed and/or enacted is in balance. This is the weakest type of enforcement (present in all states except for Vermont) because it does not stipulate what happens if revenue estimates are incorrect and a deficit is incurred. As a consequence, state legislatures have some leeway in overstating anticipated revenues in order to allow greater levels of spending. A prospective rule is unlikely to have an impact on behavior, as there is little incentive to make "honest" revenue estimates short of fearing the political costs of deficit spending or increased taxation down the road.

Retrospective rules place some requirements on what a state must do if deficits exist at the end of the fiscal year. In seven states, a carryover rule allows for deficit rollover to the next fiscal year, provided that the deficit is explicitly accounted for in next year's budget. Thirty-six states explicitly prohibit the carryover of a deficit, requiring that the state address the shortfall in the current fiscal year (or in the case of biennial budgeting, current biennium) by reducing spending, generating additional revenue, or obtaining federal aid.

Interestingly, when state budget officials are asked what motivates their governments to make ends meet, many list tradition and expectation alongside formal requirements (General Accounting Office 1993). Bohn and Inman (1996), however, find that budget deficits are smallest (i.e., balanced budget rules "bite") in states with no-carryover rules. The results of Bohn and Inman's study suggest that tradition and expectation can go only so far. Empirically, these rules matter, and states with stricter rules have lower deficit spending.

Enforcement

Most balanced budget rules are constitutional rather than statutory, meaning that the ultimate arbiter of the rule is the state's highest court.[3] Since constitutional provisions are more difficult to change than statutes, states will tend to be more successful at enforcement than the federal government because they are more willing to turn to the state constitution when implementing important laws or rules. The U.S. Constitution often changes through varying interpretations over time, while state constitutions are most often amended through direct, clear changes (Elazar 1982; Griffin 1995). Only two states (Illinois and Michigan) have adopted fewer amendments to their constitutions than the federal government has, while half have adopted at least a hundred amendments. Then there is Alabama, which has amended its constitution a whopping 743 times. The average number of state constitutional changes across all fifty states, 136, is five times more than that of the federal constitution (Council of State Governments 2005, 10–11). Moreover, by being more detailed and specific, state constitutions offer courts less interpretive leeway than the federal constitution (Elazar 1982).

Because of these different approaches to constitutional evolution, the U.S. Constitution and state constitutions differ significantly. Where state constitutions are rich, the U.S. Constitution is sparse. It follows that budget rules can be placed into state constitutions more easily than into the federal constitution. (The flipside is that, presumably, state constitutions can also be changed more easily than can the U.S. Constitution, but eliminating a balanced budget or other fiscal provision would presumably impose high constituency costs. Therefore, it is reasonable to assume that these rules are fixed in the short run.) The rise of tax and expenditure limits in the states in the 1980s and 1990s, in contrast with the failure to enact a federal balanced budget amendment, speaks to the results of these differences between state and federal constitutions.

The ultimate arbiters of constitutional rules are the courts. Certain types of judges may be more inclined to aid and abet the legislative and executive branches in playing fast and loose with constitutional budget rules. The success of balanced budget rules can be compared by distinguishing between elected and appointed jurists. The former are less likely to be beholden to the legislature or the governor, as they are selected by the electorate, and are therefore not inclined to rubber-stamp legislative actions. While budget disputes rarely wind their way to a state high court, it may be that the threat of effective enforcement is enough to obtain compliance with the rules.[4] Indeed, there is empirical evidence to suggest that states with elected high courts have lower deficits than states with appointed high courts (Bohn and Inman 1996).[5]

There is good reason to fear the involvement of the courts. As Schoenbrod, Levine, and Jung (2002) note, courts have a variety of options at their disposal to deal with claims against laws that violate constitution.[6] In theory, a state court could issue an injunction preventing the governor from spending the monies appropriated by the legislature, and it could also strike down appropriations bills that led to a violation of a balanced budget requirement.[7] Because courts may start tinkering with budgets in ways that legislatures may not like, even the possibility of court enforcement may be sufficient to induce compliance.

The tendency to place clear-cut amendments into state constitutions makes enforcement of budget rules at the state level more likely than at the federal level. Even at the state level, though, the success of the rules will depend both on how they are written and how they are enforced by the courts. To simplify matters, in the remainder of this chapter I assume that elected state courts will perfectly enforce strict balanced budget rules, while appointed state courts will shirk and ignore violations of this rule.

Connecting Model and Data

Several relationships emerged from the distributive politics model presented in chapter 3. First, spending limits were shown to have a negative effect on total spending. Second, the impact of executive veto authority was shown to depend on whether the executive (*a*) vetoed legislation and (*b*) exercised veto authority in a setting with or without a spending limit. Third, the impact of supermajority voting rules for budget passage was shown also to depend on whether such rules operated in an environment with or without a spending limit. All of these rules assumed perfect enforcement.

The discussion of enforcement and courts here needs to be connected with the model in chapter 3 and the data analysis to follow. First, there is the issue of how to operationalize a spending limit and its associated enforcement mechanism. To do this, we need to connect balanced budget rules discussed above with the spending limits introduced in chapter 3. I argue that a spending limit and a balanced budget rule are operationally equivalent if the spending limit is assumed to bind both revenues and outlays. In other words, the setting of a limit on spending also has the effect of setting an equivalent tax rate. The limit in chapter 3 is modeled in this way—as a budget constraint, where total costs (read: taxes) are shared equally across districts. Crain (2003, 112) shows that "strict balanced budget rules influence policy largely through expenditure adjustments and not through increases in taxes or other revenue sources." There is also empirical evidence showing that states tend to deal with budget shortfalls with spending cuts rather than tax increases (Bohn and Inman 1996). In other words, a balanced budget rule acts on the spending side rather than the revenue side, offering further evidence of the link between the spending limit modeled in chapter 3 and the balanced budget rules studied in this chapter.

Second, there is the matter of enforcement. I assume here that elected high courts will enforce balanced budget rules perfectly, while appointed courts will enforce them ineffectively. While admittedly a stark assertion, it nonetheless places a high burden on the spending limit variable, which is composed of both the rule component (does a state have a strict balanced budget rule?) and the status of the court (is it elected or appointed?). An additional advantage is that the elected status of the court is exogenous to a state's preferences for spending, so concerns about balanced budget rules being endogenous are mitigated, especially when combined with the fact that these rules were adopted well before the modern era under study. The same is not true of tax and expenditure limits (TELs), discussed below. If perfect enforcement is assumed, then the spending limit model can be contrasted with the unconstrained setting (i.e., no enforcement or weak enforcement). In the data analysis to follow, I will examine whether strict balanced budget rules enforced by an elected high court produce the same effects as seen in the abstract model.

There is not enough variation to examine the impact of supermajority voting rules, but the impact of executive veto authority is studied by examining the differences in spending under Democratic versus Republican governors. Recall from chapter 3 that when a spending limit is in effect, a conservative executive is expected to lead to increased spending, while the reverse is true when no such limit is present. As a result, in this case an interaction term combining spending limit with the partisanship of the governor is appropriate.[8]

Another issue is how a distributive politics model will connect up with data analysis utilizing total levels of spending as a dependent variable, since distributive politics spending will be a small part of overall budgets. First, distributive politics plays an important role in "greasing the wheels" of policymaking (Evans 2004), and to the extent that wheels are greased as part of logrolls, there is a clear link between increased distributive spending and increased spending overall. Second, if the model is made more complex, in the spirit of Primo and Snyder (2007b), by adding a public good benefiting all districts to the bargaining setting, one can show that the size of the public good is constant and does not depend on the presence of a spending limit. Therefore, if a spending limit is added to the model, in equilibrium it will affect distributive and not public goods spending (assuming distributive spending was desired to begin with). This analysis should not be taken to mean that I am arguing that only distributive spending would be influenced by a spending limit. After all, one could also add other types of goods to the model that are neither purely public nor purely distributive. For goods in between, the negative effect should be somewhat mitigated, as the inefficiencies will be less pronounced. Because they typically represent the most inefficient type of government spending, distributive goods are often the first to go when belt cinching is necessary. Anecdotally, we observed a clamoring for earmark reform in Congress in 2006, in part due to the worsening fiscal situation at the federal level.[9] In sum, if a negative effect is found in the specifications below, I will be confident that the effect is negative for distributive goods, as well.

Data Analysis

To examine the impact of state balanced budget rules on spending outcomes, I utilize spending data from 1969 to 2000 for forty-seven of fifty states.[10] The dependent variable in the analysis is per capita real direct general expenditures, measured in 2000 dollars. This category includes all state and local spending except for utilities, liquor stores, or insurance trust sectors, which the Census Bureau categorizes separately (U.S. Census Bureau 2000).

At a glance, we can see that states with spending limits, defined as having a no-carryover balanced budget rule and an elected high court, spend less than states without such rules. The mean level of state and local spending is $3,336, compared with $3,756 for states without a cap, yielding a large and statistically significant difference. Similar results hold for state-only spending, where local spending is excluded.[11] Below is a list of the seventeen states with spending limits and the thirty-three without for the time period under study.[12]

States with Spending Limits	*States without Spending Limits*
Alabama	Alaska
Arkansas	Arizona
Georgia	California
Idaho	Colorado
Kentucky	Connecticut
Minnesota	Delaware
Mississippi	Florida
Montana	Hawaii
New Mexico	Illinois
North Carolina	Indiana
North Dakota	Iowa
Ohio	Kansas
Oregon	Louisiana
Tennessee	Maine
Texas	Maryland
Washington	Massachusetts
West Virginia	Michigan
	Missouri
	Nebraska
	Nevada
	New Hampshire
	New Jersey
	New York
	Oklahoma
	Pennsylvania
	Rhode Island
	South Carolina
	South Dakota
	Utah
	Vermont
	Virginia
	Wisconsin
	Wyoming

This simple data analysis points to the need for a more in-depth study. The next step, then, is to examine whether spending levels are systematically different in states with strict balanced budget rules than in states

Table 5.1 Summary statistics

Variable	Mean	S.D.	Min	Max
State and local spending	3,613.14	1,050.81	1,604.96	7,531.09
State-only spending	1,662.10	644.12	634.26	4,903.17
State/(state + local) spending	.46	.09	.22	.81
State personal income	19,999.96	4,909.29	9,256.19	40,328.40
State and local federal aid	752.75	259.27	251.23	2,283.03
State and local debt change	220.87	276.04	−600.22	6,077.39
Unemployment rate	6.01	1.99	2.05	16.50
Population growth	1.22	1.24	−3.83	7.36
Seats in upper chamber	39.37	9.67	18.00	61.00
Seats in lower chamber	113.58	56.83	35.00	400.00
Citizen initiative	.43	.50	0.00	1.00
Spending limit	.34	.47	0.00	1.00
No-carryover rule	.72	.45	0.00	1.00
Biennial budgeting	.38	.49	0.00	1.00
Tax and expenditure limits (TELs)	.24	.43	0.00	1.00
Republican governor (modified)	.43	.50	0.00	1.00
% Democrat upper chamber	59.79	19.91	10.42	100.00
% Democrat lower chamber	59.46	19.20	14.49	100.00
Democratic unified government	.35	.48	0.00	1.00
Republican unified government	.14	.35	0.00	1.00
Normalized Democratic presidential vote share	.11	1.00	−2.56	3.05

NOTE: Financial variables in per capita real 2000 dollars. $N = 1,504$. Alaska, Minnesota, and Nebraska are omitted from the analysis.

without them, controlling for other factors that have an impact on outlays. Here I use a statistical technique known as feasible generalized least squares (FGLS). Technical details are in the appendix for this chapter. Intuitively, FGLS allows the researcher to account for the fact that budgets tend to change incrementally over time, with this year's budget bearing a close resemblance to last year's budget. Panel-corrected standard errors are used to adjust for heteroskedasticity in the data. Sources for data and summary statistics for the variables used in the analysis are located in tables 5.1 and 5.2, respectively.

There is a potential endogeneity problem in using a spending limit as an independent variable to explain state spending. This endogeneity can cut in two ways. First, fiscally conservative states may be more likely to create rules that constrain spending, thereby reinforcing preferences. If this is true, then the spending limit may reflect the preferences for spending in a state, rather than the effect of the rule. Second, a fiscally liberal state that

Table 5.2 Data sources

Variables	Source
Fiscal data and population	Census Bureau
State personal income	Bureau of Economic Analysis
Unemployment	Bureau of Labor Statistics, Department of Labor
Party variables and legislature size	Klarner (2003)
Presidential vote share	http://www.uselectionatlas.org
Citizen initiative	Matsusaka (1995)
Budget rules and procedures	Advisory Commission on Intergovernmental Relations (1987), Bohn and Inman (1996), Council of State Governments (various years), National Conference of State Legislatures (2005)

is in dire financial straits may be more likely to create rules that constrain spending, which is likely to dampen the apparent effects of such rules (as the state may have trouble living up to the rule and might have higher levels of spending due to factors unrelated to the limit). Endogeneity is always a concern in institutional analysis. Fortunately, it is less of a concern here. First, one component of the spending limit operationalization, the selection of state high court justices, is based on factors unrelated to the budget process. Second, balanced budget rules were typically implemented well before the budgetary era under study and, often, were part of a state's original constitution, thereby creating a healthy separation between the creation of the institution and spending decisions in the late twentieth century (Savage 1988; National Association of State Budget Officers 1992). The spending limit is therefore considered exogenous for the purposes of this analysis.[13]

As a robustness check, I create an alternative measure of a spending limit, defining it as the presence of a balanced budget rule with no carryover allowed. In the discussion of the results, I also note what happens when the courts measure and the balanced budget measure are separated out. A final robustness check adds tax and expenditure limits to the analysis. For reasons discussed earlier, these limits may be endogenous, but they provide insight into my claim that limits passed in the modern era are less likely to be effective than those enacted before government provided many more goods and services. Concerns about endogeneity will be mitigated if the coefficients and standard errors of other variables are largely unaffected by the inclusion of this variable.

In addition to the spending limit variable, two other variables based on the model in chapter 3 are included in the analysis.[14] The ideology of the governor is measured as an indicator variable coded 1 if the governor is a Republican, and 0 otherwise. This variable is then modified to account for budget passage and veto rules that affect the impact of the governor. It will be referred to as the "modified" Republican governor variable throughout the chapter.[15] The (modified) ideology of the governor is interacted with the spending limit variable to determine whether the influence of gubernatorial ideology is contingent on the presence of a spending limit. The analysis in chapter 3 established that given the presence of a spending limit, supermajority coalitions lead to higher spending than simple majority coalitions. Also recall that conservative governors are assumed to veto distributive politics legislation, while liberal governors are assumed to let such legislation pass. Because of this, conservative governors lead to supermajority veto override coalitions, and therefore larger spending, than their liberal counterparts in cases where a spending limit is in effect.

In this analysis I control for economic, demographic, institutional, and partisan variables that may have an impact on spending.[16] These include real per capita state personal income (the sum of all net income taken in by residents of a state [Wagner 1994]), real federal aid per capita, unemployment, population growth, the presence of citizen initiatives (Matsusaka 1995, 2000; Matsusaka and McCarty 2001; Feld and Matsusaka 2003), the change in state and local debt, the size of the state legislative chambers (Gilligan and Matsusaka 1995, 2001), biennial budgeting, the proportion of Democrats in the state legislature, the presence of unified Democratic or Republican government (Alt and Lowry 1994, 2000, 2003; Poterba 1994), and normalized state presidential vote share from the most recent election. Income and the unified government variables are interacted to determine whether unified governments respond differently to the income of a state when setting spending. Such governments may act more responsibly because blame is more easily directed to the party in power in the case of fiscal mismanagement. Also, because the Southern states were dominated by Democrats for much of the time period under study, I conduct a robustness check to see if the results are significantly affected by the elimination of the South from the analysis. Year fixed effects are estimated in order to account for any systematic shifts in spending common to all states due to changes in the economic situation or the role of the federal government. Although state fixed effects cannot be included because the presence of a spending limit in a given state does not vary across time, regional effects are included in the analysis.

The results of the FGLS analysis, along with robustness checks, are presented in table 5.3. The first column presents the baseline specification, the second column uses an alternative measure of spending limit, the third column omits the South, the fourth column adds tax and expenditure limits to the main specification, and the fifth column uses state-only spending as the dependent variable. State-only spending is significantly smaller than state plus local spending, so the coefficients for institutional variables in the last column should be of a smaller magnitude than in the first four columns.

ECONOMIC AND DEMOGRAPHIC VARIABLES. State personal income has a substantively and statistically significant effect on spending in all specifications. Specifically, state and local governments extract approximately eight cents of every dollar of state income. The effect of unemployment is statistically significant in only some specifications. In the primary specification, a one-point unemployment increase translates into a (statistically significant) increase of $14 of per capita state spending. The effect of unemployment is small when compared to the mean spending level of $3,613 and reflects only a modestly countercyclical fiscal policy. Unsurprisingly, federal aid and increases in debt consistently lead to more spending.

INSTITUTIONAL VARIABLES. Taking into account both the constitutive term (the spending limit) and the interaction term that includes the spending limit, the presence of a spending limit decreases spending, on average, by $147 per capita in the main specification when compared with spending in cases where no limit is in effect. This effect is robust across all specifications. When just state spending is examined, a smaller coefficient results; however, it is more important to consider whether spending is reduced by the same overall proportion. The mean of state and local spending in states without a limit is $3,756, while the mean of state spending is $1,710. The effect of a spending limit is to reduce both state and local spending and state-only spending by about 3.9 percent.[17] The use of the no-carryover rule as the measure of a spending limit produces a larger effect. The reason has to do with how comparisons are made with dummy variables. In the main specification, spending in states with no-carryover rules plus elected courts is compared to all other states, including those with no-carryover rules and appointed courts. In the specification with just a no-carryover rule, spending in states with such a rule is compared to states without, regardless of the composition of the courts.

One can indirectly examine enforcement success by estimating the

Table 5.3 Spending in the U.S. states, regression results

Variable	Model 1	Model 2	Model 3	Model 4	Model 5
Spending limit	-127.68*** (38.40)	...	-140.03** (63.37)	-127.97*** (38.37)	-60.59** (24.39)
No-carryover law	...	-227.81*** (47.29)	...	...	...
State income	.08*** (.01)	.08*** (.01)	.08*** (.01)	.08*** (.01)	.04*** (.00)
Federal aid	.94*** (.09)	.87*** (.08)	.90*** (.09)	.94*** (.09)	.53*** (.04)
Debt change	.03** (.01)	.03** (.01)	.03** (.01)	.03** (.01)	.02 (.02)
State/(state + local) spending	-203.13 (193.21)	-77.82 (197.04)	-183.53 (233.94)	-202.03 (192.63)	3,682.53*** (169.93)
Unemployment	14.34* (7.39)	8.95 (7.53)	12.11 (9.35)	14.41* (7.38)	6.65 (4.08)
Population growth	-22.96*** (8.26)	-22.33*** (8.22)	-23.30** (10.11)	-22.95*** (8.25)	-9.03** (4.45)
Seats in upper chamber	5.90*** (1.64)	5.75*** (1.73)	6.96*** (2.22)	5.85*** (1.64)	.97 (.74)
Seats in lower chamber	-1.70*** (.31)	-2.37*** (.37)	-2.03*** (.37)	-1.71*** (.31)	-.82 (.19)
Citizen initiative	-160.96*** (35.14)	-161.08*** (38.41)	-161.38*** (52.66)	-160.22*** (34.96)	-66.78*** (22.85)
Biennial budgeting	85.21*** (26.70)	69.72*** (25.01)	-169.70*** (39.36)	83.81*** (26.39)	37.76** (17.08)
Tax and expenditure limit	...	...	...	-11.11 (21.70)	...
% Democratic (upper)	-1.17 (.77)	-1.07 (.76)	-1.35 (.87)	-1.16 (.77)	.24 (.40)

% Democratic (lower)	1.73*	1.16	1.58	1.73*	.56
	(.92)	(.90)	(1.10)	(.92)	(.46)
Republican governor (modified)	11.34	3.85	17.45	11.47	.31
	(17.18)	(23.64)	(21.13)	(17.16)	(8.32)
Governor × limit	−44.09*	...	−54.63*	−44.28*	−15.11
	(23.77)		(32.86)	(23.74)	(12.03)
Governor × no carry	...	−11.80	...	...	...
		(27.15)			
Democratic unified	−74.57	−71.99	−117.39	−75.01	−80.53***
	(47.17)	(47.48)	(75.02)	(47.26)	(24.86)
Republican unified	−6.51	−23.35	−43.82	−6.55	35.87
	(62.71)	(62.47)	(65.31)	(62.77)	(31.40)
Democratic unified × income	.004	−.004	.006*	.004	.0042***
	(.002)	(.002)	(.003)	(.002)	(.0012)
Republican unified × income	.0003	.001	.002	.0003	−.002
	(.003)	(.003)	(.003)	(.003)	(.001)
Democratic presidential vote share	−7.34	−11.19	−17.25	−7.30	−5.72
	(8.72)	(8.66)	(16.86)	(8.72)	(5.09)
Constant	2,259.37***	2,666.71***	2,339.26***	2,263.94***	−747.63***
	(274.33)	(295.44)	(325.23)	(276.04)	(165.78)
South omitted	No	No	Yes	No	No
Estimate of ρ	.80	.82	.82	.80	.85
R^2	.81	.81	.78	.81	.82
N	1,504	1,504	1,024	1,504	1,504

NOTE: Prais-Winsten FGLS regression with regional effects and year fixed effects. Panel-corrected standard errors are in parentheses. Dependent variable is real state and local spending per capita measured in 2000 dollars, except in model 5, which uses state-only spending.

*Indicates $p < .10$

**Indicates $p < .05$

***Indicates $p < .01$

effects of the no-carryover rule, whether a court is elected, and the interaction of the two. When this is done, the three variables are jointly significant, and the impact is greatest when the no-carryover rule and elected courts are present. The impact of moving from a weak balanced budget law to a no-carryover law is greater under unelected than elected courts, in part because elected courts have a (large) independent negative effect on spending. In other words, states with unelected courts get a bigger "bump" from implementing no-carryover rules than states with elected courts. The interaction of the two features leads to the greatest effects. The upshot is that both the no-carryover law and the presence of elected courts contribute to the impact of spending limits on government expenditures.

Consistent with previous research, the presence of a citizen initiative decreases spending. Another interesting finding is that the number of seats in the lower house has a negative and significant effect on spending, while the effect of upper chamber seats is positive and significant (except in Model 5). This result stands in contrast with Gilligan and Matsusaka (1995), who find no statistically significant effect on spending in lower chambers, and demonstrates that more theoretical development of the impact of legislature size is needed.[18]

Also, the fourth column shows that not only do tax and expenditure limits have little effect on spending, they also have minimal impact on other variables, thereby allaying concerns about endogeneity. More important, the result is consistent with the fact that most of these limits, enacted since the late 1970s, were designed under circumstances where there would be clear winners and losers, depending on how they were constructed, making them less likely to be effective than balanced budget rules enacted when governments had fewer preexisting commitments.

PARTY VARIABLES. None of the party variables or citizen preferences variables is consistently statistically significant across all specifications. For instance, the percentage of Democrats in the lower house has a positive effect on spending in the baseline specification, but in no other. The party of the governor has no effect, either; the coefficient for governor is statistically insignificant, and joint significance cannot be established for the governor and (governor × limit) variables. Similarly, the interaction terms on the state income and unified government variables are not statistically significant across all specifications. An F-test of all the party variables in the primary specification does not achieve statistical significance (p = .50). Further, the condition number for the party variables in the primary specification is 11, indicating that multicollinearity is not a serious concern.

Finally, the citizen preferences variable is not statistically significant in any specification. In short, these findings are extremely robust.

The FGLS analysis tells us that states with strict balanced budget rules spend less than states without such rules. I now take the analysis one step further and examine whether states with strict balanced budget rules react differently to changes in state revenue. This hypothesis is assessed with an error correction model (ECM), which probes both long-term and short-term relationships in the data. The general error correction framework, denoting Δ as a difference operator, is

$$\Delta y_t = \alpha + \beta \Delta x_t + \rho(y_{t-1} - \theta x_{t-1}) + \varepsilon_t.$$

The β represents the short-term effects of changes in the independent variable, while θ reflects long-term effects. The rate at which long-term effects occur is represented by the absolute value of ρ. Suppose that a one-unit change in the independent variable induces a one-unit change in the dependent variable over the long term (i.e., $\theta = 1$). Then $\rho = -0.7$ means that 70 percent of the effect occurs in the first period, with 21 percent occurring in the next period $[0.7(1 - 0.7) = 0.21]$, 6.3 percent in the third period $[0.7(1 - 0.7 - 0.21)]$, and so on.[19] The ECM must include the first differences (and lagged differences) of variables that are expected to have short-run effects, and the lagged levels of variables that are expected to have long-run equilibrium effects.[20] The dependent variable is differenced and a lagged level is included as an independent variable.[21] The main insight of the ECM is that one can account for both long-term and short-term fluctuations in time series data by explicitly modeling both.

The ECM cannot adequately tap the effects of variables that do not vary temporally, so variables such as the citizen initiative and the number of seats in the state legislature are left out of the analysis. In addition, the hypothesis that "spending will be lower in states with spending limits than in states without spending limits" cannot be tested directly with an ECM. While the ECM will not allow a direct test of the effect of spending limits, it will be extremely useful in an indirect test. Specifically, this test will examine whether states without limits respond differently to an increase in state personal income than states with such spending caps. States with spending limits should not extract as much of an additional dollar of income as states without them, as such a sudden increase in the state budget would set an expectation for future budget years that would likely lead to (unallowable) deficits in the long term. Consider a state in which there is no concern about deficits because of a weak balanced budget rule. If state revenues increase, spending can be increased immediately; the legislature need not fear having to make cuts in a subsequent economic downturn because deficit spending is permissible. In contrast, a state with a strict balanced budget rule may not want to spend an additional dollar of revenue immediately because a subsequent downturn could necessitate politically unpalatable cuts. Separate ECMs are estimated for states with and without spending limits to allow for different dynamic relationships.

The error correction model produces intriguing results that offer support for the claim that states with spending limits tend to keep their fiscal houses in better order. In an effort to simplify the presentation of the results, I present selected coefficients from the error correction model — specifically, those related to how states respond to changes in income.[22] An overbar ($^{-}$) indicates that the coefficients are significant at the .05 level or better.

For states with spending limits,

$$\Delta \text{ state and local spending}_{it} = -0.005 \, \Delta \text{ state income}_{it} - \overline{0.10} \, (\text{state and local spending}_{i,t-1} - \overline{0.11} \text{ state income}_{i,t-1}) + \text{constant} + \text{other variables} + \varepsilon_{it}.$$

For states without spending limits,

$$\Delta \text{ state and local spending}_{it} = \overline{0.065} \Delta \text{ state income}_{it} - \overline{0.06} \, (\text{state and local spending}_{i,t-1} - \overline{0.14} \text{ state income}_{i,t-1}) + \text{constant} + \text{other variables} + \varepsilon_{it}.$$

These equations demonstrate that the presence of a spending limit prevents states from immediately using the additional revenues implied by an increase in state income. In states without spending limits, an additional dollar of state income translates into an immediate 6.5 cent increase in spending (indicated by the difference term). The interpretation of the state income lag term (i.e., the one with a $t-1$ subscript) is that an increase in state income increases spending in the long term by 11 cents in states with a spending limit and by 14 cents in states where a spending limit is not in place. The rate of increase is 0.10 in states with spending limits, and 0.06 in states without these limits.[23]

The ECM results point to the role of spending caps in limiting spending increases: as state personal income jumps, states without limits tend to take the resulting increase in tax revenue and spend it. If the economy subsequently falters, there is little concern about tightening the budget to adjust to hard times, since the balanced budget rule can easily be violated. States with spending limits are far more cautious about increasing spending in this manner, preferring instead to "reequilibrate" over the long run and forgo short-run increases. This result is consistent with Crain's finding that states with strict balanced budget rules exhibit less volatility in spending over time (Crain 2003).

An alternative perspective is that states without spending limits can set spending levels without regard for revenues, since they are unconcerned with deficits. Therefore, changes in state revenue should not have as much of a short-term impact in those states as in states where budgets must be balanced every year, meaning that the above results would be contrary to expectations. This alternative perspective suggests that a state without a spending limit would apply more of that shock to a rainy day fund, since it has already made spending decisions without regard to balance. The data do not support this hypothesis.

Returning to my argument, suppose that there is a positive revenue shock due to an increase in state personal income, but that spending decisions have already been made. My analysis implies that states with a spending limit that have already made their spending decisions are likely to place the surplus in a rainy day fund to be tapped in cases when negative revenue shocks occur. States without spending limits are more likely to view the revenue shock as found money and find a way to allocate some of it. Bohn and Inman (1996) find precisely this: states with stricter balanced budget rules tend to have larger rainy day funds and to put surpluses into those funds.

In short, then, there is ample evidence that strict balanced budget rules enforced by an elected high court lead to lower spending in the U.S. states. Real-world budget rules, when properly designed and enforced, are effective, just as the models in chapter 3 showed.

Constituency Costs and Budgetary Reform

Although most balanced budget rules have been on the books for decades, budgetary reform is attempted frequently in the U.S. states. Yet legislatively implemented major reforms are few and far between. New York State helps us understand why. The New York State government passed a budget on March 31, 2005. "So what?" you might say. The legal deadline for passing a budget is March 31, so the legislature and governor merely did what was required of them by law. However, because this was the first time in twenty-one years that a budget was passed on time in New York, the story received widespread attention. Legislators and the governor congratulated themselves on their timeliness, and there was general agreement that a groundswell of public dissatisfaction with Albany led to this "achievement."

In spite of this success, a battle was raging between the legislature and the governor over larger reforms to the budget process. Reform groups were divided on a provision that would shift some power in the process from the legislature to the governor. A less controversial provision would change the start of the fiscal year from April 1 to May 1, so as to increase the possibility of an on-time budget.[24]

In New York, legislators face little in the way of sanctions if they do not meet budget deadlines, leading one lawmaker to suggest sequestering legislators in Albany until they reach agreement (Gallagher 2005). Another approach, perhaps even more extreme, would be to jail all legislators and the governor until a budget agreement is reached. Of course, the legislature has little motivation to impose these requirements on itself. In fact, its preferred budgetary reform proposal would eliminate a sanction in the budget process: a provision that withholds legislator pay (temporarily) until agreement is reached.

What was the impetus for the proposed reforms? A simple model, using the concept of constituency costs introduced in chapter 3, will illustrate why a wide-ranging set of reforms was suddenly added to the agenda in New York. Suppose the median legislator (or some other representative agent of the legislature) is happy with the current budgetary status quo, which I represent as a policy of 0. Also assume that all voters agree that the budget process in New York is broken and would like reforms that amount to a policy of 1. The median legislator's utility is equal to the negative of the absolute value of the budget policy in place. For instance, if an even looser set of budget rules were enacted, taking policy to −0.5, the legislator's utility would be −0.5. If a stricter set of policies were enacted, taking policy to +0.5, the legislator's utility would also be −0.5. These single-peaked preferences indicate that the median legislator prefers budgetary policy to stay where it is and views as harmful movement in either direction from this policy. In this world, reform does not occur unless the median legislator changes.

One important impetus for reform, not factored into the model, is public clamoring for change accompanied by a threat to impose costs, presumably at the ballot box, if ignored. This is modeled as a cost c that is paid if the public's desired reform is not implemented. In the simple model under consideration, then, reform occurs only when $c > 1$. When $c < 1$, the median legislator is willing to endure constituency costs and keep his or her preferred budget rules in place because his utility of $-c$ would be greater than the −1 that would result if the demand for reform was met.

Note that this is a threshold effect. Either constituency costs are large enough to make reform worthwhile or they are not. In other words, public dissatisfaction with the budgetary process can go on for years without any action on the part of the legislature. Then, due to an exogenous shock that increases c, reform can suddenly rise to the top of the legislative agenda. This appears to be what happened in the early 2000s in New York State. While New York had been viewed for years as a laggard in the budgetary arena, it was only in 2004 that reform became a real possibility, though it was ultimately unsuccessful (as of late 2006).

This model offers an explanation for the emergence of reform proposals, though it says nothing about whether proposed reforms are meaningful or effective. For instance, an on-time budget says nothing about the content of the budget, which is what citizens presumably ought to be concerned about. The on-time budget, however, is a powerful political symbol, which explains the attention it receives from lawmakers, the press, and the public alike. And, of course, c can decline just as suddenly as it can increase, explaining why proposed reforms often fail to be enacted.

Reversion Budgets — the Design and Impact of Rules

While New York State laws make missing a budget deadline primarily a public relations issue, budget stalemates can have a greater impact elsewhere. In 2005, there were two high-profile budget standoffs. In New Jersey, intralegislative battles between Assembly and Senate Democrats led to a near government shutdown, with the budget only being signed by Democratic governor Richard Codey at the very last moment. According to one press account, Codey was willing to compromise at the end because he feared that a shutdown would remove any bargaining power he had (Whelan and Margolin 2005). In Minnesota, a state often viewed as a beacon of "good government," the government was partially shut down for eight days because a budget was not passed on time.

A budget stalemate can spell big trouble for governors and legislatures alike, as it is a visible and potent symbol of government ineptitude. Yet the consequences of a missed budget deadline vary from state to state. In some states, such as Illinois, key government services are kept running while negotiators hash things out. In others, such as New Hampshire, the legislature must pass a temporary spending measure, known as a continuing resolution, to keep government functioning in the interim. Some states have no provisions on the books. New Jersey is among these states, and the 2005 standoff produced a test case, with the Attorney General's office arguing that a shutdown was required if no agreement on a budget was reached. In 2006, the scene was replayed, this time with agreement not being reached in time. Governor Jon Corzine shut down the New Jersey government in July 2006 after the budget deadline had passed, referencing the constitutional requirements: "Our constitution doesn't allow us to spend money [in the absence of a budget agreement]. It's not like in Washington where you can just have a continuing resolution or ignore deadlines" (Hurdle 2006). In twenty-three states, such as Minnesota, the government shuts down until an agreement is reached (Grooters and Eckl 1998).

These rules change the nature of the bargaining process. Specifically, these rules imply different reversion values for spending if agreement is not reached. As a simple model will demonstrate, these values will have consequences for budgetary outcomes.[25] The following is based on Romer and Rosenthal (1978) and Primo (2002). Assume that the governor and a pivotal voter in the legislature are bargaining over the size of spending.[26] Further assume, in keeping with the view of the executive as a fiscal steward, that the governor always prefers less total spending than the legislature.

The game proceeds as follows. In the first round, the pivotal legislator proposes a budget size to the governor. This matches reality, as in forty-seven states the legislature can make most any changes it sees fit to a proposed executive budget.[27] Then, the governor can either accept it or veto it. If he accepts it, the budget is enacted and the game ends. If he rejects it, a reversion budget goes into effect, and bargaining begins again.[28] Payoffs occur in each period and are based on how far away spending is from the ideal spending level of the players. The simplest way to characterize these payoffs is to make them the negative of the distance between actual spending and the player's ideal spending level. For example, if the pivotal legislator's ideal spending level is $1 billion, and the government shuts down, implying zero spending, his payoff is −1 billion. Also, legislators and the governor discount the future, so an agreement tomorrow will be discounted relative to an agreement today.

If the reversion budget is zero, as it is in states where a shutdown occurs if agreement is not reached, then the legislature will be able to achieve its ideal budget, so long as the governor prefers it to no spending. The legislature has the bargaining advantage because the governor, when considering a spending proposal, compares it to the outcome that would be obtained if he vetoed the spending proposal. If the reversion budget is anything greater than zero (or is expected to be greater than zero on average), then spending under the reversion budget will be set either at the legislature's ideal point or lower. Therefore, in cases where shutdown provisions are in place, spending will be (weakly) higher than when they are not in place.

The pattern is also observed empirically in the U.S. states. By adding shutdown provisions to the FGLS analysis discussed earlier, I found that states with shutdown provisions spend $64 more per capita in state and local spending.[29] This effect is remarkably large, given that shutdowns occur rarely. The threat of a shutdown changes the bargaining environment. Without the model, one might not expect that a shutdown provision could under some circumstances be a pro-spending rule.[30] This finding points to the importance of accounting for strategic interactions and the institutional environment into which rules are introduced.[31]

Lessons

This chapter has explored the impact of budget rules on spending patterns in the U.S. states. A balanced budget rule that does not allow for deficit carryover and that is subject to enforcement from an elected high court was shown to be effective at holding down spending, consistent with the model in chapter 3. These large effects contrast with the negligible impact of modern institutional innovations, like tax and expenditure limits. This juxtaposition illustrates that rules designed in the modern era, when many interests have a stake in how the rules are constructed, are unlikely to reach the level of effectiveness that rules initiated in an earlier era have achieved.

This analysis also used the status of courts to gain leverage on the question of laws' effects. I showed that states with elected courts and no-carryover rules spent less than other states. A robustness check showed that this was due both to the presence of the no-carryover rule and to the presence of elected courts, so the claim that independent courts improve enforcement quality is borne out.

The second contribution of this chapter is to explain the motivation for reform proposals. Using the logic of constituency costs from chapter 3, I show that public dissatisfaction with the process may remain latent for several years, before an exogenous shock prompts reform efforts (which may or may not be successful).

I have also explained why provisions that shut down the government in the event of a budgetary stalemate advantage legislatures and lead to more government spending. This counterintuitive finding demonstrates the importance of strategic interactions in the budget process.

In sum, rule design is inherently a political process, and reforms will often occur after political pressure is applied. Because of the many competing players involved, effective rule design is a challenging endeavor. It is not surprising, then, that newer rules, like tax and expenditure limits, achieve little, while strict balanced budget rules are more effective. Nor is it surprising that many reform attempts, like those in New York State, are unsuccessful. In the final analysis, the deck is stacked against effective reform. This makes the success of balanced budget rules in the U.S. states all the more remarkable.

CHAPTER 6

The Federal Government

The problem doesn't require new legislation because the law is not the problem. We do not need legislation with teeth in it. Congress would still do what it wills, with or without teeth. The problem is the will: It's the unwillingness of Congress to commit to self-discipline. SENATOR CHARLES GRASSLEY (R-IA)

State governments can boast some success in the area of budget rules, but the federal government is not so fortunate. The history of federal budget reform is littered with unrealized dreams of balanced budget amendments to the Constitution, spending caps that merely reflected short-run preferences, and deficit reduction plans gone awry. One reason for these failures is that the U.S. federal government is under little pressure to abide by budget limitations; as a central government, it is free to inflate away many financial problems by printing more money.[1] This is just one example of the additional powers conferred on federal governments that make budgetary rule design and enforcement that much more challenging. This chapter builds on the theory developed in chapters 3 and 4 to explain why budget reform is unlikely to be implemented successfully at the federal level. In discussing both actual and proposed reforms, I will demonstrate why rules have failed in the past and why prospects for successful reform are dim.

The two primary reasons for the failure of federal budget reform are political compromise and enforcement challenges. The diversity of powerful interests at the federal level means that rules will often have to be designed suboptimally, as part of a compromise, in order to secure a winning coalition.[2] Put another way, preference heterogeneity is likely to produce ineffectively designed rules. In some cases this means that the rules will be intentionally designed with loopholes or other inefficiencies. In addition, those who want a rule to have little impact may demand certain provisions that will make successful implementation of that rule more difficult (Moe 1989). The consequence of political compromise is that rules will sometimes be doomed from their inception.

The second stumbling block to effective implementation of budget rules is the challenge of enforcement. Ex ante preferences for budgetary discipline are often inconsistent with ex post preferences for particularized spending. A well-designed rule must deal with such contingencies. The federal government is especially vulnerable to poor enforcement; Congress has fewer opportunities for external enforcement than state and local governments since constitutional amendments are difficult to enact at the federal level. Further, as we will see later in the chapter, any constitutional amendment that survives the Congress is likely to be ineffective in practice.

These two problems can be characterized as political problems and design problems. Even if the design problem is solved, the political problem will remain. Federal budget reform reflects both political and design failures. As in the model in chapter 4, I will show that Congress often does not have the desire to implement effective rules because they conflict with preferences. The result is a litany of unsuccessful reforms. Using the framework developed in chapter 3, I will explain why effective externally enforced rules are unlikely to emerge at the federal level. This chapter begins by briefly reviewing the history of federal budget reform. A detailed analysis of recent reform efforts follows, along with an analysis of several proposed reforms.

Federal Budget Reform: Problems and Possibilities

In the twentieth century, there were three major sets of reforms to the budget process.[3] The first was the 1921 Budget and Accounting Act, which reflected the beginnings of the "institutional presidency" (Moe 1985). The act, in an attempt to make budgetary policymaking holistic, directed the president to propose an executive budget every year. While not binding, the executive budget was thought to set the agenda for subsequent negotiations. As Moe (1985) notes, President Franklin Delano Roosevelt used the Bureau of the Budget (BOB) to pursue his policy ends and consolidate power. Subsequent presidents followed suit.

The modern federal budget process was born in 1974 with the Congressional Budget and Impoundment Control Act. This act had the effect of placing Congress on a level playing field with the president by creating the Congressional Budget Office as a counterweight to the executive branch's Office of Management and Budget (OMB).[4] In addition, it created congressional budget committees charged with preparing a budget resolution concerned with overall totals. The result was a two-track budget process, with the president and the Congress each developing a budget blueprint. These changes were not meant to secure any particular outcome but instead were concerned with the process surrounding budget creation.[5]

The dramatic increase in the federal budget deficit in the early 1980s prompted the passage of the Gramm-Rudman-Hollings Act, which set limits on deficit spending. This legislation and its descendant, the Budget Enforcement Act of 1990, are discussed below. Unlike previous reforms, which were concerned with process and the balance of power between the branches, these rules were focused on specific policy outcomes.

These three waves of reform indicate that reforms are divisible into two types: those with particular policy outcomes as goals and those that focus on process without concern for specific outcomes. Of the two types, it is the policy-related reforms that have been particularly unsuccessful at the federal level. Public administration scholars have tended to favor process-related reforms, focusing on the potential of rules to reinforce or facilitate an existing consensus about policy (Congressional Budget Office 1993; Schick 1996; Davis 1997; Joyce 2005). Such reforms are unlikely to improve the ability of legislators to reshape a broken system. A rule that merely reinforces existing preferences may be successful procedurally, but it may also reinforce existing pathologies in legislative decision making.

Despite this, public administration scholars caution against the use of rules to foster agreement where none exists. Yet it is precisely in these cases that rules have an impact on policy outcomes. Schick writes, "The logic of the budget process is that a willful majority should be permitted to adopt whatever budget policy it wants" (1996, 43). This view is flawed in that it portrays budget policy as a monolithic whole. In reality, budget policy is multidimensional. There is often agreement on the macro-level outcome (say, a balanced budget or reduced spending) but disagreement on micro-level outcomes (which areas to cut). It is here that a binding rule could help achieve the changes that the majority would prefer but cannot achieve through standard "process" reforms.

An apt analogy is a diet. Suppose an individual wishes to lose ten pounds. A public administration scholar might argue that an effective diet is one that sets out an eating plan that, if followed, will lead to the desired weight loss. But, while the dieter may genuinely want to lose the weight, he may still find it hard at any given moment to choose not to eat the extra slice of pizza that is tempting him. An effectively designed diet is one that not only sets out a plan for weight loss but also sets out a mechanism that reconciles one's immediate temptations with one's long-term goals. Effective design, therefore, requires attention to both process and policy (as well as their interaction).

Many, such as Schick, believe that the short-term will of the majority cannot be thwarted. They also suggest that rules that mandate certain sorts of outcomes effectively write their own obituaries, since a majority determined to violate the rules can do so through legislative sleight-of-hand. As Schick puts it, "In the long run, efforts to frustrate majority rule by dictating certain outcomes and precluding others are almost sure to fail. Even the proposed balanced budget amendment to the Constitution invites, as similar state government strictures have shown, financial legerdemain, bookkeeping gimmicks, and other ploys that enable the majority to express its will while giving lip service to the principle of budgetary balance. On matters as vital as the budget, the majority will win out, even if its hands appear to be tied" (1996, 45).

Certainly, it is well-established by the courts that entrenchment, whereby a current Congress binds the actions of a subsequent Congress, is unconstitutional (McGinnis and Rappaport 1995; Fisk and Chemerinsky 1997), and it is also thought by some that rule changes are to be voted on only by majority rule (Fisk and Chemerinsky 1997).[6] The classic statement is from jurist William Blackstone, who wrote, "Acts of parliament derogatory from the power of subsequent legislatures bind not" (1765, 90). This perspective was quickly adopted by the U.S. Supreme Court in *Fletcher v. Peck* (1810), where Chief Justice John Marshall wrote, "The principle asserted is, that one legislature is competent to repeal any act that a former legislature was competent to pass; and that one legislature cannot abridge the powers of a succeeding legislature" (10 U.S., at 135).[7]

Congress is responsible for its own fate, so Schick is correct that there is no way to thwart the will of the majority. Instead, clever mechanisms must be devised to tie the hands of legislators who *prefer* to have their hands tied. In other words, if legislators do not want to diet, no rule will make them do so. If legislators did want to diet, a rule could help reconcile their long-term goals with their short-term desires. Unfortunately, public administration scholars are correct in asserting that such nonconstitutional rules are unlikely to be successful. Moreover, constitutional rules, if produced through the legislative process, may cause more problems than they solve. This chapter reflects pessimism about the likelihood of successful federal budget reform. The remainder of this chapter explores several reforms that are illustrative of these problems and examines the pitfalls in proposed reforms.

The Cure Was Worse than the Disease: Gramm-Rudman-Hollings and Deficit Reduction

In the mid-1980s concern about the rapidly growing federal budget deficit reached a fever pitch.[8] From the 1981 to 1985 fiscal year, the total budget deficit, which includes the Social Security trust fund, ballooned from 79 to 212 billion in nominal dollars (the number most often reported by the press and elected officials).[9] As a percentage of GDP, the deficit had reached its highest level since World War II. The precarious state of the federal budget spurred calls for reform.

Three senators, Phil Gramm (R-TX), Warren Rudman (R-NH), and Ernest Hollings (D-SC), felt that the only way to force deficit reduction was to mandate it. To accomplish this, the senators tacked the change on to a "must-pass" debt ceiling increase rather than building support for the measure gradually. Many members of Congress viewed the rules as strong medicine; they would have preferred not to swallow it but still believed that it was needed if they were to have a chance of reversing the trend of worsening deficit spending. Senator John Danforth (R-MO) told his colleagues, "I cannot say that any of these proposals represents my first choice for reducing the deficit. My first choice would be responsible congressional action. But Congress has not shown itself to be willing and able to take such action, and it is for that reason that I support the institutional constraints that have been proposed" (1985). Echoing the self-enforcement argument made in this book, Senator Charles Grassley (R-IA) raised the following concerns:

> The changes outlined in this amendment are not ineffective in and of themselves. For me, it is a case of being "once bit, twice skeptical." In 1978, Congress passed a law known as the Byrd-Grassley law that mandated that no deficit spending could occur beginning in fiscal year 1981. That is now a public law. Well, obviously, we have not only deficit spend [*sic*] every year thereafter, but since 1981, we merely doubled the trillion dollar debt. Mr. President, for the past 5 years, Congress has willfully ignored a statute mandating a balanced budget. What makes us think Congress will balance its budget as a result of this amendment? Or any other bill? The problem doesn't require new legislation because the law is not the problem. We do not need legislation with teeth in it. Congress would still do what it wills, with or without teeth. The problem is the will: It's the unwillingness of Congress to commit to self-discipline (Grassley 1985).

This reform was the product of political compromise, leading to a punishment scheme that was not sustainable. Despite any misgivings, and spurred on by fears aroused by the growing deficit, the plan was enacted. President Reagan signed the Gramm-Rudman-Hollings bill (GRH) into law on December 12, 1985 (U.S. Congress 1985), less than three months after the proposal was introduced.[10] The law's main innovation was to require deficit targets for each fiscal year, though it did not specify where cuts had to be made. Under the law, the deficit would be eliminated by 1991 (later extended to 1993). A set of budget reductions was mandated for each year, beginning in fiscal year 1986. The law's deficit targets required the deficit to drop to 171 billion in fiscal year 1986 and then decline until it reached 0 in fiscal year 1991.[11] The actual deficit did not have to meet these targets; rather, the anticipated deficit based on projections at the time of budget passage had to meet the target. According to Gramm, the goal of the legislation was not to mandate a series of required cuts but, rather, to force decisions to be made: "The time has come to set out binding constraints and make Congress make hard decisions, to force the President and Congress to come to grips with a problem that the American people want to see someone come to grips with" (Gramm 1985). If deficit reduction is the goal, the most direct rule is one that mandates that the deficit be reduced.

Though legislators feared large deficits, these worries clashed with preferences for maintaining existing programs. When faced with the decision about whether to meet a deficit target or to increase spending to benefit one's district, the legislator invariably favors increased spending. The law, therefore, was intended to enforce the fiscal discipline that could not be sustained as part of the standard budget process.

The enforcement mechanism in the initial legislation came in the form of a mandatory across-the-board sequestration (i.e., set of spending cuts) if deficit targets were exceeded. Though the Social Security Trust Fund was running surpluses that had the effect of reducing the deficit, it was exempted from those cuts, as were payments on the national debt and other contractual obligations. Also exempted were veterans' pensions, the earned income tax credit, the president's compensation, the postal service, and welfare payments, among other things. In addition, cuts to Medicare were severely limited. The upshot was that most federal spending was off-limits to punitive cuts. This carve-out hastened the demise of GRH because it made enforcement threats noncredible.

Initially, the comptroller general was given the authority to order the sequestering of funds. The comptroller general, who heads the General Accountability Office (GAO), is nominated by the president and approved by the Congress.[12] Unlike other appointees, he is subject to removal not only by impeachment for "Treason, Bribery or other high Crimes and Misdemeanors" but also for other reasons by a joint resolution of Congress. The U.S. Supreme Court ruled in *Bowsher v. Synar* (1985) that this conferred unconstitutional power on Congress to control the execution of the laws, which is an executive branch function. It let stand a fallback provision that would transfer reporting authority to a joint committee of the Congress. This was viewed as constitutional because the Congress is authorized to control the direction of enacted legislation through new legislation, according to *INS v. Chadha* (1983). This fallback position was untenable, though, because it required Congress to pass legislation each time it wanted to trigger a sequester. Such an eventuality is exactly what legislators wanted to avoid in crafting the law. Congress subsequently rewrote the law to give the executive branch's Office of Management and Budget (OMB) the power to trigger the sequesters.

The Court's decision raised the bar, perhaps only slightly, for enforcement success. Congress could always change the law (as it later did). From an enforcement perspective there was little difference in having authority for enforcement in an agency subject to direct oversight by the Congress versus an executive branch–controlled group. It may have been slightly easier to fire the comptroller general than to change deficit-reduction legislation, but Congress's fundamental political control remained. In this sense, GRH relied on endogenous enforcement. For enforcement to be successful, the threat of cuts would have to be sufficient to provide legislators with the political cover to make tough spending decisions. If the threat were too great, however, it would make the punishments so incredible that they would lack a deterrent effect.

The design of the enforcement mechanism all but guaranteed that the threats would lack credibility. By exempting so much of the budget from sequestration, smaller programs (many with vocal constituencies with much to lose) would be subject to severe cuts in the event of sequestration. Legislators concerned with reelection would therefore be under severe pressure to prevent those cuts from taking place, which would in turn jeopardize the political will to continue with deficit reduction.

For GRH to work, legislators would have to be willing to make smaller cuts in a wider set of programs in order to avoid the threat of potentially devastating cuts to a smaller group of programs. It was clear that this enforcement mechanism was doomed from the get-go because reelection-motivated members of Congress could not allow such devastating cuts to occur. Remember, GRH was legislation, not a constitutional amendment, and therefore could be changed at will. At one point, GRH authorized the OMB to make cuts of over 30 percent to both defense and unprotected discretionary spending (U.S. Senate 1998, 10). Clearly, such a move would have been political suicide. Not surprisingly, the Congress subsequently scuttled the law as part of the Budget Enforcement Act (BEA) of 1990 (U.S. Congress 1990).

Gramm-Rudman-Hollings failed because the enforcement mechanism was not credible. Congress's power to change the process was unconstrained (save for a presidential veto, subject to override). As soon as punishments became too harsh, Congress could (and did) change the rules. In addition, by focusing on anticipated rather than actual deficits, the result depended heavily on budgeting assumptions. As Thurber (1995, 143) put it, "When the budget game gets too hard, the members change the rules."

To complete the analysis, I must consider the counterfactual: What would deficits have looked like had the Gramm-Rudman-Hollings legislation not been enacted? Assessing the impact of the law statistically is challenging; economists who have attempted to do so have reached widely varying conclusions (Poterba 1997). Here I will use the theory proposed in this book to assess this counterfactual. The actual and GRH-mandated deficits are plotted in figure 6.1. Two countervailing forces are at work. On the one hand, the symbolic aspects of GRH may have led legislators to reduce the deficit. The bill was a very public signal that the Congress was committed to deficit reduction. To the extent that symbolic aspects of GRH loomed large, deficits might have been lower than in the law's absence. In this way, constituency costs may have made violations of GRH undesirable.

On the other hand, the law may have led to larger deficits. Legislators could insure against enforcement by radically increasing the deficit, be-

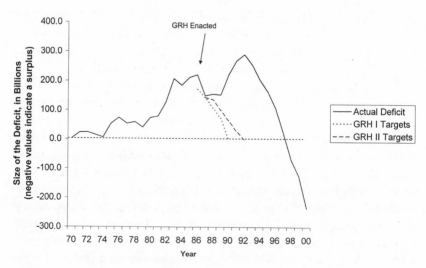

Figure 6.1 Gramm-Rudman-Hollings and deficit reduction

lieving that enforcement was unlikely to occur if the cuts required became too large. Knowing this, the logical move was to miss the budget targets by a large margin, thus simultaneously funding desired programs and avoiding harsh cuts. Thus, it is unclear whether GRH had an impact on deficits. What is clear is that it repeatedly missed its targets and was legislated out of existence in 1990 with the passage of the BEA.

The BEA did not mandate adherence to strict deficit targets, though flexible targets were a component of the law. Instead the focus was on discretionary spending caps as well as pay-as-you-go (PAYGO) procedures that prevented tax cuts or new direct spending (which is established by legislation and does not require yearly appropriations) that was not deficit-neutral. PAYGO required that additional new government programs had to be offset by equivalent cuts, and tax cuts had to be matched by spending cuts. However, the procedures did nothing to deal with increases in the costs of existing direct spending programs like Social Security or Medicare. Enforcement was via points of order, which enable a member of Congress to ask the chair for a ruling on whether legislation violates chamber rules, as well as a sequestration procedure similar to the one in GRH. This procedure was more realistic than the enforcement mechanism in GRH, because sequestration would only be utilized if new programs or spending were not offset by cuts; existing commitments were safe. In this way, the goals of the BEA were more modest than those of GRH. The impact on the overall budget was likely to be small. At the time the law was passed, mandatory spending on items like Social Security and interest on the debt consumed 60 percent of the federal budget, up from one-third in 1962. Ironically, the very line items that were consuming a (rapidly) increasing share of the federal budget were untouched by the process.

The BEA was viewed as a success in part because caps on discretionary spending were heeded in the budget process. Of course, there were loopholes in the law that enabled these caps to be avoided at times. These loopholes included changes in the timing of spending or the categorization of non-urgent spending as an exempt "emergency appropriation" (with Congress defining an emergency). For the most part, the caps were honored because the goals were more modest and the sacrifice required to adhere to the caps was minimal, as the caps required that discretionary spending increase at a lower rate than in the past.

The provisions of the BEA expired after a certain time, and needed to be renewed. Once they expired, the caps and PAYGO procedures would be reinstated only if they were consistent with current spending preferences. Not surprisingly, the statutory PAYGO rules were allowed to expire in 2002 when they conflicted with the desire to cut taxes without requiring a similar cut in spending. Even when the rules were in effect, there were ways around them, so much so that the Congressional Research Service even prepared a report for Congress titled "Techniques for Preventing a Budget Sequester" (Keith 2002). The discretionary spending caps expired, as well. This, of course, is the problem with all budget rules, belying the typically rosy view of the BEA. The BEA merely reflected existing preferences at a certain point in time, and its provisions were changed as soon as it became an inconvenience.

This analysis may strike some readers as antimajoritarian. After all, if members of Congress prefer higher spending or tax cuts and are reflecting the interests of their constituents, then altering the rules to facilitate those outcomes seems desirable. A distinction must be made, though, between preferences for spending on specific items and overall budgetary discipline. While in principle a legislator may support a PAYGO procedure, violating PAYGO when it means new spending or tax cuts for one's constituents may prove to be too great a temptation. Rational action may lead to collectively suboptimal outcomes (and rules). The bottom line is that Congress has been unable to police itself effectively and make the difficult decisions that have long-run benefits but require short-run sacrifice. Short-run gain prevails every time.

This view is not universally shared by scholars or practitioners of the budget process. A Congressional Budget Office analyst has observed, "Spending controls that have attempted to force budgetary outcomes in advance of the substantive policy changes needed to reach those outcomes have been unsuccessful, while those that have set forth and enforced budget policies forged by a consensus have proven more effective in controlling spending and reducing the deficit. Spending disciplines that require policy changes for which a consensus does not yet exist may lead to budgetary evasions and other problems that only further complicate spending control" (Davis 1997, 10–11). As a Congressional Budget Office document noted, "Budget procedures are much better at enforcing deficit reduction agreements than at forcing such agreements to be reached" (Congressional Budget Office 1993, 86). This argument mirrors the preference-reinforcement perspective described earlier in the context of BEA, and it is a concession to the enforcement problem described in this book. The ideal is a rule that would enable legislators to reach goals otherwise unobtainable through standard negotiations. For instance, a credible enforcement mechanism for GRH could potentially have led to zero deficits if legislators believed that there would be consequences for missing the targets. The failure of congressional budget reform reflects enforcement as well as design challenges.

What are the prospects, then, for effective budget rules at the federal level? The remainder of this chapter considers two possible rules, both of which rely on external enforcement. The first, a balanced budget amendment, is perennially on the congressional agenda and demonstrates the problems with political compromise. The second, a rule that requires supermajorities to increase spending year to year, was proposed by two constitutional law scholars.

Prospective Analysis: A Constitutional Balanced Budget Rule

Many observers are skeptical of Congress's ability to self-police, leading to calls for constitutional provisions to influence the budget process. One such provision, a balanced budget amendment, has been floated since the country's founding (Savage 1988), though the first real shot at passage did not arrive until the 1980s (U.S. Senate 1995). A 1995 attempt came close to overcoming the first hurdle, a two-thirds majority in the House and Senate; although the amendment handily passed the House, it failed by one vote in the Senate. Senator Mark Hatfield of Oregon, the only Republican to vote against the amendment, was excoriated by his party, with many calling for punishment to be meted out by party leaders. Consistent with the mores of the Senate, Hatfield emerged unscathed. The balanced budget amendment has since languished, coming up for a floor vote only twice since then (in 1996 and 1997). While the goal of deficit-free spending may be laudable, a constitutional amendment is unlikely to be effective at eliminating the deficit for two reasons. First, the amendment would be the product of political compromise and, as such, would contain loopholes rendering it ineffective. Second, these loopholes would render impotent the special type of enforcement implied by a constitutional amendment, leaving only the constituency costs for violating the spirit of the amendment to provide enforcement.

Over the past two decades, many variants of the balanced budget amendment have been proposed. The purpose here is not to recount the details of each iteration but, rather, to glean from the record evidence that speaks to whether such an amendment would have an effect on outcomes. In particular, a close reading suggests that the proposed amendment would routinely be violated unless its presence imposed such high constituency costs that members of Congress felt compelled to abide by it even under difficult circumstances. The 1995 version of the proposed amendment came the closest in recent memory to passing both the House and the Senate, so it is the focus here. Figure 6.2 presents its text. Subsequent versions of the amendment have remained remarkably similar.

The amendment requires that the budget be balanced in each fiscal year, except in times of war or military conflict. A supermajority is required for Congress to approve deficit spending or to increase the national debt. Other technical provisions lay out definitions of receipts and outlays and specify a date for the amendment to take effect. This proposed constitutional amendment was the product of compromise, and as we have seen, compromise often renders rules ineffective or, worse, produces perverse outcomes. Other proposed revisions, not included in this version of the amendment, include exempting Social Security and infrastructure spending from deficit calculations, and requiring a three-fifths majority in each chamber to approve tax increases.

Many of these provisions would hamper the rule's effectiveness. Exempting times of war and military conflict opens the doors to other spending increases or tax cuts. This will exacerbate the fiscal problems wrought by war, making a return to fiscal discipline in the postwar era more difficult, since the spending cuts or tax increases required may not be politically palatable. The same is true for exempting Social Security or infrastructure from deficit calculations. Perhaps most significantly, the supermajority provisions are an easy escape hatch for anyone wishing to circumvent the rule without either reducing spending or increasing taxes. If one can secure a three-fifths majority to pay for deficits by issuing debt, difficult choices are postponed. Moreover, building a three-fifths majority may require that additional goodies be doled out, thus leading to potentially higher spending and potentially greater deficits in the absence of tax increases. As the distributive politics model showed, the impact of a balanced budget rule is to decrease spending, relative to no rule. However, if we compare a balanced budget proposed under majority rule to deficit spending approved by supermajority rule, as the amendment would require, spending is considerably higher under supermajority rule. In other words, the presence of an escape hatch could worsen fiscal policy relative to an ironclad balanced budget rule. If the choice is between an austere budget that raises the ire of constituents or deficit spending with goodies for many, the (bipartisan) choice for legislators will be clear.

The amendment is also problematic for what it leaves unsaid. Section 1 is notably ambiguous about when deficits are to be measured, and a Senate committee report on the proposal notes that this omission is intentional (U.S. Senate 1995). The committee specifically envisions that Congress may allow for deficit carryovers from one fiscal year to the next or, alternatively, may require only that the budget be balanced at the beginning of a

104th CONGRESS
1st Session
H. J. RES. 1

JOINT RESOLUTION

Proposing a balanced budget amendment to the Constitution of the United States.

Resolved by the Senate and House of Representatives of the United States of America in Congress assembled (two-thirds of each House concurring therein), That the following article is proposed as an amendment to the Constitution of the United States, which shall be valid to all intents and purposes as part of the Constitution when ratified by the legislatures of three-fourths of the several States within seven years after the date of its submission to the States for ratification:

`Article--

`SECTION 1. Total outlays for any fiscal year shall not exceed total receipts for that fiscal year, unless three-fifths of the whole number of each House of Congress shall provide by law for a specific excess of outlays over receipts by a rollcall vote.

`SECTION 2. The limit on the debt of the United States held by the public shall not be increased, unless three-fifths of the whole number of each House shall provide by law for such an increase by a rollcall vote.

`SECTION 3. Prior to each fiscal year, the President shall transmit to the Congress a proposed budget for the United States Government for that fiscal year in which total outlays do not exceed total receipts.

`SECTION 4. No bill to increase revenue shall become law unless approved by a majority of the whole number of each House by a rollcall vote.

`SECTION 5. The Congress may waive the provisions of this article for any fiscal year in which a declaration of war is in effect. The provisions of this article may be waived for any fiscal year in which the United States is engaged in military conflict which causes an imminent and serious military threat to national security and is so declared by a joint resolution, adopted by a majority of the whole number of each House, which becomes law.

`SECTION 6. The Congress shall enforce and implement this article by appropriate legislation, which may rely on estimates of outlays and receipts.

`SECTION 7. Total receipts shall include all receipts of the United States Government except those derived from borrowing. Total outlays shall include all outlays of the United States Government except for those for repayment of debt principal.

`SECTION 8. This article shall take effect beginning with fiscal year 2002 or with the second fiscal year beginning after its ratification, whichever is later.'.

Figure 6.2 Proposed Balanced Budget Amendment to the U.S. Constitution, as passed by the House (U.S. House 1995)

fiscal year. After all, section 6 of the amendment specifically authorizes the Congress to enforce the provision so, in principle, Congress could waive the rule as needed. More generally, Congress can write implementing legislation that renders the requirement toothless. As long as this legislation is reasonable, the Supreme Court will be loath to intercede.[13] Even if the Court did intervene, it would be unlikely to order the Congress to engage in a specific remedy. The Senate committee report notes that members of Congress swear an oath to uphold the Constitution (U.S. Senate 1995, 9). Still, if one person's violation is another's creative accounting, this admonition becomes close to meaningless.

Constituency costs may represent another hope for enforcement, since there will often be enough wiggle room built into any amendment that one can adhere to the letter of the law while still violating its spirit. Real enforcement would come from penalties that could be incurred from the public for using budgetary gimmicks. This type of enforcement will be most effective only when the supermajorities needed to incur deficit spending are not present. Presumably, if a supermajority votes for it, the public will not punish legislators for violating the amendment. Given that the public now expects deficit spending as a matter of course, constituency costs may not be a viable enforcement mechanism.

Prospective Analysis: Supermajority Requirements for Spending Increases

As chapters 3 and 5 showed, a balanced budget rule and a spending limit are procedurally similar in many cases. If budgets must be balanced, the setting of a spending limit implies a set of tax rules that must also be implemented. In some cases, the two may diverge; a reasonable modification would be to impose spending limits, regardless of deficit spending, since in practice balanced budget amendments often can be circumvented through creative accounting. McGinnis and Rappaport (1999) suggest a constitutional amendment requiring that spending in excess of 90 percent of the previous year's budget receive a supermajority of votes. The rule works as follows, simplifying their argument for presentational ease:

1. Legislation requiring spending in fiscal year t must be approved by a simple majority if total spending in that year is no more than 90 percent of spending in year $t-1$.
2. Spending laws that do not meet requirement 1 require a supermajority vote in both houses (say, three-fifths).

3. The president reserves the right to sequester amounts in excess of 90 percent of spending if passed by simple majority rule.

I use the baseline model in chapter 3 to analyze the impact of this rule. I assume that enforcement is perfect and that the legislature does not set the size of spending in advance of the agenda setter allocating projects. For simplicity, I also assume that the 101 legislators are perfectly patient and that b and c, which appear in the net benefit function, are both 1.

Assume that the legislature began playing the game from the baseline model in chapter 3 at time t and that the new rule is implemented prior to bargaining beginning in the second period, at time $t + 1$. Based on the results from chapter 3, spending in the first period, at time t, will equal $1,325.50. (See the app. D for an explanation.) What happens in the next period?

The agenda setter has two choices. Either he can adhere to the 90 percent rule or he can build a supermajority coalition and avoid this limitation. Recall from chapter 3 that in the absence of any constraints on agenda setter behavior, supermajority coalitions will produce lower spending relative to majority coalitions. In fact, under three-fifths supermajority rule, he spends only $860.50. In addition, the agenda setter has to give out more goodies as the size of the coalition increases. Therefore, he has no incentive to build a supermajority coalition, so he builds a simple majority coalition and spends $1,192.95.

Now let's move to period $t + 2$. Here the agenda setter must decide between spending $1,192.95 × 0.9, or $1,073.66, under majority rule, or to spend $860.50, the equilibrium supermajority level of spending. Again, there is no incentive to build a supermajority coalition, since the only condition under which the agenda setter would want to do so is in order to spend more than the 90 percent rule permits.

I can calculate the level of spending at which the agenda setter is indifferent between adhering to the limit under majority rule and building a supermajority coalition, unconstrained by this limit. That value is $846.94. For the first four periods after the rule is enacted (periods 2–5), the 90 percent rule will be adhered to because spending under supermajority voting will be lower than what the 90 percent limit permits. Starting in period 6, the limit would force spending below what could be obtained by supermajority voting. The agenda setter's calculation shows that supermajority voting makes him better off in this case, so he proposes the higher spending level and secures a supermajority coalition. In period 7, the agenda setter chooses between building a majority coalition at $0.9 × $860.50 = $774.45 or violating this limit and setting spending at $860.50 again with a supermajority coalition. Again, he chooses to violate the limit, since spending under the 90 percent rule would fall below $846.94. In period 8, again the limit is $774.45, and so the legislature has reached a new "steady-state" level of spending at $860.50. The impact of the budget rule, then, is to lower spending permanently by 35 percent.

Now let's examine what happens when the size of spending is set by the legislature, with the 90 percent rule also in effect. Recall that in the model in chapter 3, the legislature will set spending at a higher level when supermajorities are required for budget passage. When faced with a new rule limiting spending to 90 percent of the previous year's expenditures, the legislature will have a choice: one option is to set spending within that limit, thereby requiring the agenda setter to enact spending under majority rule; a second option would be to set a new, higher spending limit that will require the agenda setter to build a supermajority coalition. The legislature will always prefer the latter. What is at issue is whether the agenda setter will prefer the new, higher level of spending to the lower level of spending he could obtain via majority rule (while still adhering to the cap). In simulations, I find that the agenda setter will always prefer the higher level of spending. While the agenda setter does not like to add more members to his coalition, increased spending makes it advantageous to do so.

Notice, then, that the impact of the 90 percent rule is to increase spending when the legislature sets spending in advance of allocations, but not when the agenda setter acts in the absence of legislature-imposed constraints. The rule works in the latter case because the agenda setter does not want to add members to his coalition; he will do so only when the reduction in spending becomes so significant that adding members to his coalition becomes the lesser of two evils. In the other case, the legislature wants to see supermajority coalitions built. Therefore, it sets a spending limit higher than what the 90 percent rule allows, thereby necessitating supermajorities in favor of the spending. Importantly, the welfare of the legislature increases in both cases, so this rule is welfare improving. This reinforces a point from chapter 3: the size of spending is only one piece of the puzzle. Spending at any level might be very efficient or very inefficient. Unfortunately, efficiency is not as easily measured as spending. Overall, the 90 percent rule makes effective use of the interaction between spending limits and supermajority rule. The supermajority requirement is not so much an escape hatch (as it is with a balanced budget amendment) as a means to require greater support for all spending increases. While it operates in a different way for each version of the model I considered, in both cases the supermajority requirement improves welfare.

We can also model spending with a simple spatial model, where the legislature merely sets the size of the budget and is unconcerned with the allocation of those funds. Assume that spending can range from nothing to $1, with every legislator aiming to get spending closest to his or her ideal level. Assume that 101 legislators' ideal points are evenly arrayed from 0 to 100 cents. The median voter is located at 50 cents; this voter is also the proposer. Assume that the previous year's spending level was 50 cents. In the next period, the proposer has a choice: she can offer 45 cents, or she can seek a supermajority of sixty-one legislators to secure spending larger than 45 cents. Since sixty-one legislators cannot be found who prefer some larger amount of spending to 45 cents, 45 cents will be successful. The same question will be raised in the next period: find sixty-one legislators who prefer spending more than 40.5 cents, or propose 40.5 cents. Again, 40.5 cents wins. Now sixty-one legislators prefer spending more than 36.45 cents (90 percent of 40.5). The median voter needs to secure the vote of the fortieth to hundredth legislators, so he offers 43.55 cents, which will be successful. Then, in the next period, 90 percent of this (39.2 cents) will be the spending level enacted. The process will iterate until it reaches a steady state at 42.1 cents. By effectively making the status quo lower than the previous year's budget but making upward changes more difficult due to a supermajority requirement, the rule exerts downward pressure on spending. Also, by not being too extreme, it is likely to have an impact (i.e., the punishment is not so extreme as to be impractical to mete out) without risking circumvention.

These simulations suggest a way to insulate against the perverse consequences of rules (i.e., the 90 percent rule leading to higher spending). The goal of the supermajority requirement is to either lower spending or lower the rate of increase in spending. There are two possibilities: the requirement is successful, or it is not. If it is successful, this means that legislators will find some optimal spending level, $I^{*'}$, that is below the previous spending level, I^{*}. If it is not successful, spending $I^{*''}$ is higher than the previous spending level. An easy way to insulate against $I^{*''}$ is to add a provision that spending can never exceed the previous year's outlays, adjusted for inflation, or alternatively, that spending can never increase more than some predetermined amount in any given year, regardless of supermajority requirements. This essentially puts an upper bound on $I^{*''}$, thereby minimizing the downside of any errors. The upper bound on spending prevents any unintended consequences arising from instituting the supermajority requirement.

Lessons

By analyzing both actual and proposed reforms, this chapter has illustrated the challenges of federal budget rule design and enforcement. Rule design requires political compromise, often rendering policies ineffective. This type of compromise is especially prevalent at the federal level, where preferences are typically more heterogeneous than at the local level. The many loopholes written into proposed amendments to the Constitution illustrate this point nicely. Even if the rules are designed to be effective, both exogenous and endogenous enforcement are difficult to achieve because even under the best circumstances, success requires commitment on the part of the enforcers to see that the rules are carried out. This problem is exacerbated at the federal level because fewer commitment devices are at a legislature's disposal. Often the enforcement mechanisms are too harsh, as in Gramm-Rudman-Hollings, or the rules are written so as to hamstring enforcement, as in the proposed balanced budget amendments to the Constitution. Despite the advantages of the 90 percent rule, successful implementation would likely require a constitutional amendment, subject to all of the problems discussed earlier.

The one example of a moderately successful set of spending rules — the BEA — codified the areas in which spending would be restricted and, in doing so, merely reinforced existing preferences. Public administration scholars and practitioners often argue that this is what rules ought to do — reinforce an existing consensus. However, this perspective misses what I view as a key problem in budgeting: the tension between micro-level, short-run pain and macro-level, long-run gain. The analysis in this book suggests that reformers should not be sanguine about the possibility of successfully implementing rules that address this quandary. Even if the enforcement problem is solved by a constitutional amendment, the challenge of political compromise remains. Reinforcing consensus may be the best that reformers can hope for. This hardly seems like a satisfactory outcome of rule making.

Nevertheless, possibilities remain for real and meaningful reform. For example, one means of enforcement, constituency costs, could be effective for enforcing any sort of budget rule, if awareness were high enough. Success here would require the public to reconcile its tastes for particular spending items and fiscal discipline. Another possibility would be to use the approach from chapter 4 and tie budget rules to parts of the organization that are costly to ignore. This same fear of injury has successfully prevented the Senate's filibuster rule from being eroded despite temptations to ignore it on certain key votes. The same principle could work for the design of budget rules but would suffer from the same political compromise problems facing proposals to amend the Constitution.

CHAPTER 7 Conclusion

It's like with the Ten Commandments. Everybody knows
they should abide by it, but everybody is a sinner.
IRISH FINANCE MINISTER CHARLIE MCCREEVEY, DISCUSSING
FAILURES IN EUROPEAN UNION BUDGET RULES

Why mandate deficit reduction when there is already unanimous agreement that deficits are too high? Why write balanced budget amendments into state constitutions when a norm of balanced budgets exists there already? The answers to these questions reflect the main findings of this book. Budget rules act as a constraint on behavior in situations where macro-level and micro-level preferences clash or where preferences are time inconsistent. They are effective when they are designed to account for the larger institutional environment in which they operate and are attached to credible enforcement mechanisms, as state balanced budget rules show. They are ineffective when political compromise produces a rule filled with loopholes or implausible enforcement techniques, as the history of federal budget reform demonstrates.

In this concluding chapter, I will summarize my findings, tying together the various theoretical and empirical results and providing answers to the puzzles introduced in the first chapter. I will then investigate the implications of my findings for reform efforts at the state, federal, and international levels, as well as for policy analysts and legislative practitioners. This chapter concludes with thoughts on the implications of the analysis for institutional design more generally.

Lessons

Institutions are effective only when constraints are properly designed given the environment in which they are operating and when credible external or internal enforcement exists. The central argument of this book is that the conditions required for budget rules to be effective — an appropriate design and a credible enforcement mechanism—will rarely be realized in practice. While theoretical models can point us in the direction of effective budget rules, as chapters 3 and 4 demonstrated, political compromise, unintended consequences, a lack of attention to institutional interactions, and a desire to see rules fail keep theory and practice from meeting.

In chapter 2, I developed the idea that to understand institutional design we must consider both the provisions of a rule and its associated enforcement mechanism. Enforcement can either be external to the organization promulgating the rule or occur within the organization. External enforcement is simple to capture theoretically. Either one can assume perfect enforcement or one can assume that the enforcer has objectives. Internal, or endogenous, enforcement is achieved via repeated interactions or by tying rules to a stable aspect of the organization that is altered only at considerable cost. This framework was utilized to understand budgetary bargaining in the chapters that followed.

Chapters 3 and 4 used distributive politics bargaining models to study the impact of spending limits, supermajority voting rules, and executive veto authority on budgetary outcomes. I first established that, without any of these institutions, distributive politics bargaining produced outcomes that were very inefficient. By focusing on the case of perfect enforcement in chapter 3, I was able to establish that each of the above institutions mitigated these inefficiencies and improved legislative welfare as a consequence. I also demonstrated that spending declined with the presence of spending limits but that the impact of rules requiring the building of supermajority coalitions depended on whether a spending limit was in place. This result demonstrated that institutional interactions are an important component of any study of budget rules. In chapter 5, I demonstrated that the spending limit result matched what we observe in U.S. state spending patterns. Those states with a strict balanced budget rule, enforced by an elected high court, spend less than states without such institutions. In addition, states with strict balanced budget rules react less sharply in the short run to changes in state revenue. Given my argument that rules that work in theory may nonetheless fail in practice, this result may be surprising. But most of these rules were enacted well before the era of the modern state, where existing governmental commitments to varied constituencies fortify the status quo. A recent reform, the tax and expenditure limit, was shown to have little impact on spending outcomes, reinforcing this point.

Suppose a perfect external enforcer is not present. In chapter 3, I showed that courts or agencies may still, even if they have their own interests, act as imperfect enforcers of rules. Moreover, if the public has well-articulated preferences for spending, they may impose constituency costs on legislators who overspend. The more conservative the public relative to the legislature, though, the less likely such a procedure will have any impact. Conversely, for any given spending preference, the more costs the public imposes for exceeding this threshold, the more likely the threshold is to be effective. Constituency costs were used in chapter 5 to explain why reform proposals may emerge suddenly.

The next question is how to understand internal enforcement of budget rules, which is necessary when external enforcement is not viable or is ineffective. In chapter 4, I established the conditions under which the agenda setter's incentive to overspend is tempered by offering him a closed rule on legislation, which gives him a bargaining advantage over an open rule setting. I show that this is only possible under limited conditions, one of these being simple majority rule, which is when the distributive politics problem is at its worst. By tying adherence to a spending limit to fundamental procedures, implementation is sometimes successful. The requirements for success — that the legislature has an incentive to create such a rule to begin with and that the agenda setter will want to abide by it — are often not met in practice.

Chapter 6 demonstrated the problems with internal enforcement, using modern federal budget history as an exemplar. The federal government offers up many examples of unsuccessful attempts at internal enforcement of budget rules. Gramm-Rudman-Hollings legislation was supposed to eliminate the deficit, but it had little effect because too many programs were exempt from mandatory sequestration. This made enforcement of the rules unrealistic. Its replacement, the Budget Enforcement Act of 1990, merely codified existing preferences, and so it did little to change the trajectory of policy.

In all, the empirical evidence demonstrates that, in modern politics, the design of budget rules is a challenging task. Data from the U.S. states show that balanced budget rules enforced by an independent state high court will keep spending down, relative to states without such provisions. Yet these provisions were often in state constitutions from their inception. Modern reforms, like state tax and expenditure limits, were shown to have little impact on spending patterns. Attempts at federal budget reform read like a litany of failures, demonstrating the challenge of effective design there as well.

Given these results, we can return to the puzzles raised in chapter 1.

In 1985, the U.S. Congress passed and President Ronald Reagan signed into law new budget rules designed to eliminate the deficit by the 1990 fiscal year (U.S.

Congress 1985). While the deficit declined initially, by 1991 it had shot up to a level higher than before the law took effect, and the reform is widely considered to have been a colossal failure. On the surface it was deceptively simple, with clear guidelines and a straightforward enforcement procedure. Why did this law fail?

The legislation fell short of reformers' goals in part because the enforcement mechanism was not credible. At one time they required that draconian budget cuts be implemented to enforce the rules. A rule that works well in theory may not work in practice if the punishments are not credible.

Nearly all states have some form of a balanced budget requirement on the books, yet the magnitude of deficits and spending varies greatly across the states. What explains this variation?

Both the details of the rules and the enforcement of the rules have an impact. In some states, budgets need only be balanced in the initial proposals, while in others they must be balanced at the end of a fiscal year. One rule has real bite, the other does not. Similarly, in some states elected courts rule on constitutional matters; in other states appointed courts do. My analysis shows that elected courts tend to keep spending down.

Some states have rules that shut down government if a budget deadline is missed; others do not. Why do states with shutdown provisions spend more than states without such laws?

This finding relies on a result, first shown by Romer and Rosenthal (1978), that the more extreme a status quo or reversion point, the more advantaged is the proposer in bargaining settings with take-it-or-leave-it offers. By making the reversion point, in effect, zero, states that do not allow for some reasonable level of spending in the absence of budgetary agreement advantage the proposer in the process (in this case, the legislature). This result demonstrates the sometimes surprising effects of budget rules.

Why are certain legislative rules, like the Senate filibuster, treated as if they are sacrosanct, while budget rules are often ignored?

Rules like the Senate filibuster affect almost all legislation, while budget rules affect only specific provisions. It stands to reason, then, that the stakes are higher for ignoring basic organizational procedures. The long-term benefits to maintaining the rule will usually outweigh any short-term benefit that is garnered by violating it. It is for this reason that I used a stable aspect of legislatures — amendment procedures — as an enforcement mechanism for a budget rule. By tying the budget rule to an aspect of the organization that is highly valued, the stakes are raised for violations.

Despite the success of constitutional balanced budget rules at the state level, a comparable amendment to the U.S. Constitution is unlikely to be successful at lowering spending or eliminating deficits. Why might we expect rules successful at the state level to falter at the federal level?

The states may have a different set of norms or interests regarding fiscal discipline. For example, states incur a higher cost for deficit spending since they cannot mint money. Though they vary in their success, all states have zero deficits at least as a goal; the same cannot be said for the federal government. The next section provides more detail.

This book has demonstrated both theoretically and empirically that budget rules, whether enforced externally or internally, can be effective. In practice rules may lose some effectiveness because they are not designed by impartial arbiters seeking to maximize social welfare. Rather, they are designed by those with interests that may cause them to derail reform. Add this to the fact that rules are often designed in complex institutional environments, and prospects for success are indeed dim. The one area where budget rules have been successful has been in the U.S. states. One reason for this is that balanced budget rules were constructed in times when governments — for better or worse — did less. The upshot of this is that fewer entrenched interests had a desire to block reform. As chapter 6 demonstrated, constitutional amendments offer the promise of effective enforcement but also the peril of institutional lock-in, as amendments are difficult to alter once enacted. Policymakers must consider these difficult trade-offs when considering new rules. In a time when government provides many goods and services, interested parties may derail reform. It is to this and other consequences of the argument that I now turn.

Consequences of the Argument

Constitutional Budget Reform: Potential and Pitfalls

The findings presented here present a conundrum for policymakers. On the one hand, the evidence from the U.S. states suggests that constitutional rules offer the best opportunity for external enforcement. On the other hand, the evidence from previous attempts to institute a balanced budget amendment at the federal level is not encouraging. This somewhat pessimistic analysis in chapter 6 needs to be reconciled with the relative success of balanced budget provisions in the states, as demonstrated in chapter 5. Why might we expect rules that are successful at the state level to falter at the federal level?

Observers of state governments have argued that balanced budget rules are effective at the state level not because of enforcement but because there is a norm of balanced budgets, as well as market-based limitations on state debt. States have fewer policy instruments at their disposal to engage in deficit spending. As legal scholar Richard Briffault put it, "States balance their budgets not because of their constitutions but because they have little practical alternative" (1996, 63). Unlike the federal government, states have debt ratings to worry about, as well as limits on debt issuance. The norm of balanced budgets is ingrained at the state level, leading to higher constituency costs for continued large deficits. In contrast, deficits are not unusual at the federal level. While the evidence I have presented supports the claim that enforcement matters, these other factors may also work in tandem with state constitutional provisions.[1] Even if an effective constitutional rule is developed at the federal level, its expected impact will be dampened relative to a state rule.

Moreover, the successful passage of a federal balanced budget amendment would require a supermajority in Congress in its favor. To construct such a supermajority would require significant political compromise, which often results in ineffectively designed rules. The design of a constitutional amendment is itself a political process. The seeds of failure may be sown in the negotiations. Earlier, I discussed the balanced budget rule as a policy that garners widespread support. Why, then, would such rancor emerge during the design of a constitutional balanced budget rule? While a legislator may prefer a balanced budget, balanced budget rules are enacted against a backdrop of current circumstances. A given set of spending priorities is already in place, and a balanced budget rule will operate with respect to this starting point. For this reason, legislators may want to insert provisions protecting spending that benefits their constituents or may oppose a balanced budget precisely because it forestalls new types of spending programs due to existing commitments. The success of balanced budget rules at the state level varies based on their severity as well as their enforcement mechanisms. The federal balanced budget amendment that is typically proposed resembles a weak law rather than a strict one.

The third reason why success at the federal level may prove elusive relates to uncertainty. It may not be possible to anticipate all possible institutional interactions, making the impact of a balanced budget rule somewhat unpredictable. This creates a problem when combined with the ability of constitutions to lock in a policy. The risk of locking in a policy that is the product of political compromise and that may lead to unanticipated consequences is therefore large. Briffault (1996) predicts that just as state balanced budget rules are subject to evasion and unintended consequences, behavior at the federal level would be no different. In addition, Briffault (2003) argues that courts may be inappropriate venues to resolve the fundamentally political issues that are at the heart of many budgetary matters. This would be as true at the federal level as it is at the state level.

The very advantages of a constitutional amendment—relative permanency and authoritativeness—can also be drawbacks in a world where political battles will shape the nature of rules. Those who advocate constitutional balanced budget reform as a panacea for all that ails budgeting tend to ignore the risks of such reform. Those who criticize such reforms as unworkable tend to ignore the consequences of inaction. The truth is more complicated than either of these extremes. The associated risks and rewards of a particular constitutional budget reform need to be carefully weighed. Only then can a reasonable assessment of the reform's impact be formulated.

Amendments related to spending are different than other types of amendments that might be added to the Constitution. Budget rules relate directly to how Congress conducts business, and Congress guards its legislative prerogatives jealously. How else can one explain a constitutional amendment prohibiting deficits that may be waived by a supermajority in Congress, when the major purpose of a constitutional provision is to insulate it from change in the short run? Any sort of regulation of congressional behavior, from ethics to elections to campaign finance, suffers from the same problem.

There is an alternative that may offer the benefits of constitutional lock-in without the costs of congressional compromise. The argument above implicitly assumes that a balanced budget amendment would be added to the Constitution via congressional passage followed by ratification by three-fourths of the states. But there are two formal routes to amendment, according to article 5 of the Constitution. The other is for two-thirds of the states to propose a constitutional convention.[2] Amendments that make it through the convention then must be approved by three-fourths of the states. This route has never been used successfully, so there is a great deal of uncertainty surrounding it (Almond 1975). Putting aside these concerns, a convention would solve the problem of members of Congress wishing to protect themselves from outside intervention into internal rules. A convention would not solve the problem of self-interested behavior, though. For instance, states with a large elderly population may attempt to include a provision exempting Social Security from deficit calculations. Still, if state delegates bring to the convention the norms in the states for balanced budgets, they may be more likely to enact a rule that has some teeth.

Of course, other types of budget rules, such as the 90 percent rule discussed in chapter 6 or a budget rule permitting some limited amount of debt, might be considered as part of a constitutional convention, as well. Balanced budget rules might be viewed as too severe a constraint on a government that must be prepared to fight expensive wars, and in fact, some amount of debt may be economically optimal. These sorts of issues will need to be debated as part of the amending process. A constitutional convention may sound like an extreme idea, but it has been proposed from time to time on the issue of term limits and balanced budgets, among other subjects. In the 1970s, thirty-one states called for a convention on the subject of a balanced budget, and Missouri did so in 1983. Since then, three states (Alabama, Florida, and Louisiana) have rescinded this request, though it is unclear whether they can do so. Depending on how the counting is done, then, only two to five more states are needed for a convention to be called.[3] Of course, should a convention be called (or come close to being called), the Congress may preemptively act and pass a balanced budget amendment of their own, so that they can control the design.

Calls for constitutional conventions that have won the support of a significant number of states relate to balanced budgets, legislative apportionment, and the direct election of Senators. On matters related to spending, elections, and campaign finance, Congress has been unable to enact meaningful reforms. Whether the risks of a convention outweigh the potential benefits is a question that is beyond the scope of the present discussion. However, the debate is one worth having.

International Agreements

The arguments in this book, though focused on U.S. policymaking, extend naturally to a comparative context, as well as to international agreements. The challenges of budgetary rule enforcement faced by the European Union (EU) are illustrative in this regard. The 1997 Stability and Growth Pact (SGP) was enacted with the goal of limiting deficits in European Monetary Union (EMU) countries to 3 percent of GDP in difficult economic times, with near-balanced budgets expected in general. In addition, it required that debt not exceed 60 percent of GDP. These were significant hurdles for European countries struggling with bloated budgets.

The creation of a European Central Bank (ECB) and a common monetary unit—the Euro—led to a situation where the EMU countries had a unified monetary policy in conjunction with disparate, nationally controlled fiscal policies. Thus, there was a collective action problem inherent in the EMU. While all countries benefited from fiscal discipline in other countries, each had an incentive to deviate unilaterally and free ride on the discipline of others. This also posed a challenge for the ECB, since the only way it could punish a country engaging in inflationary policy was to raise interest rates across the EMU, thereby punishing all countries (Hancke 2003).

The requirements for admission into the EMU were set as part of the 1992 Maastricht Treaty. One of these requirements was that countries demonstrate that they were on the path toward achieving the economic goals described above. Once countries had been admitted into the EMU, however, there were no provisions for their expulsion. The SGP was put in place as a way to ensure that countries maintained fiscal discipline once admitted.[4] The policy was very straightforward. Countries were required to maintain deficits below 3 percent of GDP except in extraordinary circumstances, such as a fall in real GDP of over 2 percent. Alternatively, countries could show that they were moving toward a deficit below 3 percent of GDP. The underlying theory was that in normal times, the national deficit should be close to zero. This would still allow for greater spending during downturns, which might increase the deficit. The SGP threshold was set so that in moderate downturns countercyclical fiscal policy could be pursued without leading to high deficits.

An International Monetary Fund (IMF) report praised the SGP for being "simple, clearly defined, and transparent" (Annett, Decressin, and Deppler 2005, 7).[5] But as I have shown, the rules are only part of the puzzle. Unfortunately, in the case of the SGP, the other part, enforcement, was poorly designed. Specifically, the SGP's enforcement component, the Excessive Deficit Procedure (EDP), collapsed quickly. Its replacement gave more, not less, discretion to enforcement authorities, thereby making the SGP essentially toothless.

The initial EDP was supposed to work as follows: If triggered by the existing fiscal situation in a given country, the European Commission (EC) would prepare a report on that country's financial situation for submission to the EU's Economic and Financial Affairs Council (ECOFIN). The council's members represent the interests of EU member countries (as opposed to the EC, which represents the interests of the EU). The council then would determine whether an excessive deficit existed. If it determined that no such deficit existed, the procedure came to an end. If it determined that such a deficit did exist, ECOFIN then would require that the excessive deficit be eliminated, typically within one year. If after ten months from the initial report the country in question was determined to still be in violation of the SGP, it would be required to make a deposit based on a formula.[6] If the excessive deficit persisted, the component of the formula directly tied to the size of the deficit would be applied in subsequent years.[7] Deposits would be converted into fines if the country was not in compliance within two years of the deposit being made. There were no sanctions for violating the debt to GDP ratio requirement.

Because ECOFIN is the body authorized to enact fines, the SGP is essentially self-policing. The question becomes whether internal enforcement will succeed here. On the positive side, fines would be levied against individual countries, with the other countries (who are not running excessive deficits) receiving a share of those fines, proportional to their GDP. This provides countries with an incentive to act as effective enforcers. Unfortunately, enforcement of the SGP is not so simple. Enforcement instead is part of a larger set of EU member interactions. This naturally will advantage larger, more powerful countries. Enforcement of the SGP in practice bears this out.

In 2001, Portugal was the first country to miss the 3 percent target, and it was immediately subject to the Excessive Deficit Procedure. In 2002 and 2003, as Europe struggled economically, deficits exceeded the 3 percent benchmark in several key countries, including France and Germany. However, when France and Germany violated the caps, political pressure was enough to prevent enforcement of the rules. The SGP was ignored when it was no longer in the interests of major powers to abide by it. Powerful countries like Germany and France will follow international rules only if it is in their interests to do so. That these countries chose short-term domestic political gain over the long-run benefits of monetary union is not a hopeful sign for the future of international monetary agreements in Europe.

Is this assessment too harsh? One criticism of the SGP is the inflexibility of its rules in combination with harsh punishments. Instead of, say, requiring that deficits average no more than 3 percent of GDP over a certain time period to allow for increased spending in deficit years, the rules mandate deficits less than 3 percent of GDP at all times no matter the circumstances. In addition, fines are substantial. Thus, the problem lies in both design and enforcement.

The Stability and Growth Pact deficit rules have since been rewritten so as to be toothless (or as supporters might say, more flexible). Exceptions for violating the 3 percent cap are more numerous and include spending that aids in European unification and fosters international solidarity. In addition, any economic downturn has become sufficient to justify deficits in excess of 3 percent of GDP. If an excessive deficit is found to exist, the timeline for addressing the deficit is longer than under the original SGP, as well. In short, the EDP no longer has viable threats associated with it. The European Central Bank has harshly criticized these changes.

Despite this seemingly clear failure, many commentators have claimed that the SGP has been a success. The IMF notes that, in anticipation of the EMU, countries dramatically reduced their deficits (Annett, Decressin, and Deppler 2005, 7). An ECB central banker commented that fiscal policy is better with SGP than without it (Gonzalez-Paramo 2005).

Moreover, Rosendorff (2005) argues for a system where deviations due to domestic political considerations are permitted with little or no punishment, in what he refers to as tolerated defection. Given that incentives for rule violations exist, states can implicitly agree to accept certain sorts of defections (with little to no sanctions) with the understanding that they will not be punished either for undertaking similar actions. Rosendorff posits a trade-off, then, between the rigidity of a rule in the short term and its long-run stability. He provides a concrete example of an effective system that allows for deviations: World Trade Organization (WTO) dispute resolution. If countries violate WTO rules, they can pay a fine and promise to bring their actions back into conformity. The rulings are made by an independent body, largely in accordance with well-defined procedures.

In the SGP case, however, sanctions and enforcement were asymmetric and were done "in house" to a large degree. When it became inconvenient, major powers like Germany and France felt free to thumb their noses at the rules. The SGP, in other words, is convenient window dressing for the larger set of negotiations and interactions between sovereign states.

International agreements are fragile and will tend to collapse in the long run unless countries are willing to accept punishments when meted out. France and Germany calculated that they were better off violating the SGP and, in the process, rendering it meaningless, than accepting the pain of abiding by it. No enforcement mechanism can change that. The challenge for Europe is to design a rule that countries will adhere to, even if it means accepting punishments from time to time.

Understanding Reform

My findings also have implications for those who design or evaluate budget rules. Since budget rules may represent the product of compromise, rules are particularly sensitive to the institutional interactions among different provisions. With this in mind, there are some simple but important questions that one can ask when designing or evaluating institutions. Of course, this discussion assumes that the designer is interested in effective rule design. As I have shown, this is often not the case. These questions, while focused on budgeting, apply to the analysis of rules in other domains, as well.

What is the problem to be addressed?

The question sounds obvious, but motivations for reform vary and may work at cross-purposes. For example, in the case of distributive politics, is the problem the size of spending or inefficiency (or both)? As the institutional interactions section of chapter 3 demonstrated, in some cases an increase in total spending mitigates inefficiencies; in other cases inefficiencies are exacerbated.

Rules that solve one problem may lead to new problems. For instance, sales taxes on food are thought to be regressive because they affect the poor more than the relatively well-off. If a sales tax on food is eliminated, then assuming the need to replace that revenue, another tax may be implemented that creates greater distortions and inefficiencies. While eliminating the sales tax on food could still be worthwhile, one cannot ignore the other consequences of such a decision.

What are the preferences of relevant decision makers in the legislative process, and what domains do decision makers care about?

One role of institutions is to take preferences and map them into policy outcomes. As those preferences change, the optimal institutions change as well. The impact of the executive veto on spending depends on the executive's preferred level of spending, relative to the legislature. A liberal executive is unlikely to produce lower spending if his preference is for more spending than what the legislature would spend in the absence of a veto. This principle holds for other sorts of budgetary bargaining.

Moreover, legislators and executives may differ in whether they care about total spending, the allocation of spending, or both. In chapter 3, the executive cared only about the size of spending, not the distribution of spending. The impact of the executive veto on bargaining would be different if he or she had preferences over both the size and distribution of spending. In that case, a line-item veto, under which the executive could strike particular spending items while approving the remainder of the budget, might be a more effective institutional tool.

What is the existing institutional environment like?

The impact of a rule is often contingent on what other institutions are in place. Because organizations are typically complex, with layers of rules, determining which rules will interact is no simple task. Determining where interactions are likely is perhaps more an art than a science. Trial-and-error may be the only way to proceed, and often unintended consequences of reform reflect an unanticipated institutional interaction. For example, if one's goal is to keep spending down, then moving from simple majority rule to a supermajority rule in distributive politics bargaining when a spending limit is in place will not be an effective innovation.

An additional complication is that rules are often enacted piecemeal, rather than as part of a coherent reform effort. The end result can be a hodgepodge of rules that work at cross-purposes and generate complications when attempting to isolate a rule's impact. Moreover, even if a significant reform is proposed, with many different rules, only some components may survive the bargaining process. Due to institutional interactions, the surviving rule may accomplish little or perhaps even backfire.

What are the possible loopholes that might be exploited by those who wish to circumvent the rule?

Modeling loopholes is difficult. No rule is ironclad, and often loopholes are explicitly added into a rule as part of a compromise. That said, when examining a rule, one can think strategically and imagine that working around the rule is a goal for some parties. A researcher studying an existing rule will want to examine how it was implemented, looking for such loopholes. Importantly, a loophole is different from a violation. Loopholes stay within the letter, if not the spirit, of a rule.

Loopholes can take many forms. The rule may have exceptions, or situations under which it does not apply. An example of an exception is a statement of the form: Budgets shall be balanced, except in times of war. The vaguer the language, the less likely the rule is to be effective. Another loophole involves interpreting an action as falling outside the purview of the rule. For instance, in an effort to get around a balanced budget requirement, one can incur an expense today but not pay the bill until the next fiscal year. That spending, therefore, falls outside of the balanced budget rule. A third type of loophole involves creating an organization that is not subject to the rule. For example, governments often create "special purpose" entities to skirt limits on debt issuance and other requirements that apply to routine government spending.

What is the likely impact of the rule, given existing institutional arrangements, preferences, and assuming strategic behavior on the part of those involved in the budgeting process?

While game theory is useful for answering such a question, even a nontechnical analysis that takes into account that individuals are strategic is superior to a naive analysis that assumes that individuals do not respond to incentives or institutional arrangements. For example, a naive perspective on the executive line-item veto would suggest that spending declines as a result of such a rule, since the executive could strike specific line items out of the budget. This view, of course, assumes that proposers do not alter policy proposals in response to the executive's new power.

Legislators may also respond to rules by changing how they vote on proposals, if by doing so they obtain a better outcome. A rule that changes the status quo in the event of a stalemate from a government shutdown to a mostly functioning government will lead some legislators to vote against many more extreme proposals, the drawback to doing so (a shutdown) being eliminated. If a proposal is rejected, the reversion outcome is no longer as bad.

If external enforcement is prescribed, what are the incentives of the enforcers? If internal enforcement is prescribed, is it credible?

While many analyses of a rule's impact assume perfect external enforcement, enforcers may have their own incentives and act accordingly. The proper design of a rule is a necessary but not sufficient condition for effectiveness. Success also requires adequate enforcement. To the extent that the enforcer has incentives at odds with the rules or the wishes of the enforced, enforcement may not be perfect. We saw that courts or bureaucracies would ignore spending limits under certain conditions. We also observed that the public's outrage is only somewhat effective at putting the brakes on spending.

In terms of internal enforcement, the enforcer must have an incentive to police the organization. In legislative settings, the enforcer is a (super)majority of legislators, meaning that following the rules must be in the interests of a majority of legislators at all points in time. If this is not the case, then rules violations will occur. Perhaps some positive number of violations is optimal to ensure the long-run stability of a rule (see the earlier discussion of tolerated defection), but then the question becomes whether the rule binds behavior or is merely a guideline.

What is the procedure for rule enactment? Who is responsible for creating and enacting the rule? If one person is not given unilateral authority to enact rules, is political compromise likely to produce ineffectual rules?

Typically, legislative budget rules emerge within the legislature, and the very preferences that create common pool problems (wanting to secure benefits for one's district at the expense of all other districts) may prevent legislators from enacting effective rules. Most laws affecting the operation of Congress or the behavior of legislators are examples of such rules. Campaign finance law, ethics law, budgetary rule making — all have done little (if anything) to improve the functioning of elections or the legislative process. If the rules are created outside of the legislature, they are more likely to be crafted by individuals who may be able to consider the entire budgetary picture and not suffer from the "common pool disease" afflicting legislators.

In addition, Riker's inheritability problem takes center stage when answering this set of questions. Rule design "inherits" the instability problems prevalent in the policymaking process. For example, if majority rule is used to make decisions on budget rules via a series of votes pitting two alternatives against each other, then the order of votes will sometimes affect the outcome. The procedures used to enact rules matter just as much as, and perhaps more than, preferences in determining the make-up of budget rules.

Distilling these seven sets of questions into three, one can ask, Will the rule work if perfectly enforced? Is rule enforcement likely to be successful? What rule is likely to emerge from the rule selection process? These questions highlight the intimate link between the design and enforcement of rules. The nature of the rule may influence the answers one receives to the question of whether internal enforcement is credible or whether external enforcers have the incentive to enforce the rule. For example, a rule that requires balanced budgets, even in times of war, may not be credibly enforced within an organization composed of hawks. By thinking about questions of design and enforcement simultaneously, a more complete understanding of institutions results. The final question, regarding the identity of the designers, is often overlooked. A bureaucrat or academic can sit in a room and design the perfect rule, but if elected officials must pass the rule into law, their tinkering will ultimately determine the rule's success or failure.

Implications for Institutional Design

INTERNAL RULES. This study has implications for institutional design beyond the realm of budget rules. Most legislative rules are not externally enforced, so legislative enforcement is largely an internal affair. My study points to the importance of examining both the provisions of a rule and its enforcement mechanism. A rule that does not improve outcomes on average (with improvement defined by members of the organization) is not worth enforcing. An effective rule is enforced, even in cases where it leads to a subpar outcome in the short run, when the long-run advantages of seeing the rule remain in place outweigh the short-run harms. From this perspective, then, rules will be enforced when they improve outcomes or when members of the organization are willing to incur short-run pain for long-run improvements. As I have shown, these conditions are rarely met in the case of budget rules.

Rules affecting all aspects of an organization's functioning, however, should do better because the long-run benefits are presumably larger. A criticism of the Congress from 1995–2006, when it was primarily under Republican rule, is that it did not play by its own rules (Mann and Ornstein 2006). In the House, an increasing number of bills reached the floor under closed or restrictive rules with little debate permitted. The leadership held open votes until its preferred outcome was reached, in violation of House norms (though not House rules). In the Senate, the nuclear option is held up by Mann and Ornstein as an omen of impending changes in this chamber. Are these changes cause for concern? In my view, they are not, and they are perfectly consistent with the evolution of Congress over time.

The perspective that rules are inviolate (or ought to be) places the organization above outcomes. Real-world politics never has, and never will, operate in this way. Legislators must balance a desire to obtain particular policy outcomes with the need to maintain an organization. While some legislators, like Robert Byrd, may place the rules first (or use rhetoric to that effect), a strategic politician will view the rules as means to an end. Rules, of course, must have a certain level of support or else the organization will collapse. This explains why rules are mostly followed even in dysfunctional legislatures. It also explains why rules may be ignored and may be changed, and why this does not portend the end of democracy as we know it. As Binder (1997) notes in her sweeping study of congressional rules changes over time, the majority party often alters rules when such changes are likely to lead to favorable changes in policy. Put simply, "political bodies are designed and altered to secure their members' most preferred outcomes" (Binder 1997, 3). Another important factor is that legislative rules are altered and adapted piecemeal via battles among competing interests, leading to a Congress full of "tensions and contradictions" (Schickler 2001). Because of this, it is not surprising that rules sometimes fail to serve their intended purposes over time or that we have observed periods of great institutional change as well as periods of relative stability in the rules.

The following example illustrates the challenge of maintaining rules over time. During the debate over whether filibusters were permitted on judicial nominees, a concern was raised that the filibuster may be in jeopardy and that the nuclear option, discussed in chapter 2, might be used effectively to kill the filibuster for all legislation. Yet it did not, and it has not. So we can ask, then, under what conditions do the advantages of the filibuster decline so that using the nuclear option becomes an attractive option? To answer this question, one must know both (*a*) the impact of the filibuster on policy and (*b*) the perceived benefits of seeing the rule remain in place. Most studies of legislative rules assume that *b* is high, but this value may change over time. Moreover, as the composition of the Senate changes relative to the status quo, *a* will change.

CONSTITUTIONS. This study is also a cautionary tale about institutional fragility. The challenges of budget rule design underscore how remarkable it is that institutions persist at all. Constitutions are thought to be the surest way to achieve a well-functioning state, yet governments are prone to collapse and most constitutions fail (Weingast 2005). The reason is that for constitutions to survive, they must satisfy some stringent conditions, identified by Weingast (2006): limits on the state must be specified; the constitution must make all parties at least as well off as under the status quo; parties agreeing to the constitution must believe the other parties will abide by it; and the parties to the agreement must be willing to challenge leaders who violate the constitution.

Weingast's perspective is complementary with the argument presented here. His conditions relate to the creation of constitutions; as the key players change, the constitution is threatened as interests may develop that want to move to a new institutional arrangement. For a constitution to remain in force, then, its provisions must continue to serve the interests of the population; it must make them collectively better off than they would be with some other arrangement. In the language of this book, the constitution must still be effective. It also must continue to have a credible enforcement mechanism. In the U.S. case, that mechanism is a Supreme Court that has the (moral) authority to issue rulings that are largely implemented by the other branches of government. Those in power will adhere to court rulings if any short-run policy costs of doing so are outweighed by the prospect of a constitutional crisis.

It is the relative permanence of the U.S. Constitution that makes the American experiment so noteworthy. This stability may be due in part to the creation of a society so wealthy that any damage to its basic foundations would come at too high a cost. This phenomenon is not unlike the tying of budget rules to amendment procedures discussed in chapter 4.

The long-run benefits of seeing the Constitution remain in force outweigh any gains from seeing it fall, both for citizens and for leaders. In developing countries, constitutions are much more fragile.

The lessons of budget rule design can be used to understand constitutions, but this book makes another connection by offering some possibilities for effective institutional design in the budgetary arena. Implementing effective rules is challenging even for well-run governments. Bringing fiscal reform to countries with unstable governments is that much more difficult, since they have yet to solve the constitutional problem. International organizations that attempt to bring American-style fiscal reform to developing countries may be putting the cart before the horse.

Final Words

Too often practitioners and scholars talk past one another. In this book I have connected real-world budgetary institutions and theoretical models to offer a more complete understanding of how budgetary processes work. Practitioners of budgeting often focus on its technical aspects and emphasize process over politics. Scholars often focus on artificial worlds without linking those worlds to real-world budgeting. I have bridged these two perspectives to show how real-world budgetary politics can inform models of the process. This in turn offers new insights into the process itself.

This book has offered a more complete picture of budgetary institutions and their impact on spending outcomes by exploring their design and enforcement. In the process, I hope that I have convinced readers that design and enforcement matter. Perhaps the best evidence for this claim are the pitched battles we have observed over what rules should look like. Battles rage over seemingly technical provisions because in reality, rules matter. Constitutional amendments are debated vociferously because they may alter the nature of bargaining. Rules typically require restraint, and restraint is inimical to an elected official's desire to satisfy constituents. That struggle characterizes budgetary politics in the past and present, and will continue to do so in the future.

Technical Material
for Chapter 3

Description of Model

ACTORS AND PREFERENCES

A legislature L comprises n identical legislators (where n is odd for convenience), who have preferences over a vector of district-specific projects $X = (x_1 \quad x_2 \quad x_3 \ldots x_n)$, $x_i \in [0, \infty]$, indexed by $i \in \{1, 2, 3, \ldots, n\}$.[1] The net benefits of a project for a legislator in district i are

$$bx_i - \frac{1}{2}cx_i^2, b > 0, c > 0.[2]$$

The social net benefit (i.e., social welfare) function for the legislature is

$$\sum_{j=1}^{n} bx_j - \frac{1}{2}c\sum_{j=1}^{n} x_j^2.$$

The social net benefit function implies that the optimal project scale is b/c for each district and that the net benefits of a project decline monotonically as projects move away from b/c (i.e., the function is single peaked).[3] The net benefits from X for legislator i are

$$NB_i(X) = bx_i - \frac{1}{2n}c\sum_{j=1}^{n} x_j^2.$$

The benefits of the projects do not spill over into other districts (i.e., no positive externalities are present), and districts share the total cost of projects equally. Given this function, legislator i's ideal vector of projects consists of $x_i = nb/c$ and $x_j = 0 \; \forall j \neq i$. The legislators in this model, therefore, prefer projects that are larger and more expensive than the efficient level, b/c.

LEGISLATIVE ORGANIZATION

A legislature L must select a vector of projects $X = (x_1 \quad x_2 \quad x_3 \ldots x_n)$. The game is an infinite-horizon bargaining model with the following structure. Voting takes place via a q-rule, $q \geq (n + 1)/2$, where q is the minimum number of legislators who must approve a proposal for it to pass. For example, simple majority rule is reflected by $q = (n + 1)/2$ and unanimity rule is reflected by $q = n$. Let x represent the size of the proposer's project, and y the size of projects for those members who receive an offer from the proposer.[4]

At the beginning of every period, nature selects a legislator at random to serve as an agenda setter. Each legislator's probability of being selected is $1/n$. The agenda setter makes a proposal that consists of a project for each district, with a possible project size being zero. The legislature, operating under a closed rule (i.e., no amendments allowed), then votes on the proposal. If the proposal receives at least q votes, it is accepted, and the game ends. If the proposal is rejected, nature selects a new agenda setter at random, and he offers a new proposal. The game continues indefinitely until an agreement is reached. In the spending limit version of the model, the legislature selects the size of spending, I, before the agenda setter is chosen.

Delay in bargaining is accounted for by a discount factor, $\delta \in (0, 1]$, with a payoff in period t ($t = 1, 2, \ldots, \infty$) being discounted by δ^{t-1}. Discounting occurs in the closed rule model after a bill is rejected. The discount factor is assumed to be 1 in the constituency costs model. A legislator who is indifferent between voting for or against a proposal is assumed to vote for it. To eliminate equilibria that involve legislators voting against legislation that gives them higher utility than the alternative or voting for legislation that gives them lower utility than the alternative, weakly dominated strategies are also ruled out.

EQUILIBRIUM CONCEPT

The equilibrium concept is symmetric subgame perfect Nash restricted to the consideration of stationary strategies, in which players must take the same actions at every node in which the game is structurally identical.[5] This means that in every period, the same equilibrium offers will be made.[6]

Propositions and Proofs

The proof of proposition 1 solves the baseline model for a general q-rule. Substituting $(n + 1)/2$ for q gives the result for the baseline simple majority rule case. Letting q vary allows one to consider the supermajority case. Proposition 2 solves the baseline model with a spending limit, again for any q-rule. The comparative statics discussed in the main text are based on a computer simulation in some cases and on analytical solutions in others. The proof of Proposition 3 solves the baseline model with the addition of constitutency costs and a spending limit exogenously given as V. In this model, the discount factor is assumed to be 1 (i.e., legislators are perfectly patient).

PROPOSITION I: BASELINE CLOSED RULE MODEL WITH q-RULE. *The symmetric subgame perfect Nash equilibrium in stationary strategies is as follows. Define*

$\lambda^* =$

$$\frac{2\delta(q-1)-n+\sqrt{[2\delta(q-1)-n]^2-(q-1)[2\delta+(1-\delta)n][n(\delta+1)-2\delta(q-1)]}}{n+\delta n-2\delta(q-1)}.$$

In every period, the agenda setter proposes $y^* = \lambda^* bn/[(1+\lambda^*)(q-1)c]$ *to* $(q-1)$ *legislators and* $x^* = bn/[(1+\lambda^*)c]$. *In every period, those members who receive an offer of at least* y^* *vote for it, and all other legislators vote against it. The agenda setter accepts offers of at least* y^*, *and since* $x^* \geq y^*$, *the agenda setter votes for the proposal.*

PROOF OF PROPOSITION I (BASELINE CLOSED RULE MODEL WITH q-RULE). The agenda setter chooses x and y to maximize

$$bx - \frac{c}{2n}[x^2 + (q-1)y^2]$$

$$\text{subject to} \quad by - \frac{c}{2n}[x^2 + (q-1)y^2] - \delta v \geq 0,$$

where v is the equilibrium continuation value of a legislator receiving an offer of y. In addition,

$$v = \frac{bx^*}{n} + \frac{(q-1)by^*}{n} - \frac{c[x^{*2}+(q-1)y^{*2}]}{2n}.$$

The Lagrangian is

$$L = bx - \frac{c}{2n}[x^2 + (q-1)y^2] + \lambda\left\{by - \frac{c}{2n}[x^2+(q-1)y^2]-\delta v\right\},$$

which gives three first-order conditions:

$$\frac{\partial L}{\partial x} = b - (1 + \lambda^*)\frac{cx^*}{n} = 0,$$

$$\frac{\partial L}{\partial y} = -(1 + \lambda^*)\frac{(q-1)cy^*}{n} + \lambda^* b = 0, \text{ and}$$

$$\frac{\partial L}{\partial \lambda} = by^* - \frac{c}{2n}[x^{*2} + (q-1)y^{*2}] - \delta v = 0.$$

Solving for x^* and y^* in terms of λ^* gives

$$x^* = \frac{bn}{(1+\lambda^*)c} \text{ and}$$

$$y^* = \frac{\lambda^* bn}{(1+\lambda^*)(q-1)c}.$$

The third first-order condition and the definition of v gives

$$2\delta bx^* + (1-\delta)cx^{*2} = 2by^*[n - \delta(q-1)] + c(q-1)y^{*2}(\delta - 1). \tag{1}$$

Substituting the relations for x^* and y^* into (1) implies that

$$\lambda^* = \frac{2\delta(q-1) - n + \sqrt{[2\delta(q-1) - n]^2 + (q-1)[2\delta + (1-\delta)n][n(\delta + 1) - 2\delta(q-1)]}}{n + \delta n - 2\delta(q-1)}.$$

Finally, it can easily be verified that neither defection nor building a larger than minimum-winning coalition is ever optimal. ∎

PROPOSITION 2: CLOSED RULE MODEL WITH SPENDING LIMIT. *The symmetric subgame perfect Nash equilibrium in stationary strategies is as follows. Define*

$$\lambda^* = \{2b^2\delta(q-1)[n - \delta(q-1)] + (q-1)(1-\delta)$$

$$\cdot \sqrt{2b^2c[n - \delta(q-1)]^2 I^* + (q-1)2b^2\delta^2 cI^* - c^2(q-1)(\delta-1)^2 I^{*2}}\}$$

$$\div \{2b^2[n - \delta(q-1)]^2 - c(q-1)(\delta-1)^2 I^*\}.$$

In every period, the agenda setter proposes $y^* = (\lambda\sqrt{2I^*})/\sqrt{c(q-1)(q-1+\lambda^{*2})}$ *to* $(q-1)$ *legislators and* $x^* = \sqrt{2I^*(q-1)}/\sqrt{c(q-1+\lambda^{*2})}$. *In every period, those members who receive an offer of at least* y^* *vote for it, and all other legislators vote* *against it. The agenda setter accepts offers of at least y*, and since x* ≥ y*, the agenda setter votes for the proposal. The legislature selects the value I* that maximizes expected net benefits in the model.*

PROOF OF PROPOSITION 2: CLOSED RULE MODEL WITH SPENDING LIMIT. The agenda setter chooses x and y to maximize

$$bx - \frac{c}{2n}[x^2 + (q-1)y^2]$$

subject to $\quad by - \frac{c}{2n}[x^2 + (q-1)y^2] - \delta v \geq 0$ and

$$I - \frac{c}{2}[x^2 + (q-1)y^2] \geq 0,$$

where v is the equilibrium continuation value of a legislator receiving an offer of y, and I is the budget selected by the legislature in the first period. In addition,

$$v = \frac{bx^*}{n} + \frac{(q-1)by^*}{n} - \frac{c[x^{*2} + (q-1)y^{*2}]}{2n}.$$

The Lagrangian is

$$L = bx - \frac{c}{2n}[x^2 + (q-1)y^2] + \lambda\left\{by - \frac{c}{2n}[x^2 + (q-1)y^2] - \delta v\right\}$$
$$+ \gamma\left\{I - \frac{c}{2}[x^2 + (q-1)y^2]\right\},$$

which gives four first-order conditions:

$$\frac{\partial L}{\partial x} = b - (1 + \lambda^*)\frac{cx^*}{n} - \gamma^* cx^* = 0,$$

$$\frac{\partial L}{\partial y} = -(1 + \lambda^*)\frac{(q-1)cy^*}{n} + \lambda^* b - \gamma^* c(q-1)y^* = 0,$$

$$\frac{\partial L}{\partial \lambda} = by^* - \frac{c}{2n}[x^{*2} + (q-1)y^{*2}] - \delta v = 0, \text{ and}$$

$$\frac{\partial L}{\partial \gamma} = I - \frac{c}{2}[x^{*2} + (q-1)y^{*2}] = 0.$$

Solving for x^* and y^* in terms of λ^* and γ^* gives

$$x^* = \frac{bn}{(1 + \lambda^* + \gamma^* n)c} \text{ and}$$

$$y^* = \frac{\lambda^* bn}{(1 + \lambda^* + \gamma^* n)(q - 1)c}.$$

This implies that $y^* = [\lambda^*/(q - 1)]x^*$.

To calculate γ^*, substitute the relations for x^* and y^* into the fourth first-order condition. Algebraic simplification implies that

$$\gamma^* = \frac{1}{n}\left[-1 - \lambda^* + bn\sqrt{\frac{(q - 1) + \lambda^{*2}}{2cI^*(q - 1)}}\right].$$

Substituting this back into the relation for x^* and y^* gives the equilibrium values

$$y^* = \frac{\lambda^*\sqrt{2I^*}}{\sqrt{c(q - 1)(q - 1 + \lambda^{*2})}} \text{ and}$$

$$x^* = \frac{\sqrt{2I^*(q - 1)}}{\sqrt{c(q - 1 + \lambda^{*2})}}.$$

The third first-order condition and the definition of v gives

$$2\delta bx^* + (1 - \delta)cx^{*2} = 2by^*[n - \delta(q - 1)] + c(q - 1)y^{*2}(\delta - 1). \tag{2}$$

Substituting the relations for x and y into (2) implies that

$$\lambda^* = \{2b^2\delta(q - 1)[n - \delta(q - 1)] + (q - 1)(1 - \delta)$$

$$\cdot \sqrt{2b^2c[n - \delta(q - 1)]^2 I^* + (q - 1)2b^2\delta^2 cI^* - c^2(q - 1)(\delta - 1)^2 I^{*2}}\}$$

$$\div \{2b^2[n - \delta(q - 1)]^2 - c(q - 1)(\delta - 1)^2 I^*\}.$$

In the first period, the legislature selects I^* that makes it best off, given expectations about the agenda setter's behavior in the distributive game. Since all legislators are equally likely to be either an agenda setter or a member of the coalition receiving projects, consider the decision of a generic legislator. All legislators will vote identically.

Formally, a legislator's problem is to choose the I that maximizes

$$\frac{b}{n}\frac{\sqrt{2I(q-1)}}{\sqrt{c(q-1+\lambda^2)}}+\frac{b(q-1)}{n}\frac{\lambda\sqrt{2I}}{\sqrt{c(q-1)(q-1+\lambda^2)}}$$

$$-\frac{c}{2n}\left[\frac{2I(q-1)}{c(q-1+\lambda^2)}+\frac{2I\lambda^2}{c(q-1+\lambda^2)}\right].$$

Simplifying gives

$$\frac{b}{n}\frac{\sqrt{2I(q-1)}}{\sqrt{c(q-1+\lambda^2)}}(1+\lambda)-\frac{I}{n}.$$

Note that $\lambda^* = f(I^*)$, so λ^* cannot be treated as a constant here. This maximization problem is not readily solvable analytically but has well-defined properties.

Finally, it can easily be verified that neither defection nor building a larger than minimum-winning coalition is ever optimal. ∎

PROPOSITION 3: BASELINE CLOSED RULE MODEL, SPECIAL CASE (δ = 1) WITH CONSTITUENCY COSTS. *The symmetric subgame perfect Nash equilibrium in stationary strategies is as follows. Let V be the spending threshold given exogenously. If spending exceeds V, all legislators who vote for the bill pay a constituency cost z. In each period, the agenda setter compares the net benefits he receives from the model outlined in Proposition 2, assuming I = V and δ = 1, with the net benefits obtained by ignoring V and paying constituency costs of z. If he receives higher net benefits by ignoring V, then he proposes x* and y* as given in Proposition 2. Those members who receive an offer of at least y* vote for it, and all other legislators vote against it. The agenda setter accepts offers of at least y*, and since x* ≥ y*, the agenda setter votes for the proposal. If he receives higher net benefits by adhering to V, then he proposes x* = (n − q + 1) (b/c) − (q − 1) [z(n − q)/(bn)] and y* = (b/c) + [z(n − q)/(bn)].*

PROOF OF PROPOSITION 3: BASELINE CLOSED RULE MODEL, SPECIAL CASE (δ = 1) WITH CONSTITUENCY COSTS. If the agenda setter ignores the limit, then he chooses x and y to maximize

$$bx-z-\frac{c}{2n}[x^2+(q-1)y^2]$$

subject to $$by-z-\frac{c}{2n}[x^2+(q-1)y^2]-v\geq 0,$$

where v is the equilibrium continuation value of a legislator receiving an offer of y, and where

$$v = \frac{bx^* - z}{n} + \frac{(q-1)(by^* - z)}{n} - \frac{c[x^{*2} + (q-1)y^{*2}]}{2n}.$$

The Lagrangian is

$$L = bx - z - \frac{c}{2n}[x^2 + (q-1)y^2] + \lambda\left\{by - z - \frac{c}{2n}[x^2 + (q-1)y^2] - v\right\}$$

which gives three first-order conditions:

$$\frac{\partial L}{\partial x} = b - (1 + \lambda^*)\frac{cx^*}{n} = 0,$$

$$\frac{\partial L}{\partial y} = -(1 + \lambda^*)\frac{(q-1)cy^*}{n} + \lambda^*b = 0, \text{ and}$$

$$\frac{\partial L}{\partial \lambda} = by^* - z - \frac{c}{2n}[x^{*2} + (q-1)y^{*2}] - v = 0.$$

Solving for x^* and y^* in terms of λ^* gives $x^* = [bn]/[(1 + \lambda^*)c]$ and $y^* = [\lambda^*bn]/[(1 + \lambda^*)(q-1)c]$.

Substituting these values, as well as the value of v, into the third first-order condition and solving for λ^* gives

$$\lambda^* = \frac{(q-1)[cz(n-q) + b^2n]}{b^2n(n-q+1) - z(n-q)(q-1)c}.$$

Substituting back into x^* and y^* gives

$$x^* = (n-q+1)\frac{b}{c} - (q-1)\frac{z(n-q)}{bn} \text{ and}$$

$$y^* = \frac{b}{c} + \frac{z(n-q)}{bn}.$$

By construction, legislators offered y^* will accept, since they can do no better by rejecting. Further, the agenda setter always accepts his own offer, since $x^* \geq y^*$. That a supporter never wants to deviate from the equilibrium strategy is obvious.

To show that the agenda setter would never want to offer something different than x^* in any round, note that to offer $\tilde{y} < y^*$ or $\tilde{x} > x^*$ would make him worse off. If $\tilde{y} > y^*$ or $\tilde{x} < x^*$ were offered, then the supporters would reject the offer, which would make the agenda setter worse off. This shows that no defection with regard to project scales is rational.

If the agenda setter abides by the threshold V, then he acts as in Proposition 2. Letting $\delta = 1$ implies that $\lambda^* = [(q-1)/(n-q+1)]$. Substituting this as well as $I = V$ into the values of x^* and y^* implies that

$$y^* = \sqrt{\frac{2V}{c[(n-q+1)^2 + (q-1)]}} \text{ and}$$

$$x^* = (n-q+1)\sqrt{\frac{2V}{c[(n-q+1)^2 + (q-1)]}}.$$

To determine whether to abide by V or not, the agenda setter compares his net benefits from abiding by V to the net benefits from ignoring V and incorporating constituency costs z into his decision-making process. ∎

APPENDIX B ## Technical Material for Chapter 4

Description of Baseline Open Rule Model

For a description of the closed rule model, see appendix A. For the open rule model, everything is identical about the game except the amendment procedure. In the open rule model, at the beginning of every period, nature selects a legislator at random to serve as an agenda setter. Each legislator's probability of being selected is $1/n$. After the agenda setter proposes legislation, a legislator is selected randomly either to propose an amendment to the legislation or to ask that the bill be voted on, what we will term (in a slight abuse of terminology) "moving the previous question" (MPQ).

If she moves the previous question, then the previous question (PQ) comes up for a vote. If it receives at least $q \in [(n + 1)/2, n]$ votes, it is accepted, and the game ends. If it is rejected, a new agenda setter is chosen and play proceeds as above.

If she offers an amendment, then the proposal and the amendment are pitted against each other. The proposal receiving the most votes is then subject to amendment by another randomly chosen agenda setter, as before. The game continues indefinitely until the previous question is moved and receives q votes. Let $k \geq q$ be the number of members that receive projects in equilibrium. Unlike under a closed rule, k may be larger than a minimum winning coalition, since the agenda setter may want to insure against amendments being made to his proposal. Discounting occurs in the open rule model whenever an amender chooses not to move the previous question or the legislature rejects a bill on a previous question vote.

Propositions and Proofs

PROPOSITION 4: OPEN RULE MODEL. *The following characterizes a symmetric subgame perfect Nash equilibrium in stationary strategies. In the first period, the agenda setter chooses (k^*, x^*, y^*) that maximizes*

$$\frac{k-1}{n-1}\left\{ bx - \frac{c}{2n}[x^2 + (k-1)y^2] \right\} + \delta v_1(z^m)$$

subject to $$by - \frac{c}{2n}[x^2 + (k-1)y^2] - \delta v_1(z^1) \geq 0,$$

where $v_1(z^1)$ and $v_1(z^m)$ are continuation values determined in equilibrium. The player selected to make an amendment then moves the previous question if she was offered y^* by the agenda setter, and the bill passes. If she was not offered a project, she makes an amendment where she offers y^* to the $(n-k)$ members who did not receive a project initially, and then allocates the other $(2k - n - 1)$ projects of size y^* randomly to the other members, except for the first agenda setter. She offers herself a project of size x^*. Then another player is selected to make an amendment or to move the previous question, and he follows the same strategy given above. Legislators vote for any bill giving them a project of at least y^*. Project sizes are $x^* = [bn(k^* - 1)]/\{c[(k^* - 1) + \lambda^*(n-1)]\}$ and $y^* = [bn(n-1)\lambda^*]/\{c(k^* - 1)[(k^* - 1) + \lambda^*(n-1)]\}$, where

$$\lambda^* =$$
$$\frac{(k-1)2\delta v_1(z^1)ck^* - b^2n - 2\delta v_1(z^1)c + (k-1)\sqrt{b^2nk^*[b^2n - 2\delta v_1(z^1)ck^* + 2\delta v_1(z^1)c]}}{(n-1)[2\delta v_1(z^1)c - 2\delta v_1(z^1)ck^* + b^2n]},$$

$v_1(z^1)$ is defined in the proof, and $k^* \geq q$ is the coalition size that maximizes the agenda setter's expected utility (typically the minimum winning condition).

PROOF OF PROPOSITION 4: OPEN RULE MODEL. This proof has elements that are similar to the Baron and Ferejohn (1989) proof of the open rule model. An additional assumption, left out of their proof, is made here: when building a coalition, an amender must always "buy" members without a project in the existing bill before buying others (Primo 2007). Also, for simplicity, let $NB(\cdot)$ denote the net benefits to a player reflecting the benefits of receiving an equilibrium project of size $(\cdot)$, along with the costs associated with that project and all other equilibrium projects in the bill. Finally, assume that a legislator votes for the most recently proposed bill when indifferent between two pieces of legislation.

Before solving the agenda setter's maximization problem, the continuation values for various players in the model are calculated. Let $v_i(z^j)$ be the value to player i of an offer z by a player j, where z is shorthand for the set of projects offered by a player. Denote the first player chosen as the agenda setter "player 1." Then $v_1(z^1)$ is the value of the game to player 1 when he has the ability to make an offer.

I proceed by constructing $v_1(z^1)$. To forestall an amendment, the agenda setter must provide a project large enough that the player receiving the project has no incentive to amend the bill. (Players receiving no project will propose an amendment.) Thus he must pay these project players, call a single one p, $\delta v_1(z^1)$. The size of the agenda setter's coalition is determined in equilibrium. Let $k^* \geq q$ be the number of players receiving a project in the equilibrium, including the agenda setter.

This implies that

$$v_1(z^1) = \frac{k^*-1}{n-1} NB(x^*) + \left(1 - \frac{k^*-1}{n-1}\right)\delta v_1(z^m),$$

where $[1 - (k^*-1)/(n-1)]$ reflects the probability that a player m not offered a project is selected to amend the agenda setter's bill, in which case the agenda setter expects to receive $v_1(z^m)$ in the next period, therefore causing a one-period discount. Because the agenda setter here is too costly to buy relative to others, he will not receive a project offer from m and is therefore in the same position as m was at the beginning of the game, so $v_1(z^m) = v_m(z^1)$.

Next,

$$v_m(z^1) = \frac{k^*-1}{n-1}NB(0) + \frac{\delta}{n-1}v_1(z^1) + \left(1 - \frac{k^*}{n-1}\right)\delta v_p(z^1).$$

This follows from the fact that m receives no project if the amender moves the previous question. He has a small chance of being selected to make an amendment, therefore putting him in the same situation as the present agenda setter, in which case he receives $v_1(z^1)$. Finally, there is a $\{1 - [k^*/(n-1)]\}$ chance that another player lacking a project will be chosen to be the agenda setter, which guarantees that he'll be selected to get a project, by the assumption about coalition building given at the beginning of the proof, thereby giving him a continuation value similar to a player offered a project in period 1.

Similarly,

$$v_p(z^1) = \frac{k^*-1}{n-1}NB(y^*) + \delta\left(1 - \frac{k^*-1}{n-1}\right)v_p(z^m).$$

Next,

$$v_p(z^m) = \frac{2k^*-n}{k^*-1}\left[\delta\frac{k^*-1}{n-1}v_1(z^1) + \delta\left(1 - \frac{k^*-1}{n-1}\right)v_p(z^m)\right]$$

$$+ \frac{n-k^*-1}{k^*-1}\left[\frac{k^*-1}{n-1}NB(0) + \frac{\delta}{n-1}v_1(z^1) + \left(1 - \frac{k^*}{n-1}\right)\delta v_p(z^1)\right].$$

This follows from the fact that player p has a $(2k^*-n)/(k^*-1)$ chance of receiving a project, in which case he is in the same position as when he was offered a project by player 1. This probability comes from the rule that player m follows when building a coalition. First he makes offers to players without projects, and then he gives the remaining projects to players who received projects in the earlier bill. Player p has a $\{1 - [(2k^* - n)/(k^*-1)]\}$ chance of not receiving a project, in which case he is in the same position as m was when player 1 made an offer, or $v_m(z^1)$.

Next, let $\alpha = \{1 - \delta[1 - (k^*-1)/(n-1)][(2k^*-n)/(k^*-1)]\}^{-1}$.

Let $\beta = \{1 - \alpha\delta^2[1 - (k^*-1)/(n-1)][(n-k^*-1)/(k^*-1)][1 - (k^*/(n-1))]\}^{-1}$.

Let

$$\psi = \left\{1 - \delta^2\left(1 - \frac{k^*-1}{n-1}\right)\left(\frac{1}{n-1}\right)\right.$$

$$\left. - \alpha\beta\delta^4\left(1 - \frac{k^*-1}{n-1}\right)^2\left[\frac{(2k^*-n)(k^*-1)+n-k^*-1}{(k^*-1)(n-1)}\right]\left(1 - \frac{k^*}{n-1}\right)\right\}^{-1}.$$

Next, by substituting $v_p(z^m)$ into the expression for $v_p(z^1)$, then substituting $v_p(z^1)$ into the expression for $v_m(z^1)$, and then finally substituting $v_m(z^1)$ into $v_1(z^1)$, we obtain

$$v_1(z^1) = \psi\left[\frac{k^*-1}{n-1}NB(x^*) + \beta\delta^2\left(1 - \frac{k^*}{n-1}\right)\left(\frac{k^*-1}{n-1}\right)\left(1 - \frac{k^*-1}{n-1}\right)NB(y^*)\right.$$

$$+ \delta\left(1 - \frac{k^*-1}{n-1}\right)\left(\frac{k^*-1}{n-1}\right)NB(0)$$

$$\left. + \delta^3\alpha\beta\left(1 - \frac{k^*-1}{n-1}\right)^2\left(1 - \frac{k^*}{n-1}\right)\left(\frac{k^*-1}{n-1}\right)\left(\frac{n-k^*-1}{k^*-1}\right)NB(0)\right], \text{ or}$$

$$v_1(z^1) = \psi \left[\frac{k^*-1}{n-1} \left\{ bx - \frac{c}{2n}[x^{*2} + (k^*-1)y^{*2}] \right\} \right.$$

$$+ \beta\delta^2 \left(1 - \frac{k^*}{n-1}\right)\left(\frac{k^*-1}{n-1}\right)\left(1 - \frac{k^*-1}{n-1}\right)\left\{ by - \frac{c}{2n}[x^{*2} + (k^*-1)y^{*2}] \right\}$$

$$+ \delta\left(1 - \frac{k^*-1}{n-1}\right)\left(\frac{k^*-1}{n-1}\right)\left\{-\frac{c}{2n}[x^{*2} + (k^*-1)y^{*2}] \right\}$$

$$+ \delta^3\alpha\beta\left(1 - \frac{k^*-1}{n-1}\right)^2\left(1 - \frac{k^*}{n-1}\right)\left(\frac{k^*-1}{n-1}\right)\left(\frac{n-k^*-1}{k^*-1}\right)$$

$$\left. \cdot \left\{-\frac{c}{2n}[x^{*2} + (k^*-1)y^{*2}] \right\}\right].$$

The agenda setter picks (x, y) that maximizes

$$\frac{k-1}{n-1}\left\{ bx - \frac{c}{2n}[x^2 + (k-1)y^2] \right\} + \left(1 - \frac{k-1}{n-1}\right)\delta v_1(z^m)$$

subject to $\quad by - \dfrac{c}{2n}[x^2 + (k-1)y^2] - \delta v_1(z^1) \geq 0.$

The Lagrangian is

$$L = \frac{k-1}{n-1}\left\{ bx - \frac{c}{2n}[x^2 + (k-1)y^2] \right\} + \left(1 - \frac{k-1}{n-1}\right)\delta v_1(z^m)$$

$$+ \lambda\left\{ by - \frac{c}{2n}[x^2 + (k-1)y^2] - \delta v_1(z^1) \right\},$$

which gives three first-order conditions:

$$\frac{\partial L}{\partial x} = \left(\frac{k-1}{n-1}\right)b - \frac{c}{n}\left(\frac{k-1}{n-1} + \lambda^*\right)x^* = 0,$$

$$\frac{\partial L}{\partial y} = \lambda^* b - \frac{(k-1)c}{(n-1)n}[\lambda^*(n-1) + (k-1)]y^* = 0, \text{ and}$$

$$\frac{\partial L}{\partial \lambda} = by^* - \frac{c}{2n}[x^{*2} + (k-1)y^{*2}] - \delta v_1(z^1) = 0.$$

Rearranging terms in the first two first-order conditions gives

$$x^* = \left(\frac{bn}{c}\right) \frac{k-1}{(k-1) + \lambda^*(n-1)}$$

and

$$y^* = \left(\frac{bn}{c}\right)\left(\frac{n-1}{k-1}\right) \frac{\lambda^*}{(k-1) + \lambda^*(n-1)}.$$

Equilibrium values of x and y can be determined by substituting the equations for x^*, y^*, and $v_1(z^1)$ into the third first-order condition and finding λ^* that satisfies the constraint, for a given k.

The agenda setter also must determine the size of the coalition to build. As opposed to the closed rule case, where it is straightforward that a minimum winning coalition is optimal, there may be reason to build oversized coalitions in the open rule case to forestall amendments.

To check whether a coalition of size k_0 forms an equilibrium, solve the above maximization problem for $k = k_0$ and note the continuation values. Then, plug those continuation values into the maximization problem. Maximize again, this time with respect to k as well as x and y (restricting k to be an integer in $[q, n]$). If the maximization gives a different solution, then k_0 was not an equilibrium, since the continuation values were not consistent with utility-maximizing behavior on the part of the agenda setter. If the equilibrium values are unchanged, then $k_0 = k^*$. Do this for all possible k_0. ∎

Technical Material
for Chapter 5

Feasible Generalized Least Squares

The baseline feasible generalized least squares (FGLS) model, with financial variables in per capita real 2000 dollars, omitting time and unit subscripts for convenience, is

> state and local spending = α + β_1 spending limit + β_2 GOP governor (modified) + β_3 cap × gov + β_4 federal aid + β_5 state income + β_6 change in state and local debt + β_7 unemployment + β_8 population growth + β_9 upper house size + β_{10} lower house size + β_{11} initiative + β_{12} biennial budgeting + β_{13} proportion Dem lower + β_{14} proportion Dem upper + β_{15} unified Dem govt + β_{16} unified GOP govt + β_{17} normalized Dem pres. vote + β_{18} unified Dem govt × state income + β_{19} unified GOP govt × state income + year fixed effects + regional effects + ε,

where $\varepsilon_{i,t} = \rho\varepsilon_{i,t-1} + v_{i,t}$, and ρ is a serial correlation parameter in [0, 1].

This is estimated via FGLS, assuming a common serial correlation parameter and AR(1) process across states and utilizing panel-corrected standard errors to account for panel heteroskedasticity. Wooldridge's (2002) test for the presence of an AR(1) process in panel data rejects the null hypothesis of no first-order correlation with a p value of less than .001.

Error Correction Model

Separate ECMs are estimated via ordinary least squares (OLS) with panel-corrected standard errors for states with and without spending limits to allow for different dynamic relationships.

The error correction model can be written as

Δ state and local spending = α + β_1 state and local spending$_{t-1}$ + β_2 state income$_{t-1}$ + β_3 federal aid$_{t-1}$ + β_4 change in state and local debt$_{t-1}$ + β_5 unemployment$_{t-1}$ + β_6 population growth$_{t-1}$ + β_7 proportion Dem lower$_{t-1}$ + β_8 proportion Dem upper$_{t-1}$ + β_9 GOP governor (modified)$_{t-1}$ + β_{10} normalized Dem pres. vote$_{t-1}$ + β_{11} unified Dem govt$_{t-1}$ + β_{12} unified GOP govt$_{t-1}$ + β_{13} unified Dem govt $\times$ state income$_{t-1}$ + β_{14} unified GOP govt $\times$ state income$_{t-1}$ + β_{15} Δ state income$_t$ + β_{16} Δ federal aid$_t$ + β_{17} Δ change in state and local debt$_t$ + β_{18} Δ unemployment$_t$ + β_{19} Δ population growth$_t$ + β_{20} Δ proportion Dem lower$_t$ + β_{21} Δ proportion Dem upper$_t$ + β_{22} Δ GOP governor (modified)$_t$ + β_{23} Δ normalized Dem pres. vote$_t$ + β_{24} Δ unified Dem govt$_t$ + β_{25} Δ unified GOP govt$_t$ + β_{26} Δ unified Dem govt $\times$ state income$_t$ + β_{27} Δ unified GOP govt $\times$ state income$_t$ + additional differences of political variables (up to 4th seasonal difference) + year fixed effects + ε

Technical Material for Chapter 6

Agenda Setter Unconstrained by Legislature

To examine the impact of the 90 percent rule on spending, I will make use of the model introduced in chapter 3 and the proofs of Propositions 1 and 2. Assume that $\delta = 1$ and $b = c = 1$. Let me begin with the baseline model, where the agenda setter is unconstrained and assuming simple majority rule [i.e., $q = (n + 1)/2$]. The results from Proposition 1 imply that the agenda setter's project will be of size $(n + 1)/2$, while the other members of the majority coalition will receive a project of size 1. Letting $n = 101$, this implies that the baseline level of spending, using the cost function of $0.5(x^2 + 50y^2)$, will be $0.5(51^2 + 50)$, or \$1,325.50. To analyze the impact of a requirement that spending be 90 percent or less of last year's spending to avoid a supermajority voting requirement, we can compare the benefits from adhering to the implicit spending limit by looking to the results of Proposition 3, assuming that the limit is being set by the rule rather than the legislature. We can then find the indifference budget limit — that budget limit where the agenda setter is indifferent between building a supermajority coalition and busting the limit, and adhering to the limit. By assuming that legislators are perfectly patient (i.e., $\delta = 1$), it is straightforward to generate closed-form solutions for Proposition 2. Some algebraic manipulation shows that the agenda setter's net benefits under a spending limit I, as a function of that limit and letting $b = c = 1$, equal $[(n + 1)/2] \sqrt{2I/[(n-q+1)^2 + (q-1)]} - I/n$. Substituting $n = 101$ and $q = 51$ gives $51\sqrt{2I/(51^2 + 50)}$. Using Proposition 1, and letting $\delta = 1$ and $b = c = 1$, we can calculate the agenda setter's net benefits under supermajority rule. In this special case, the impact of supermajority rule is to keep the size of y constant at 1 and decrease x. The net benefits for the agenda setter will be $(n - q + 1) - (0.5n)[(n - q + 1)^2 + (q - 1)]$, with spend-

Table D.1 Spending patterns under the 90 percent rule

Period	90% Option ($)	Supermajority Option ($)	Chosen Spending ($)	Supermajority?
1	n.a.	. . .	1,325.50	No
2	1,192.95	. . .	1,192.95	No
3	1,073.66	. . .	1,073.66	No
4	966.29	. . .	966.29	No
5	869.66	. . .	869.66	No
6	782.69	860.50	860.50	Yes
7	774.45	860.50	860.50	Yes
. . .				
∞	774.45	860.50	860.50	Yes

NOTE: Supermajority spending is not a credible option until after the 90 percent option dips below 860.5.

ing equal to $0.5[(n - q + 1)^2 + (q - 1)]$. Substituting $q = 61$ and $n = 101$ gives net benefits of $41 - (1/202)(41^2 + 60)$, or $32.38. At what point will the agenda setter be indifferent between the two alternatives? We can set $51\sqrt{2I}/(51^2 + 50) = \$32.38$, solve for I, and obtain $I^* = \$846.94$. For values above $846.94, the agenda setter wishes to abide by the limit. For values below this threshold, building a supermajority coalition is optimal. If we examine a table of values (table D.1), beginning with the first period, where spending is $1,325.50, we see that when we get to period 6 spending would move to $0.9 \times \$870$, or $783. This is the period in which the agenda setter moves spending to $861. But now note that in the next period, 90 percent of this value will be $774, which is below the threshold, meaning that again the agenda setter will opt for a supermajority coalition at $861. This becomes the "steady-state" level of spending.

Agenda Setter Constrained by Legislature

Now suppose that the legislature sets the level of spending, as in the spending limit model, before the agenda setter moves. The legislature as a whole now must determine whether the agenda setter will abide by the 90 percent rule or violate it. Recall from chapter 3 that when a spending limit is in effect, spending is higher under majority rule than supermajority rule and, also, that the legislature's welfare is enhanced by supermajority rule. This implies that the legislature would always want to induce "overspending" in every period. The question is whether the agenda setter would undercut the legislature by spending 90 percent of the initial level of spending. Several lines of algebra and computation establish that he would not. Therefore, in every period after period 1, the legislature will set spending at a higher level than that which would have obtained in period 1.

Spatial Setting

To arrive at the steady state for the one-dimensional spatial model discussed in the text, note that if the 90 percent spending level is below the ideal point of the fortieth legislator (who is pivotal), then the median voter can propose a policy to the right of this legislator, equidistant from this level, thereby making the pivotal legislator indifferent between the alternatives. If the 90 percent spending level is above the ideal point of the fortieth legislator, then no movement can occur, since any move that makes the median voter better off makes the fortieth voter worse off. (We always assume that spending is to the left of or at the ideal point of the median voter.) This means, essentially, that policy will ping-pong back and forth until the distance between the 90 percent value and the ideal point of the fortieth legislator is the same as the distance between x and the fortieth legislator's ideal point. Formally, we write $40 - 0.9x = x - 40$. This gives $x^* = 42.1$, which is reached in period 312 of this model.

CHAPTER I

1. McCarty, Poole, and Rosenthal (2006) document the increase in party and preference polarization in recent years, and Binder (2003) shows that legislative gridlock has increased in Washington in recent years, as well.

2. Here we must rely on qualitative observation instead of quantitative data, as time-series measures of state-level gridlock or party polarization are not readily available.

3. What explains this increase at the federal level? Entitlements. Entitlements refer to government programs that one receives automatically by virtue of being in a particular class (e.g., retired, income below a given threshold). Entitlements are written into law and stay in effect unless changed. In theory, entitlement growth could be stemmed tomorrow with significant reforms to Medicare or Social Security. The problem with entitlements is that, once enacted, they are very difficult to change. Individuals with a vested interest in seeing those programs continue will fight hard to keep them, and thoroughly inefficient or poorly designed programs can survive as a consequence. The rise of entitlements since the Great Society reforms of the 1960s has biased government in favor of increased spending. According to data from the Office of Management and Budget, in 1962, as Great Society initiatives were getting underway, mandatory spending, in the form of entitlements such as Social Security, as well as interest payments on the national debt, comprised about one-third of the budget. By 2004 that figure was over 60 percent and is expected to exceed two-thirds of the budget by 2009.

4. Moe (1989) makes a similar argument in the context of agency design.

5. In reality, committees generally do not possess this absolute power to block legislation, though it is costly to discharge a bill from committee onto the floor. Moreover, whether the delegation of such authority from the legislature to the committee is optimal for the entire chamber is the subject of much de-

bate in the literature (e.g., Kim and Rothenberg 2005; Crombez, Groseclose, and Krehbiel 2006).

6. Bach (1991) shows that votes on points of order are consistent with existing procedures more often that not.

7. See Garand and Blais (2003) for a discussion of public opinion on spending and taxation.

8. Interestingly, the President's Advisory Panel on Federal Tax Reform did just that in 2005. Of course, this panel is not up for election, enabling it to propose politically suicidal provisions. Admittedly, there would be a significant short-term cost to eliminating this deduction, since it would lead to a radical restructuring of the housing market. In the long run, though, the market would "capitalize" this change.

9. For instance, increased taxation may cause consumers to spend less.

10. For the standard theoretical reference on how electoral and governmental structures shape outcomes, see Persson and Tabellini (2000). For the most comprehensive empirical work linking electoral and organizational structure to economic outcomes, see Persson and Tabellini (2003). See also Persson and Tabellini (2004b) for a more concise overview.

11. Incorporating malapportionment into the model would affect the results, though only in certain cases (Ansolabehere, Snyder, and Ting 2003; Cutrone and McCarty 2006).

12. One could also imagine a metainstitutional interaction, such as whether the impact of a budget rule changes when moving from a unicameral to a bicameral system. This is beyond the scope of the present study.

13. For a basic introduction to positive political theory, see Hinich and Munger (1997) and Shepsle and Bonchek (1997).

14. To be sure, models are often complex, with equilibrium solutions requiring many calculations. The claim is not that individuals literally make these calculations. Rather, models help illuminate patterns of interactions by focusing on a limited set of choices in a well-defined strategic environment.

15. For instance, the interaction between supermajority voting rules and spending limits, which is an implication of the model in chapter 3, is not one that is immediately obvious.

16. For instance, it is well-established that candidates do not take identical positions in elections, contrary to Downs's (1957) famous argument. Yet Downs's model remains enormously useful because it helps us understand why candidates move toward the center. Also, his framework serves as the foundation for further model building that predicts divergence from the median. See Clarke and Primo (2006) for a discussion of the purposes of models in political science.

17. In some cases efficiency is not the relevant standard. For example, in bargaining over a single policy, so long as alternatives are not restricted, outcomes will always be Pareto optimal.

18. See U.S. House (2003, 2004, 2005) and U.S. Senate (2004).

19. See Diermeier and Krehbiel (2003) for further discussion of this issue.

CHAPTER 2

The epigraph is from Hamilton, Jay, and Madison ([1818] 2001, 269).

1. This definition undoubtedly borrows heavily from the multitude of definitions I have read over the years and is similar to the definition adopted by North (1990).

2. Of course, one reason why central planning is useful merely as a thought experiment rather than as a governmental system is that it is not possible to acquire enough information to engage in central planning of any sort successfully. For the classic articulation of this argument, see Hayek (1945).

3. For a clear discussion of these problems, see Riker (1982). Wittman (1995), to the contrary, argues that the political marketplace is efficient.

4. To see this, suppose that all citizens, including Jones, have stated their true valuations, and further assume that all have the same preferences for the public good, represented by a utility function $u(x)$, where u is increasing in x at a declining rate. Assume that the cost of the good is one dollar, implying a social welfare function of $nu(x) - x$, where $nu(x)$ is the utility that n individuals receive from a public good of size x (which also costs x). The omniscient social planner maximizes the social welfare function and solves $u'(x^*) = 1/n$ for x^*, with every citizen paying a tax share, $t^* = 1/n$. To see why Jones has an incentive to change his valuation, note that if he says he values the good at 0, the new maximization solves $u'(\hat{x}) = 1/(n-1)$, the tax share for all other citizens becomes $1/(n-1)$, and the public good drops in size. Jones's utility net of taxes changes from $u(x^*) - 1/n$ to $u(\hat{x})$ as a result, making Jones better off under a wide variety of conditions. For example, suppose $u(x) = \sqrt{x}$. Then $x^* = n^2/4$ and $t^* = 1/n$. If Jones lies and states his valuation is $u(x) = 0$, then $\hat{x} = (n-1)^2/4$ and his $t = 0$. The utility loss is 0.5, but the tax savings is $n/4$. For $n > 2$, the tax savings outweigh the utility loss.

5. See Feldman (1980) for a nontechnical discussion, and Fudenberg and Tirole (1991) for a more technical introduction.

6. This analysis assumes that buyers are risk-neutral. A simple illustration of risk-neutrality is the following: If given the choice between receiving 50 cents for certain or receiving a lottery ticket that pays nothing with probability 0.5 and pays a dollar with probability 0.5, a risk-neutral individual will be indifferent between the two.

7. Similarly, when Congress delegates regulatory authority to the Environmental Protection Agency (EPA), it does so because the agency has expertise. The downside for Congress is that the EPA may use its informational advantage to undertake or recommend actions at odds with congressional preferences.

8. This idea, of giving agents incentives to adhere to and enforce rules, is closely related to Weingast's (2005, 2006) notion of self-enforcing constitutions, a topic I return to in the concluding chapter.

9. For an overview of rational-choice institutionalism, see Weingast (2002).

10. For instance, a balanced budget rule imposes a constraint on the budgets that pass — namely, they must equate revenues and outlays. Unanimity rule is a procedure requiring that all voters approve of a measure for it to pass.

11. While few if any chambers have de jure gatekeeping power (Crombez, Grose-close, and Krehbiel 2006), in principle the floor could grant a committee such a power. I am putting aside enforcement issues, so there is no risk of the floor undoing the rule whenever the committee "gatekeeps" a bill the floor would like to see reported out.

12. One can argue that a closed rule is a type of gatekeeping authority. See Kim and Rothenberg (2005).

13. One problem with incorporating fixed proposers in infinite horizon bargaining models is that the equilibrium often will involve all legislators except for the proposer receiving nothing. In short, fixing proposal power offers little analytical leverage in these types of models.

14. A filibuster occurs when a senator or group of senators control the floor, typically by speechmaking. To invoke cloture and end a filibuster requires sixty votes.

15. See Primo, Binder, and Maltzman (2007) for a discussion of different models of judicial appointments.

16. Of course, it may be that those designing the rules want them to fail. The same mode of analysis would be appropriate in this situation, but the reason for failure would be intent, rather than the lack of careful analysis.

17. I put aside implementation problems, which refer to day-to-day administrative issues. Nor do I consider bureaucratic incompetence; even without incompetence, enforcement is challenging enough.

18. For other possible tactics that could kill the filibuster, see Gold and Gupta (2003). Theoretically, a similar strategy could be used to kill almost any rule in the Senate.

19. The specter of the nuclear option remains, but as of early 2007, it has not been exercised.

20. The factual information presented here is drawn in part from Winerip (2003).

21. For an introduction to the states and constitutions, see Squire and Hamm (2005).

22. One reason for these findings may be that these studies, except for Rueben, did not address the endogeneity of these limits. Specifically, the adoption of these limits may reflect preferences for lower spending, therefore biasing the results upward. Alternatively, adoption may reflect existing preferences for high spending and a desire to reduce it, therefore biasing results downward (or making them the wrong sign). Rueben's study, which finds that limits are effective, uses the presence of a citizen initiative as an instrument. However, this variable has been shown in several studies to have an impact on spending, therefore calling into question these results. In another study, Poterba and Rueben (1999) show that this is a poor instrument to use. For a reform that is heralded for reducing spending, the existing evidence is sparse in this regard. See chapter 5 for more details.

CHAPTER 3

The epigraph is from Clement (1991).

1. Of course, the Constitution itself is subject to change, but at much higher cost

than a statute or a norm. Therefore, at any given point in time, the Constitution is considered stable.

2. Technical details of the models in this chapter are presented in appendix A; the focus in the text is on intuition.

3. For a brief but fascinating history of the federal pork barrel, see Wolfensberger (2001).

4. Regrettably, Rhode Island politicians' propensity for bad humor continued. In response, St. Germain aired an ad rebuking Machtley, noting that surely Les knows "hogwash when he sees it" (Sullivan 1988). Continuing the bad puns, Machtley's opponent, Scott Wolf, complained in 1990 that since arriving in DC, Machtley had turned "Les Pork" into a "jumbo frank" (Wilbanks 1990). Perhaps sensing that the puns and metaphors had gotten out of control, First Congressional District voters handed Wolf a defeat.

5. See Collie (1988) for further discussion.

6. Implicit in this discussion is that legislators act as perfect agents of their constituents. Legislator preferences and district preferences are therefore coincident, and the terms are used interchangeably.

7. Fiorina and Noll (1978, 1979) offer one possible explanation for the development of inefficient norms. An inefficient bureaucracy rewards bureaucrats and increases constituent demand for "facilitation services" to help deal with an agency. Because all legislators benefit from this system, and because no single member of Congress (or group of voters) may change it, it is maintained. Fiorina and Noll's argument hinges on a bureaucracy with its own preferences. Parties may offer one possibility for the development of efficient norms. Primo and Snyder (2007b) show that party organizations that facilitate electoral success may induce legislators to seek less distributive spending and more public goods spending, even under unanimity rule. Rodden (2005) finds empirical support for the claim by Riker and Schaps (1957) that unified political parties may solve some of the fiscal tensions inherent in federalism.

8. The majority-rule version of the baseline model was introduced by Baron (1993).

9. Formally, efficiency and welfare maximization coincide when preferences are quasilinear and utility is transferable (Milgrom and Roberts 1992). The assumption of transferable utility through cash transfers is needed for efficiency and welfare maximization to be one and the same in the model presented in this chapter.

10. Formally, this is referred to as a stationary subgame perfect Nash equilibrium. Further details are located in this chapter's technical appendix.

11. Recall that legislators are selected to receive projects at random.

12. Some of the results in the remainder of the chapter are based on comparative statics; others are based on simulations using specific values for legislator patience, the size of the legislature, and the size of the majority required for budget passage.

13. One interpretation of discount factors for elected officials is that they reflect

one's expectation of being reelected. On this interpretation, 0.8 is a conservative expectation.

14. Wicksell (1958, 91) argues that unanimity rule may in fact lead to higher spending than simple majority rule. By giving everybody a veto, the fear that new programs might continue to expand far beyond their initial levels would be allayed. This might lead programs that would not be enacted under majority rule to be enacted under unanimity rule. See Buchanan and Tullock (1962), who also reference Wicksell's argument, for further discussion about the advantages and disadvantages of unanimity rule.

15. With random recognition, another way to select the budget is to assume that the executive is the first mover and selects the size of spending before it is allocated. So long as the executive wants to maximize aggregate welfare, the same result obtains. See Persson, Roland, and Tabellini (1997).

16. These are stark cases meant to illustrate the impact of veto authority versus its absence.

17. For a discussion of different perspectives on the motivations of judges, see Segal (1997).

18. See Inman (1998) for another perspective on judicial enforcement of budget rules.

19. Sellers (1997) finds that liberal legislators who bring home pork are better off than conservative legislators who do so because they are perceived to be more "fiscally consistent." To make the model tractable, I assume here that voters hold liberal and conservative legislators equally responsible for excessive spending, and I further assume that all districts like pork equally.

20. Constituency costs are akin to Fearon's (1994) concept of audience costs in international relations crises. See Groseclose and McCarty (2001) for an application of audience costs to executive veto threats. Basinger and Hallerberg (2004) introduce the term constituency costs in the context of a discussion of domestic political costs that are incurred in the legislative process. I adopt the term constituency cost because it is more appropriate for my purposes.

21. If a legislator does not receive a project, she votes against the bill and can easily blame those who voted for the legislation for the deficit. For this reason, only legislators who receive a project pay z. If we require all legislators to pay z, the only difference in the results is that spending is unaffected when the cap is ignored.

22. If we complicate the model by tying the constituency costs to the size of the deviation from the public's ideal level of spending, rather than letting the costs be constant, the results go through so long as we assume that the agenda setter's benefits to adhering to the cap increase in V at a greater rate than his benefits from ignoring the cap increase in V. This is a fairly weak assumption, requiring that the costs of a violation are not excessive and that the "punishment fits the crime." For analytical tractability, I also assume in this version of the model that all legislators bear these constituency costs, not just those who receive projects.

23. The reverse may be true. Presidents who have to veto legislation do so because of their inability to work with Congress or their poor information regarding congressional preferences.

CHAPTER 4

The epigraph is from Boxer (2005).

1. In the U.S. House of Representatives, rules can be separated into open, closed, modified open, and modified closed (or structured) rules. In practice, amendments are not unlimited. I posit a very simple distinction between closed and open rules. Naturally, this framework can be made more complicated as necessary to study particular legislatures. For further information on amendments and rules in the U.S. House, see Davis and Bach (2003). For further discussion of state legislative rules, see Grooters and Eckl (1998).

2. Cho and Duggan (2004) demonstrate that even under closed rules, the median voter outcome obtains under some very weak conditions, provided that all legislators have a positive probability of making a proposal. Of course, in some cases proposal power is prefixed, as in the case of presidential appointments; it is in these cases that a proposer shifts policy away from the median.

3. This terminology is used to remain consistent with Baron and Ferejohn (1989). But according to *Robert's Rules of Order,* when a legislator proposes to move the previous question, this does not bring the bill up for an immediate vote (Robert 2000). Rather, the vote is on whether to move the previous question. The previous question motion must be passed by a two-thirds vote; if successful, then votes are taken on the outstanding measure. In the House of Representatives, a simple majority vote is used to move the previous question. Baron and Ferejohn combine these two steps. Also, most amending takes place in the U.S. House of Representatives in the Committee of the Whole. Once the Committee of the Whole has voted on amendments, the bill is then sent to the House floor and typically the previous question is moved, and then the amendments approved in the Committee of the Whole are voted on followed by a vote on the final bill. This is done because the rules for considering amendments in the House are more onerous than in the Committee of the Whole, complicating matters even further. (See Davis and Bach [2003] for further details.) I thank Bill Heniff and Tim Groseclose for helpful discussions on the previous question motion.

4. The computation of the open rule equilibrium is more involved than the closed rule result, which is why a numerical example is not presented here.

5. The technical solutions to these models do not provide intuitive results, so formal statements of the equilibria and proofs appear in the appendix.

6. The expected value of the game refers to the value of the game before it is played. It will be the same for all players, since proposers are chosen at random. This value will be referred to with the modifier "ex ante" to distinguish it from expected payoffs that may be calculated after the game has begun.

7. As before, the parameters b and c were set to 1 and then δ was set from 0.2 to 1

in increments of 0.08. For each of these values of δ, n was set from 25 to 505 in increments of 20. For each of these values of n, all q rules from $q = (n + 1)/2$ to $q = n$ were considered.

8. Larger coalitions also lower the probability of costly delay. Under an open rule, costly delay occurs with probability $(n - k)/(n - 1)$, or the probability that a member not given a project is selected to make an amendment. The likelihood of delay therefore is declining in q.

9. For sufficiently high n and δ, the agenda setter always builds minimum winning coalitions (i.e., $k^* = q$).

10. Under an open rule, the agenda setter often builds supermajority coalitions when the legislature is small and legislators are very impatient. These supermajority coalitions make the open rule that much more attractive to the legislature in selecting rules. This means that for sufficiently small n and δ, increasing legislator patience may have the effect of reducing the size of the coalition the agenda setter builds under the open rule, thereby making implementation of the spending limit relatively more likely. The implications of these results for small groups, like committees or city councils, merit further scrutiny.

CHAPTER 5

The epigraph is from Kettl (2003).

1. When budgeting decisions occur on multiple dimensions (say, defense and welfare), then the effect of a spending limit (read: balanced budget rule) depends on the arrangement of legislator preferences (Ferejohn and Krehbiel 1987; Serritzlew 2005). And as Battaglini and Coate (2006) show in a dynamic model of spending (composed of a national public good plus local pork), taxation, and debt, the welfare effects of a balanced budget requirement depend on the size of the tax base compared with how much the citizenry wishes to spend on public goods.

2. These descriptions draw in part from Bohn and Inman (1996) and Advisory Commission on Intergovernmental Relations (1987).

3. Because so few balanced budget rules are statutory, I combine the two categories in the data analysis. The results are unaffected by doing so.

4. For a detailed argument about court enforcement, see Inman (1998). For a skeptic's view on whether such a threat exists in practice, see Briffault (1996). According to the General Accounting Office (1993), the threat of court enforcement is not viewed by most budget officials as a reason to keep budgets in check, and none reported enforcement occurring through the courts. There is some evidence that courts will intercede in spending matters, though. Examples, drawn from Dellinger (1995), include a Florida decision striking down the governor's restructuring of appropriations, a Massachusetts case regarding the ability of courts to oversee the governor's impoundment authority, and a Michigan case evaluating the governor's authority to cut funds for local governments to comply with a state balanced budget rule. In 2002, in seeming violation of the state constitution, the New Jersey Supreme Court allowed debt

issuance without a referendum because it was to be paid back through appropriations and therefore was not backed by the full faith and credit of the state (New Jersey Supreme Court 2002, 2003). In 2003 the Nevada Supreme Court set aside a constitutional provision requiring a two-thirds supermajority vote for tax increases (Nevada Supreme Court 2003a, 2003b). Governor Kenny Guinn filed suit because this hurdle had delayed the passage of the state budget. The Court argued that this delay had violated another provision of the state constitution, which mandated that the state fund education. In response, the Court altered the voting rule for the current session to simple majority rule. Ironically, days after this decision, the legislature passed the budget by the required supermajority margin, thereby casting into doubt the court's rationale for nullifying the amendment. And in 2005, the New Jersey Supreme Court ruled, in what Briffault (2006) calls the first decision of its kind, that the state acted unconstitutionally when it borrowed money to generate funds needed to balance the budget.

5. A state's selection procedure for high court justices is coded based on initial selection to the bench. Therefore, appointed justices who face retention elections are coded as appointed.

6. Williams (1987) and Eskridge, Frickey, and Garrett (2002) note that courts differ in how they evaluate whether constitutionally mandated legislative procedures have been violated. The weakest form of supervision, the "enrolled bill" rule, examines only the final, enacted bill and does not probe the enactment process. The enrolled bill rule gives legislature significant leeway on most legislation. Because budgetary procedures, such as a balanced budget rule, are relatively clear-cut, spending and taxing legislation is amenable to evaluation even under the weakest standard.

7. The court has more difficulty in *compelling* spending because appropriations authority rests solely with the legislature, and courts are limited in their ability to order appropriations, as state legislators are immune from suit and other state officials cannot be ordered to spend money that only legislators have the authority to appropriate. See chapter 3 of Schoenbrod, Levine, and Jung (2002) for more details.

8. Admittedly, this is not a perfect setup, since Democrats in Rhode Island and in Texas may look very different ideologically, but it is the best measure available for the time period under study.

9. Earmarks refer to adding projects or other perks for specific states or districts to legislation in a less-than-transparent fashion.

10. Alaska is left out of the analysis because it is an extreme outlier on all matters financial. As Kiewiet and Szakaly (1996, 75) colorfully put it, "The state of Alaska has a financial structure that, for not unsimilar reasons, bears more resemblance to that of Saudi Arabia than to that of any other state in the union." Dropping Alaska is the norm in public finance analyses of the states. Hadi's multivariate outlier test (1992, 1994) confirms that Alaska is an outlier when real federal aid per capita, real personal income per capita, and real state and

local spending per capita are considered. The Hadi test implies that some years of data for Wyoming are also outliers, and this is most likely due to the large amount of federal aid given to the state for mineral land management. Wyoming is left in the analysis because its status as an outlier is less clear-cut, and throwing away data is to be avoided whenever possible. Minnesota and Nebraska are omitted because, in the case of Nebraska, it has only one nonpartisan legislative chamber, and in the case of Minnesota, because for several years in the dataset, it also had a nonpartisan legislature.

11. State and local spending are combined in the analysis because local governments are not sovereign and are extensions of the state. States will often shift financial responsibilities to local governments in order to keep the state fiscal house in order. By including local spending, this shift is accounted for. As a robustness check, I also present the results for state-only spending. I also measure the proportion of state and local spending done at the state level in order to account for the differential tendencies of states to shift spending mandates to the local level. The proportion variable ranges from 0.22 to 0.81, showing that the states vary widely in this regard.

12. A state is defined as having a spending limit if it has a no-carryover allowed balanced budget rule and an elected state high court. This list is based on my interpretation of state law, as well as the Advisory Commission on Intergovernmental Relations (1987); Bohn and Inman (1996); Council of State Governments (various years).

13. Matsusaka (1995) makes a related argument in his work on citizen initiatives. Rueben (1995) accounts for endogeneity of tax and expenditure limits by using the presence of the initiative as an instrument and finds that tax and expenditure limitations have a small but real negative effect on state spending. Poterba and Rueben (1999) have less success when using similar instruments to study state bond markets. I attempted to use similar instruments to those used by Rueben (1995) and by Poterba and Rueben (1999); specifically, I considered whether a recall provision for elected officials, the signature requirement for getting initiatives onto the ballot, the presence of the initiative, and the year a state entered the union predicted whether a state would have a spending limit, using my primary measure. The R^2 on the linear probability model I estimated was approximately 0.05, with none of the variables having a statistically significant effect on the presence of a spending limit. Previously utilized instruments, therefore, are inappropriate for use when working with the primary definition of a spending limit considered here. A likely reason is that the definition I use includes an exogenous factor—whether high court justices are elected or appointed—and therefore directly addresses the endogeneity concern. These instruments are likely inappropriate in general because the citizen initiative has been shown to have an impact on spending.

14. As a robustness check, the presence of just a no-carryover rule is also used in the FGLS specifications to code whether a spending limit is present in a state.

15. This variable is used in the generalized least squares and error correction models

presented later in this chapter to account for some unique cases. The variable is created as follows. Suppose it takes m out of n legislators to pass the budget and s legislators to override the governor's veto, where m and s vary by state. In states where $s > m$, the governor's ideology is measured as above. In most states, a two-thirds vote is required to override a veto, and a majority vote is required to pass the budget. States in which $0.5n < m = s$ are observationally equivalent to states where a conservative governor is always in office, since coalitions larger than a majority are always predicted. Therefore, such states are coded as having a conservative governor in all cases. In states where $0.5n = m = s$, the governor is presumed to have little power, and the variable is always set to 0.

16. Because the spending data are for state fiscal years, most of which begin in July, timing becomes an issue. Whenever possible, fiscal year data are used. When not possible, it is assumed that decisions for fiscal year t were made in calendar year $t - 1$, and variables are matched up accordingly.

17. In an earlier version of this analysis (Primo 2006), I presented calculations that did not utilize the interaction term.

18. See Primo and Snyder (2007a) for a start down this path.

19. In this scenario, ρ will typically be negative. To see why, rewrite the left-hand side of the question as $y_t - y_{t-1}$. Moving y_{t-1} to the right-hand side means that the coefficient on y_{t-1} will be $1 + \rho$, which in most time series implies that $\rho < 0$.

20. The first difference of a variable at time t is calculated as $x_t - x_{t-1}$. A lagged level of a variable at time t is defined as x_{t-1}.

21. Error correction models are often discussed in the context of cointegration, or variables that move in tandem. In the seminal paper on error correction, Davidson et al. (1978) showed that an error correction mechanism enables the analyst to understand the long- and short-term effects of variables, even when series are not cointegrated, with only minor bias and a slight loss in efficiency. Beck (1991) and De Boef and Granato (1999) argue that error correction models are appropriate when theoretically justified, whether series are cointegrated or not.

22. The differenced party variables have no statistically significant effect in the ECMs, and the lags of Democrats in the upper and lower chambers have oppositely signed coefficients. Therefore, just as with FGLS, there is little evidence of any party effects.

23. The coefficient outside the parentheses is negative, but so is the coefficient inside the parentheses, making the impact positive.

24. Interestingly, twelve of the past twenty budgets would still have been late had this date been in effect in the past.

25. Another way to model this interaction is to argue that legislators and governors pay constituency costs for delay. See Kousser and Phillips (2005) for an analysis of this idea.

26. It is convenient to assume that the legislature speaks with one voice. As the New Jersey example makes clear, this is not always the case.

27. The three exceptions are Maryland, West Virginia, and as of a 2004 court deci-

sion, New York (Grooters and Eckl 1998; New York State Court of Appeals 2004). In the empirical analysis below, these states are omitted.

28. This gives the governor, in effect, an absolute veto. In reality, most vetoes are subject to override. The assumption of an absolute veto gives the executive even more authority, making any finding of legislative agenda-setting power that much stronger.

29. The effect is $48 per capita, as opposed to $64, when considering state-only spending.

30. The shutdown model also illustrates the importance of institutional interactions, as the impact of a shutdown provision will depend on the identity of the proposer. The model implies that if executives were the proposers, then spending would be lower in states with shutdown provisions than in states without. Unfortunately, there is no way to assess whether this is the case; I am not aware of any states with shutdown provisions and executive budgets that are not subject to alteration in the legislature.

31. One might think that shutdown rules were designed to advantage the legislature (i.e., this effect is not unintended), but this is an unlikely explanation because, without a law or constitutional provision to the contrary, a government shutdown provision is the default outcome. Therefore, the puzzle is why provisions allowing the government to remain open for business ever emerged; this is certainly a topic that future research should explore.

CHAPTER 6

The epigraph is from Grassley (1985).

1. Federal Reserve Chairman Ben Bernanke once noted that the federal government could deal with deflation in precisely this way (Bernanke 2002).

2. To be sure, this is also an issue at the subnational level.

3. For detailed overviews and histories of the budget process, see Schick (2000), Wildavsky and Caiden (2004), and LeLoup (2005).

4. The Office of Management and Budget was the "new-and-improved" version of the BOB.

5. For a contrary perspective, see Fisher (1985).

6. See Posner and Vermeule (2002) for a dissenting viewpoint and McGinnis and Rappaport (2003) for a reply. An interesting hypothetical is whether the House or the Senate can pass a rule that prevents votes on rule changes (or, to be less extreme, requires a supermajority for a vote to be taken on a rule change). For instance, in the U.S. Senate a rules change that is filibustered will require, in essence, sixty-seven votes to come up for a vote. There is disagreement about whether such a policy is permissible. See McGinnis and Rappaport (1995) for a discussion.

7. Both of these statements are cited by Justice Antonin Scalia in *Lockhart v. United States* (2005), indicating their staying power.

8. All deficit data are taken from the *Historical Tables, Budget of the United States Government, Fiscal Year 2006* (U.S. Office of Management and Budget 2005).

9. The increase was severe even in constant fiscal year 2000 dollars, moving from 142 to 313 billion.
10. For a behind-the-scenes discussion of the bargaining over deficit reduction, see Miller (1994).
11. Details are taken from U.S. Congress (1985).
12. At the time, the GAO was known as the General Accounting Office.
13. Some wanted to leave the courts out explicitly, and in 1995 an amendment by Sam Nunn (D-GA) passed the Senate ninety-two to eight. It stated, "The judicial power of the United States shall not extend to any case or controversy arising under this Article except as may be specifically authorized by legislation adopted pursuant to this section" (Nunn 1995). This was, in fact, the only amendment that was successful during Senate debate.

CHAPTER 7

The epigraph is from Rhoads (2003).

1. To take another example, Makinen (2001) finds that European countries with constitutionally mandated social security rights tied to judicial review tend to spend more on these rights than other countries. Though European preferences for significant social welfare spending may explain much of this, Makinen's finding accounts for additional variation across these countries.
2. A third route, changing interpretations of the Constitution, is informal, though Ackerman (1991) argues that it is just as legitimate as changes made under article 5.
3. This assumes that requests do not expire, and legal scholars disagree on this point.
4. For more detail on the creation of the Stability and Growth Pact, see Brunila, Buti, and Franco (2001). Details in this section come from various EU documents as well as various press reports. Only information that is unique to a particular source is cited.
5. See Kopits and Symansky (1998) for a discussion of fiscal policy rule effectiveness.
6. The deposit is equal to 0.2 percent of its GDP plus one-tenth of the difference between the deficit and 3 percent of GDP, with a ceiling of 0.5 percent of GDP. Suppose the deficit is 50 cents and the GDP of a country is $5. Then using the formula the deposit would be $0.002 \times 0.5 + 0.10 \times (0.50 - 0.15)$, or 4.5 cents. Because this figure exceeds the cap of 0.5 percent of GDP, or 2.5 cents, the deposit would be set at 2.5 cents.
7. So if the deficit remained unchanged, in the example in the previous note, the deposit could be as much as 3.5 cents, again reduced because the maximum would still be 2.5 cents, or 0.5 percent of GDP.

APPENDIX A

1. The closed rule, simple majority rule version of this model was first presented in Baron (1993).

2. This functional form, also used in Baron (1993), implies that the type of good being distributed is closer to a private than a public good. This is a plausible assumption if we think of traditional pork-barrel projects that benefit a narrow group of individuals in a district. See Primo and Snyder (2007a) for a discussion of how functional forms have an impact on the relationship between legislature size and government spending.

3. Put another way, marginal utility is declining in project size (as evidenced by a negative second derivative of the net benefit function). For example, suppose that $b = c = 1$. Then the optimal project size is 1, which provides a social net benefit $1 - 0.5 = 0.5$. Note that the social marginal benefit from moving from a size 0 project to a size 0.5 project is 3/8, but the marginal utility of moving from a size 0.5 project to a size 1 project is only 1/8.

4. In equilibrium, y will be the same for all legislators receiving an offer.

5. Under a closed rule, it is straightforward to establish that the symmetry of the legislature implies the symmetry of the equilibrium. See Baron (1991) for a discussion of this result.

6. See Baron and Kalai (1993) for a discussion of the "focal quality" of the stationary equilibrium. They show that the stationary equilibrium is the "simplest" equilibrium of a Baron-Ferejohn game with infinitely many subgame perfect Nash equilibria.

Abrams, Burton A., and William R. Dougan. 1986. "The Effects of Constitutional Restraints on Government Spending." *Public Choice* 49:101–16.

Ackerman, Bruce. 1991. *We the People: Foundations*. Cambridge, MA: Harvard University Press.

Advisory Commission on Intergovernmental Relations. 1987. *Fiscal Discipline in the Federal System: National Reform and the Experience of the States*. Washington, DC: Advisory Commission on Intergovernmental Relations.

Akerlof, George A. 1970. "The Market for 'Lemons': Quality Uncertainty and the Market Mechanism." *Quarterly Journal of Economics* 84:488–500.

Almond, Michael A. 1975. "Amendment by Convention: Our Next Constitutional Crisis?" *North Carolina Law Review* 53:491–533.

Alt, James E., and Robert C. Lowry. 1994. "Divided Government, Fiscal Institutions, and Budget Deficits: Evidence from the States." *American Political Science Review* 88:811–28.

——— . 2000. "A Dynamic Model of State Budget Outcomes under Divided Partisan Government." *Journal of Politics* 62:1035–69.

——— . 2003. "Party Differences in State Budget Outcomes Are There after All: Response to 'Reexamining the Dynamic Model of Divided Partisan Government.'" *Journal of Politics* 65:491–97.

Alvarez, Lizette. 1999. "Congress on Record Course for 'Pork,' with Alaska in a Class of Its Own." *New York Times,* November 19, A32.

Annett, Anthony, Jorg Decressin, and Michael Deppler. 2005. "Reforming the Stability and Growth Pact." IMF Policy Discussion Paper PDP/05/2.

Ansolabehere, Stephen, James M. Snyder, Jr., and Michael M. Ting. 2003. "Bargaining in Bicameral Legislatures: When and Why Does Malapportionment Matter?" *American Political Science Review* 97:471–81.

Arnold, R. Douglas. 1990. *The Logic of Congressional Action*. New Haven, CT: Yale University Press.

Arrow, Kenneth J., and Gerard Debreu. 1954. "Existence of an Equilibrium for a Competitive Economy." *Econometrica* 22:265–90.

Bach, Stanley. 1991. "The Senate's Compliance with Its Legislative Rules: The Appeal of Order." *Congress and the Presidency* 18:77–92.

Bails, Dale. 1990. "The Effectiveness of Tax-Expenditure Limitations: A Reevaluation." *American Journal of Economics and Sociology* 49:223–38.

Barbera, Salvador, and Matthew O. Jackson. 2004. "Choosing How to Choose: Self-Stable Majority Rules and Constitutions." *Quarterly Journal of Economics* 119:1011–48.

Baron, David P. 1991. "Majoritarian Incentives, Pork Barrel Programs, and Procedural Control." *American Journal of Political Science* 35:57–90.

——— . 1993. "A Theory of Collective Choice for Government Programs." Research Paper No. 1240. Stanford Graduate School of Business.

Baron, David P., and John A. Ferejohn. 1989. "Bargaining in Legislatures." *American Political Science Review* 83:1181–1206.

Baron, David P., and Ehud Kalai. 1993. "The Simplest Equilibrium of a Majority-Rule Division Game." *Journal of Economic Theory* 61:290–301.

Basinger, Scott J., and Mark Hallerberg. 2004. "Remodeling the Competition for Capital: How Domestic Politics Erases the Race to the Bottom." *American Political Science Review* 98:261–76.

Battaglini, Marco, and Stephen Coate. 2006. "A Dynamic Theory of Public Spending, Taxation, and Debt." Working Paper, Cornell University.

Beck, Nathaniel. 1991. "Comparing Dynamic Specifications: The Case of Presidential Approval." In *Political Analysis*, ed. James A. Stimson. Vol. 3. Ann Arbor: University of Michigan Press, pp. 51–87.

Bednar, Jenna. 2005. "Federalism as a Public Good." *Constitutional Political Economy* 16:189–205.

——— . In press. *The Robust Federation*. Cambridge: Cambridge University Press.

Bernanke, Ben S. 2002. "Deflation: Making Sure 'It' Doesn't Happen Here." Remarks by Governor Ben S. Bernanke before the National Economists Club, Washington, DC, November 21. Federal Reserve Board. http://www.federalreserve.gov/boardDocs/speeches/2002/20021121/default.htm.

Besley, Timothy, and Stephen Coate. 2003. "Centralized versus Decentralized Provision of Local Public Goods: A Political Economy Approach." *Journal of Public Economics* 87:2611–637.

Binder, Sarah A. 1997. *Minority Rights, Majority Rule: Partisanship and the Development of Congress*. New York: Cambridge University Press.

——— . 2003. *Stalemate: Causes and Consequences of Legislative Gridlock*. Washington, DC: Brookings Institution Press.

Blackstone, Sir William. 1765. *Commentaries on the Laws of England*. Oxford: Clarendon Press.

Bohn, Henning, and Robert P. Inman. 1996. "Balanced Budget Rules and Public Deficits: Evidence from the U.S. States." *Carnegie Rochester Conference Series on Public Policy* 45:13–76.

Boxer, Barbara. 2005. "Department of Defense Appropriations Act, 2006—Conference Report—Resumed." *Congressional Record* 151 (167): S14221.

Briffault, Richard. 1996. *Balancing Acts: The Reality behind State Balanced Budget Requirements*. New York: Twentieth Century Fund Press.

——. 2003. "The Disfavored Constitution: State Fiscal Limits and State Constitutional Law." *Rutgers Law Journal* 34:907–57.

——. 2006. "Courts, Constitutions, and the Fisc: Some Recent Experiences from the States." Paper presented at the conference "Fiscal Challenges: An Interdisciplinary Approach to Budget Policy," University of Southern California, February 10–11.

Brunila, Anne, Marco Buti, and Daniele Franco, eds. 2001. *The Stability and Growth Pact: The Architecture of Fiscal Policy in EMU*. New York: Palgrave.

Buchanan, James, and Gordon Tullock. 1962. *The Calculus of Consent*. Ann Arbor: University of Michigan Press.

Buchanan, James E., and Richard E. Wagner. 1977. *Democracy in Deficit*. San Diego, CA: Academic Press.

Byrd, Robert. 2005. "Department of Defense Appropriations Act, 2006—Conference Report—Resumed." *Congressional Record* 151 (167): S14221.

Calvert, Randall L. 1995. "Rational Actors, Equilibrium, and Social Institutions." In *Explaining Social Institutions*, ed. Jack Knight and Itai Sened. Ann Arbor: University of Michigan Press, pp. 57–93.

CBS News and the *New York Times*. 1995. "National Telephone Poll." Poll Conducted February 22, Released February 27.

Chari, V.V., Larry E. Jones, and Ramon Marimon. 1997. "The Economics of Split-Ticket Voting in Representative Democracies." *American Economic Review* 87:957–76.

Cho, Seok-ju, and John Duggan. 2004. "Bargaining Foundations of the Median Voter Theorem." Paper presented at the annual meeting of the Midwest Political Science Association.

Clarke, Edward H. 1971. "Multipart Pricing of Public Goods." *Public Choice* 11:17–33.

Clarke, Kevin A., and David M. Primo. 2006. "Modernizing Political Science: A Model-Based Approach." Working Paper. University of Rochester.

Clement, Robert. 1991. "Coast Guard Authorization Act of 1991." *Congressional Record* 137 (110):H5605.

Coase, R. H. 1937. "The Nature of the Firm." *Economica* 4:386–405.

Collie, Melissa P. 1988. "The Legislature and Distributive Policy Making in Formal Perspective." *Legislative Studies Quarterly* 13:427–58.

Congressional Budget Office. 1993. *The Economic and Budget Outlook: Fiscal Years 1994–1998*. Washington, DC: U.S. Government Printing Office.

Council of State Governments, comp. *Book of the States*. Various years. Lexington, KY: Council of State Governments.

Cox, Gary W. 2000. "On the Effects of Legislative Rules." *Legislative Studies Quarterly* 25:169–92.

Cox, James, and David Lowery. 1990. "The Impact of the Tax Revolt Era State Fiscal Caps." *Social Science Quarterly* 71:492–509.

Crain, W. Mark. 2003. *Volatile States: Institutions, Policy, and the Performance of American State Economies*. Ann Arbor: University of Michigan Press.

Creelan, Jeremy M., and Laura M. Moulton. 2004. *The New York State Legislative Process: An Evaluation and Blueprint for Reform*. New York: Brennan Center for Justice at NYU School of Law.

Cremer, Jacques, and Thomas R. Palfrey. 1999. "Political Confederation." *American Political Science Review* 93:69–83.

Crombez, Christophe, Tim Groseclose, and Keith Krehbiel. 2006. "Gatekeeping." *Journal of Politics* 68:322–34.

Cutrone, Michael, and Nolan McCarty. 2006. "Does Bicameralism Matter?" In *Oxford Handbook of Political Economy*, ed. Barry R. Weingast and Donald Wittman. New York: Oxford University Press, pp. 180–95.

Danforth, John. 1985. "Increase of Permanent Public Debt Limit." *Congressional Record* 131 (133):S12954.

Davidson, James E. H., David F. Hendry, Frank Srba, and Steven Yeo. 1978. "Econometric Modelling of the Aggregate Time-Series Relationship between Consumers' Expenditure and Income in the United Kingdom." *Economic Journal* 88:661–92.

Davis, Christopher M., and Stanley Bach. 2003. "The Amending Process in the House of Representatives." Report for Congress Received through the CRS Web, Order Code 98-995 GOV, April 16.

Davis, Edward. 1997. "The Evolution of Federal Spending Controls: A Brief Overview." *Public Budgeting and Finance* 17:10–24.

De Boef, Suzanna, and Jim Granato. 1999. "Testing for Cointegrating Relationships with Near-Integrated Data." *Political Analysis* 8:99–117.

de Figueiredo, Rui J. P., Jr., and Barry R. Weingast. 2005. "Self-Enforcing Federalism." *Journal of Law, Economics, and Organization* 21:103–35.

Dellinger, Walter. 1995. "The Balanced Budget Amendment." Statement before the Joint Economic Committee, U.S. Congress, January 23.

Denzau, Arthur T., and Robert J. Mackay. 1983. "Gatekeeping and Monopoly Power of Committees: An Analysis of Sincere and Sophisticated Power." *American Journal of Political Science* 27:740–61.

Diermeier, Daniel, Hulya Eraslan, and Antonio Merlo. 2002. "Bicameralism and Government Formation." Working Paper, University of Pennsylvania.

Diermeier, Daniel, and Timothy J. Feddersen. 1998. "Cohesion in Legislatures and the Vote of Confidence Procedure." *American Political Science Review* 92:611–21.

Diermeier, Daniel, and Keith Krehbiel. 2003. "Institutionalism as Methodology." *Journal of Theoretical Politics* 15:123–44.

Diermeier, Daniel, and Roger B. Myerson. 1999. "Bicameralism and Its Consequences for the Internal Organization of Legislatures." *American Economic Review* 89:1182–96.

Downs, Anthony. 1957. *An Economic Theory of Democracy*. New York: Harper & Row.

Druckman, James N., and Michael F. Thies. 2002. "The Importance of Concurrence: The Impact of Bicameralism on Government Formation and Duration." *American Journal of Political Science* 46:760–71.

Eggertsson, Thrainn. 2005. *Imperfect Institutions: Possibilities and Limits of Reform.* Ann Arbor: University of Michigan Press.

Elazar, Daniel J. 1982. "The Principles and Traditions Underlying State Constitutions." *Publius* 12:11–25.

Epstein, David, and Sharyn O'Halloran. 1999. *Delegating Powers: A Transaction Cost Politics Approach to Policy Making under Separate Powers.* New York: Cambridge University Press.

Eskridge, William N., Jr., Philip P. Frickey, and Elizabeth Garrett. 2002. *Legislation: Statutes and the Creation of Public Policy.* 3d ed. St. Paul, MN: West Group.

Evans, Diana. 2004. *Greasing the Wheels: Using Pork Barrel Projects to Build Majority Coalitions in Congress.* New York: Cambridge University Press.

Fearon, James D. 1994. "Domestic Political Audiences and the Escalation of International Disputes." *American Political Science Review* 88:577–92.

Feingold, Russell. 2005. "Department of Defense Appropriations Act, 2006 — Conference Report — Resumed." *Congressional Record* 151 (167):S14221.

Feld, Lars P., and John G. Matsusaka. 2003. "Budget Referendums and Government Spending: Evidence from Swiss Cantons." *Journal of Public Economics* 87:2703–24.

Feldman, Allan M. 1980. *Welfare Economics and Social Choice Theory.* Boston: Kluwer.

Fenno, Richard F., Jr. 1978. *Home Style: House Members in Their Districts.* Boston: Little, Brown.

Ferejohn, John, and Keith Krehbiel. 1987. "The Budget Process and the Size of the Budget." *American Journal of Political Science* 31:296–320.

Ferejohn, John, and Charles Shipan. 1990. "Congressional Influence on Bureaucracy." *Journal of Law, Economics, and Organization* 6:1–20.

Fiorina, Morris P., and Roger G. Noll. 1978. "Voters, Bureaucrats, and Legislators: A Rational Choice Perspective on the Growth of Bureaucracy." *Journal of Public Economics* 9:239–54.

———. 1979. "Majority Rule Models and Legislative Elections." *Journal of Politics* 41:1081–1104.

Fisher, Louis. 1985. "Ten Years of the Budget Act: Still Searching for Controls." *Public Budgeting and Finance* 5:3–8.

Fisk, Catherine, and Erwin Chemerinsky. 1997. "The Filibuster." *Stanford Law Review* 49:181–54.

Fitts, Michael A., and Robert P. Inman. 1992. "Controlling Congress: Presidential Influence in Domestic Fiscal Policy." *Georgetown Law Journal* 80:1737–85.

Fudenberg, Drew, and Jean Tirole. 1991. *Game Theory.* Cambridge, MA: MIT Press.

Gallagher, Jay. 2005. "Need a Budget? Block the Exit." *Rochester Democrat and Chronicle,* March 3, A5.

Garand, James C., and Andre Blais. 2003. "Understanding Joint Support for Government Spending and Taxes: Linking Benefits and Costs in the Mass Public." Paper presented at the annual meeting of the American Political Science Association.

Garrett, Elizabeth. 2004. "The Purposes of Framework Legislation." ISC Public Policy Research Paper No. 04-3.

General Accounting Office. 1993. "Balanced Budget Requirements: State Experiences and Implications for the Federal Government." GAO Report AFMD-93-58BR.

Gilligan, Thomas W., and Keith Krehbiel. 1987. "Collective Decisionmaking and Standing Committees: An Informational Rationale for Restrictive Amendment Procedures." *Journal of Law, Economics, and Organization* 3:287–335.

Gilligan, Thomas W., and John G. Matsusaka. 1995. "Deviations from Constituent Interests: The Role of Legislative Structure and Political Parties in the States." *Economic Inquiry* 33:383–401.

———. 2001. "Fiscal Policy, Legislature Size, and Political Parties: Evidence from the First Half of the Twentieth Century." *National Tax Journal* 54:57–82.

Gilmour, John B. 1990. *Reconcilable Differences?* Berkeley: University of California Press.

Gold, Martin B., and Dimple Gupta. 2003. "The Constitutional Option to Change Senate Rules and Procedures: A Majoritarian Means to Overcome the Filibuster." *Harvard Journal of Law and Public Policy* 28:205–72.

Gonzalez-Paramo, Jose Manuel. 2005. "The Reform of the Stability and Growth Pact: An Assessment." Speech before the conference "New Perspectives on Fiscal Sustainability," October 13.

Gramm, Phil. 1985. "Increase of Permanent Public Debt Limit." *Congressional Record* 131 (133):S12954.

Grassley, Charles. 1985. "Increase of Permanent Public Debt Limit." *Congressional Record* 131 (133):S12954.

Green, Edward J., and Robert H. Porter. 1984. "Noncooperative Collusion under Imperfect Price Information." *Econometrica* 52:87–100.

Griffin, Stephen M. 1995. "Constitutionalism in the United States: From Theory to Politics." In *Responding to Imperfection*, ed. Sanford Levinson. Princeton, NJ: Princeton University Press, pp. 37–61.

Grooters, Jennifer, and Corina Eckl. 1998. *Legislative Budget Procedures*. Denver: National Conference of State Legislatures.

Groseclose, Tim, and Nolan McCarty. 2001. "The Politics of Blame: Bargaining before an Audience." *American Journal of Political Science* 45:100–119.

Groves, Theodore. 1973. "Incentives in Teams." *Econometrics* 41:617–31.

Haber, Stephen, Armando Razo, and Noel Maurer. 2003. *The Politics of Property Rights: Political Instability, Credible Commitments, and Economic Growth in Mexico, 1876–1929*. New York: Cambridge University Press.

Hadi, Ali S. 1992. "A Modification of a Method for the Detection of Outliers in Multivariate Samples." *Journal of the Royal Statistical Society*, Series B (*Methodological*) 54:761–71.

———. 1994. "Identifying Multiple Outliers in Multivariate Data." *Journal of the Royal Statistical Society*, Series B (*Methodological*) 56:393–96.

Hamilton, Alexander, John Jay, and James Madison. [1818] 2001. *The Federalist*, ed. George W. Carey and James McClellan. Gideon ed. Indianapolis: Liberty Fund.

Hancke, Bob. 2003. "The Political Economy of Fiscal Policy in EMU." *European Political Economy Review* 1:5–14.

Hayek, F.A. 1945. "The Use of Knowledge in Society." *American Economic Review* 35:519–30.

———. 1973. *Law, Legislation, and Liberty*. Vol. 1. Chicago: University of Chicago Press.

Heller, William B. 1997. "Bicameralism and Budget Deficits: The Effect of Parliamentary Structure on Government Spending." *Legislative Studies Quarterly* 22:485–516.

Hinich, Melvin J., and Michael C. Munger. 1997. *Analytical Politics*. New York: Cambridge.

Huber, John D., and Charles R. Shipan. 2002. *Deliberate Discretion? The Institutional Foundations of Bureaucratic Autonomy*. New York: Cambridge University Press.

Hurdle, Jon. 2006. "NJ Budget Crisis Threatens Atlantic City Casinos." *boston.com News*, July 3. http://www.boston.com/news/nation/articles/2006/07/03/nj_governor_urges_lawmakers_to_end_budget_crisis.

Inman, Robert P. 1998. "Do Balanced Budget Rules Work? U.S. Experience and Possible Lessons for the EMU." NBER Reprint No. 2173.

———. 2003. "Transfers and Bailouts: Enforcing Local Fiscal Discipline with Lessons from U.S. Federalism." In *Fiscal Decentralization and the Challenge of Hard Budget Constraints*, ed. Jonathan Rodden, Gunnar S. Eskeland, and Jennie Litvack. Cambridge, MA: MIT Press, pp. 35–84.

Inman, Robert P., and Michael A. Fitts. 1990. "Political Institutions and Fiscal Policy: Evidence from the U.S. Historical Record." *Journal of Law, Economics, and Organization* 6:79–132.

Ippolito, Dennis. 2003. *Why Budgets Matter*. University Park: Pennsylvania State University Press.

Joling, Dan. 2005. "Alaska in Line for Increase in Highway Spending Increase." *Associated Press State and Local Wire*, August 1.

Joyce, Philip. 2005. "Federal Budgeting after September 11th: A Whole New Ballgame, or Is It Déjà Vu All over Again?" *Public Budgeting and Finance* 25:15–31.

Kalandrakis, Tasos. 2004. "Bicameral Winning Coalitions and Equilibrium Federal Legislatures." *Legislative Studies Quarterly* 29:49–79.

Keefer, Philip, and David Stasavage. 2003. "The Limits of Delegation: Veto Players, Central Bank Independence, and the Credibility of Monetary Policy." *American Political Science Review* 97:407–23.

Keith, Robert. 2002. "Techniques for Preventing a Budget Sequester." CRS Report for Congress, RL31155, March 8.

Kettl, Donald F. 2003a. *Deficit Politics: The Search for Balance in American Politics*. 2d ed. New York: Longman.

———. 2003b. "Innovation Freeze." *Governing* (October), p. 12.

Kiewiet, D. Roderick, and Mathew D. McCubbins. 1991. *The Logic of Delegation.* Chicago: University of Chicago Press.

Kiewiet, D. Roderick, and Kristin Szakaly. 1996. "Constitutional Limitations on Borrowing: An Analysis of State Bonded Indebtedness." *Journal of Law, Economics, and Organization* 12:62–97.

Kim, Jaehoon, and Lawrence S. Rothenberg. 2005. "Foundations of Legislative Organization and Committee Influence." Working Paper, University of Rochester.

Klarner, Carl. 2003. "The Measurement of the Partisan Balance of State Government." *State Politics and Policy Quarterly* 3:309–19.

Kopits, George F., and Steven A. Symansky. 1998. "Fiscal Policy Rules." IMF Occasional Paper No. 162.

Kousser, Thad, and Justin Phillips. 2005. "Who Sets the Size of State Government? Comparing Models of Interbranch Conflict." Paper presented at the annual meeting of the Midwest Political Science Association.

Krehbiel, Keith. 1998. *Pivotal Politics.* Chicago: University of Chicago Press.

Kydland, Finn E., and Edward C. Prescott. 1977. "Rules Rather Than Discretion: The Inconsistency of Optimal Plans." *Journal of Political Economy* 85:473–91.

Lee, Frances. 2000. "Equal Votes for Unequal Demands: Senate Representation and Coalition Building in Distributive Politics." *American Political Science Review* 94:59–72.

LeLoup, Lance T. 2005. *Parties, Rules, and the Evolution of Congressional Budgeting.* Columbus: Ohio State University Press.

Lizzeri, Alessandro, and Nicola Persico. 2001. "The Provision of Public Goods under Alternative Electoral Incentives." *American Economic Review* 91:225–39.

Mackay, Robert J., and Carolyn L. Weaver. 1979. "On the Mutuality of Interests between Bureaus and High Demand Review Committees." *Public Choice* 34:481–91.

———. 1983. "Commodity Bundling and Agenda Control in the Public Sector." *Quarterly Journal of Economics* 98:611–35.

Makinen, Amy K. 2001. "Rights, Review, and Spending: Policy Outcomes with Judicially Enforceable Rights." *European Journal of Political Research* 39:23–52.

Mann, Thomas E., and Norman J. Ornstein. 2006. *The Broken Branch.* New York: Oxford University Press.

Martin, Lisa L. 2000. *Democratic Commitments: Legislatures and International Cooperation.* Princeton, NJ: Princeton University Press.

Matsusaka, John G. 1995. "Fiscal Effects of the Voter Initiative: Evidence from the Last 30 Years." *Journal of Political Economy* 103:587–623.

———. 2000. "Fiscal Effects of the Voter Initiative in the First Half of the Twentieth Century." *Journal of Law and Economics* 43:619–50.

Matsusaka, John G., and Nolan M. McCarty. 2001. "Political Resource Allocation: Benefits and Costs of Voter Initiatives." *Journal of Law, Economics, and Organization* 17:413–48.

McCain, John. 2004. "Statement of Senator John McCain on the FY '04 Omnibus." http://mccain.senate.gov (accessed July 6, 2005).

——. 2005. "Pork Statements." http://mccain.senate.gov (accessed July 6, 2005).

McCarty, Nolan, Keith Poole, and Howard Rosenthal. 2006. *Polarized America: The Dance of Ideology and Unequal Riches*. Cambridge, MA: MIT Press.

McGinnis, John O., and Michael B. Rappaport. 1995. "The Constitutionality of Legislative Supermajority Requirements: A Defense." *Yale Law Journal* 105:483–511.

——. 1999. "Supermajority Rules as a Constitutional Solution." *William and Mary Law Review* 40:365–470.

——. 2003. "Symmetric Entrenchment: A Constitutional and Normative Theory." *Virginia Law Review* 89:385–445.

McManus, John C. 1975. "The Costs of Alternative Economic Organizations." *Canadian Journal of Economics* 8:334–50.

Milesi-Ferretti, Gian Maria, Roberto Perotti, and Massimo Rostagno. 2002. "Electoral Systems and Public Spending." *Quarterly Journal of Economics* 117:609–57.

Milgrom, Paul R., Douglass C. North, and Barry R. Weingast. 1990. "The Role of Institutions in the Revival of Trade: The Law Merchant, Private Judges, and the Champagne Fairs." *Economics and Politics* 2:1–23.

Milgrom, Paul R., and John Roberts. 1992. *Economics, Organization and Management*. Englewood Cliffs, NJ: Prentice-Hall.

Miller, James C., III 1994. *Fix the U.S. Budget*. Stanford, CA: Hoover Institution Press.

Moe, Terry M. 1984. "The New Economics of Organization." *American Journal of Political Science* 28:739–77.

——. 1985. "The Politicized Presidency." In *The New Direction in American Politics*, ed. John E. Chubb and Paul E. Peterson. Washington, DC: Brookings Institution Press, pp. 235–71.

——. 1989. "The Politics of Bureaucratic Structure." In *Can the Government Govern?* ed. John E. Chubb and Paul E. Peterson. Washington, DC: Brookings Institution Press, pp. 267–329.

Morton, Rebecca B. 1999. *Methods and Models: A Guide to the Empirical Analysis of Formal Models in Political Science*. Cambridge: Cambridge University Press.

National Association of State Budget Officers. 1992. "State Balanced Budget Requirements: Provisions and Practice." National Association of State Budget Officers, Washington, DC.

National Conference of State Legislatures. 2000. *Mason's Manual of Legislative Procedure*. Denver: National Conference of State Legislatures.

——. 2005. "State Tax and Expenditure Limits–2005." http://www.ncsl.org/programs/fiscal/tels2005.htm (accessed May 5, 2006).

Nevada Supreme Court. 2003a. *Guinn v. Legislature*. 71 P.3d 1269.

——. 2003b. *Guinn v. Legislature*. 76 P.3d 22.

New Jersey Supreme Court. 2002. *Lonegan v. State.* 809 A.2d 91.

——— . 2003. *Lonegan v. State.* 819 A.2d 395.

New York State Court of Appeals. 2004. *George E. Pataki, as Governor of the State of New York v. New York State Assembly; Sheldon Silver v. George E. Pataki, Governor.* Case No. 171/172.

North, Douglass C. 1990. *Institutions, Institutional Change, and Economic Performance.* New York: Cambridge University Press.

North, Douglass C., and Barry R. Weingast. 1989. "Constitutions and Commitment: The Evolution of Institutions Governing Public Choice in Seventeenth-Century England." *Journal of Economic History* 49:803–32.

Nunn, Sam. 1995. "Recognition of the Democratic Leader." *Congressional Record* 141 (37):S3231.

Oates, Wallace E. 1972. *Fiscal Federalism.* New York: Harcourt Brace Jovanovich.

——— . 2005. "Toward a Second-Generation Theory of Fiscal Federalism." *International Tax and Public Finance* 12:349–73.

Oleszek, Walter J. 2004. *Congressional Procedures and the Policy Process.* 6th ed. Washington, DC: CQ Press.

Persson, Torsten, and Guido Tabellini. 1996a. "Federal Fiscal Constitutions: Risk Sharing and Moral Hazard." *Econometrica* 64:623–46.

——— . 1996b. "Federal Fiscal Constitutions: Risk Sharing and Redistribution." *Journal of Political Economy* 104:979–1009.

——— . 1999. "The Size and Scope of Government: Comparative Politics with Rational Politicians." *European Economic Review* 43:699–735.

——— . 2000. *Political Economics: Explaining Economic Policy.* Cambridge, MA: MIT Press.

——— . 2003. *The Economic Effects of Constitutions.* Cambridge, MA: MIT Press.

——— . 2004a. "Constitutional Rules and Fiscal Policy Outcomes." *American Economic Review* 94:25–45.

——— . 2004b. "Constitutions and Economic Policy." *Journal of Economic Perspectives* 18:75–98.

Persson, Torsten, Gerard Roland, and Guido Tabellini. 1997. "Separation of Powers and Political Accountability." *Quarterly Journal of Economics* 112:1163–1202.

Posner, Eric A., and Adrian Vermeule. 2002. "Legislative Entrenchment: A Reappraisal." *Yale Law Journal* 111:1665–1705.

Poterba, James M. 1994. "State Responses to Fiscal Crises: The Effects of Budgetary Institutions and Politics." *Journal of Political Economy* 102:799–821.

——— . 1997. "Do Budget Rules Work?" In *Fiscal Policy: Lessons for Empirical Research,* ed. Alan Auerbach. Cambridge, MA: MIT Press, pp. 53–86.

Poterba, James M., and Kim Rueben. 1999. "State Fiscal Institutions and the U.S. Municipal Bond Market." In *Fiscal Institutions and Fiscal Performance,* ed. James M. Poterba and Juergen von Hagen. Chicago: University of Chicago Press, pp. 181–208.

Primo, David M. 2002. "Rethinking Political Bargaining: Policymaking with a Single Proposer." *Journal of Law, Economics, and Organization* 18:411–27.

———. 2006. "Stop Us Before We Spend Again: Institutional Constraints on Government Spending." *Economics and Politics* 18:269–312.

———. 2007. "A Comment on Baron and Ferejohn (1989): The Open Rule Equilibrium and Coalition Formation." *Public Choice* 130:129–35.

Primo, David M., Sarah A. Binder, and Forrest Maltzman. 2007. "Who Consents? A Theoretical and Empirical Examination of Pivotal Senators in the Judicial Confirmation Process." Working Paper, University of Rochester.

Primo, David M., and James M. Snyder, Jr. 2007a. "Distributive Politics and the Law of 1/n." Working Paper, University of Rochester.

———. 2007b. "Party Strength, the Personal Vote, and Government Spending." Working Paper, University of Rochester.

Proxmire, William. 1988. "The Gold Medalists of the Golden Fleece Awards." *Newsday,* May 31, 50.

Qian, Yingyi, and Barry R. Weingast. 1997. "Federalism as a Commitment to Preserving Market Incentives." *Journal of Economic Perspectives* 11:83–92.

Rhoads, Christopher. 2003. "Europe's Division over Deficit Rules Is Intensifying." *Wall Street Journal,* July 16, A12.

Riker, William H. 1962. *The Theory of Political Coalitions.* New Haven, CT: Yale University Press.

———. 1980. "Implications for the Disequilibrium of Majority Rule for the Study of Institutions." *American Political Science Review* 74:432–46.

———. 1982. *Liberalism against Populism.* Prospect Heights, IL: Waveland Press.

Riker, William H., and Ronald Schaps. 1957. "Disharmony in Federal Government." *Behavioral Science* 2:276–90.

Robert, Henry M. 2000. *Robert's Rules of Order.* 10th ed. Cambridge: Perseus.

Rodden, Jonathan. 2002. "The Dilemma of Fiscal Federalism: Grants and Fiscal Performance around the World." *American Journal of Political Science* 46:670–87.

———. 2005. *Hamilton's Paradox: The Promise and Peril of Fiscal Federalism.* New York: Cambridge University Press.

Rodden, Jonathan, Gunnar S. Eskeland, and Jennie Litvack, eds. 2003. *Fiscal Decentralization and the Challenge of Hard Budget Constraints.* Cambridge, MA: MIT Press.

Rogers, James R. 2003. "The Impact of Bicameralism on Legislative Production." *Legislative Studies Quarterly* 28:509–28.

Romer, Thomas, and Howard Rosenthal. 1978. "Political Resource Allocation, Controlled Agendas, and the Status Quo." *Public Choice* 33:27–43.

Rosendorff, B. Peter. 2005. "Stability and Rigidity: Politics and Design of the WTO's Dispute Resolution Procedure." *American Political Science Review* 99:389–400.

Rosenthal, Alan. 1996. "State Legislative Development: Observations from Three Perspectives." *Legislative Studies Quarterly* 21:169–98.

Rueben, Kim S. 1995. "Tax Limitations and Government Growth: The Effect of State Tax and Expenditure Limits on State and Local Government." Unpublished paper, MIT.

Safire, William. 1993. *Safire's New Political Dictionary: The Definitive Guide to the New Language of Politics*. New York: Random House.

Samuelson, Paul A. 1954. "The Pure Theory of Public Expenditure." *Review of Economics and Statistics* 36:387–89.

Savage, James D. 1988. *Balanced Budgets and American Politics*. Ithaca, NY: Cornell University Press.

Schelling, Thomas C. 1960. *The Strategy of Conflict*. Cambridge, MA: Harvard University Press.

Schick, Allen. 1996. "The Majority Rules." *Brookings Review* 14:42–45.

——— . 2000. *The Federal Budget: Politics, Policy, Process*. Washington, DC: Brookings Institution Press.

Schickler, Eric. 2001. *Disjointed Pluralism*. Princeton, NJ: Princeton University Press.

Schoenbrod, Angus Macbeth, David I. Levine, and David J. Jung. 2002. *Remedies: Public and Private*. 3d ed. St. Paul, MN: West Group.

Segal, Jeffrey A. 1997. "Separation-of-Powers Games in the Positive Theory of Congress and Courts." *American Political Science Review* 91:28–44.

Sellers, Patrick J. 1997. "Fiscal Consistency and Federal District Spending in Congressional Elections." *American Journal of Political Science* 41:1024–41.

Serritzlew, Soren. 2005. "The Perverse Effect of Spending Caps." *Journal of Theoretical Politics* 17:75–105.

Shepsle, Kenneth A. 1991. "Discretion, Institutions, and the Problem of Government." In *Social Theory for a Changing Society*, ed. Pierre Bourdieu and James S. Coleman. Boulder, CO: Westview Press, pp. 245–63.

Shepsle, Kenneth A., and Mark S. Bonchek. 1997. *Analyzing Politics*. New York: Norton.

Shepsle, Kenneth A., and Barry R. Weingast. 1981. "Political Preferences for the Pork Barrel: A Generalization." *American Journal of Political Science* 25:96–111.

Sinclair, Barbara. 2000. *Unorthodox Lawmaking*. 2d ed. Washington, DC: CQ Press.

Smith, Adam. [1776] 1999. *The Wealth of Nations*. Books 1–3. London: Penguin Classics.

Squire, Peverill, and Keith E. Hamm. 2005. *101 Chambers*. Columbus: Ohio State University Press.

Sullivan, Kevin. 1988. "St. Germain Tries to Make Bacon of Les Pork." *Providence Journal*, September 28, A3.

Thurber, James A. 1995. "If the Game Is Too Hard, Change the Rules." In *Remaking Congress: Change and Stability in the 1990s*, ed. James A. Thurber and Roger H. Davidson. Washington, DC: CQ Press, pp. 130–44.

Tiebout, Charles M. 1956. "A Pure Theory of Local Expenditures." *Journal of Political Economy* 64:416–24.

Tsebelis, George, and Jeannette Money. 1997. *Bicameralism*. New York: Cambridge University Press.

U.S. Census Bureau. 2000. *Government Finance and Employment Classification Manual*. Washington, DC: U.S. Government Printing Office.

U.S. Congress. 1985. *Balanced Budget and Emergency Deficit Control Act of 1985*. Title II of Public Law 99-177. *U.S. Statutes at Large* 90:1038–1101.

——. 1990. *Budget Enforcement Act of 1990*. Title XIII of Public Law 101-508. *U.S. Statutes at Large* 104:1388-57–1388-630.

U.S. House. 1995. *Proposing a Balanced Budget Amendment to the Constitution of the United States*. HJ Res. 1.EH. 104th Cong., 1st sess.

——. 2003. *Family Budget Protection Act of 2003*. HR 3358. 108th Cong., 1st sess.

——. 2004. *Family Budget Protection Act of 2004*. HR 3800. 108th Cong., 2d sess.

——. 2005. *Family Budget Protection Act of 2005*. HR 2290. 109th Cong., 1st sess.

U.S. Office of Management and Budget. 2005. *Historical Tables, Budget of the United States Government, Fiscal Year 2006*. Washington, DC: U.S. Government Printing Office.

U.S. Senate. 1995. "Balanced-Budget Constitutional Amendment." 104th Cong., 1st sess., report 104-5, calendar no. 16.

——. 1998. *The Congressional Budget Process*. Washington, DC: U.S. Government Printing Office.

——. 2004. *Family Budget Protection Act of 2004*. S2752. 108th Cong., 2d sess.

U.S. Supreme Court. 1810. *Fletcher v. Peck*. 10 U.S. 87.

——. 1983. *INS v. Chadha*. 462 U.S. 919.

——. 1985. *Bowsher v. Synar*. 478 U.S. 714.

——. 2005. *Lockhart v. United States*. 546 U.S.

Vickrey, William. 1961. "Counterspeculation, Auctions, and Competitive Sealed Tenders." *Journal of Finance* 16:8–37.

Wagner, Adolph. 1994. "Three Extracts on Public Finance" (1883). In *Classics in the Theory of Public Finance*, ed. Richard A. Musgrave and Alan T. Peacock. New York: St. Martin's Press, pp. 1–15.

Walras, Leon. 1954. *Elements of Pure Economics*. Translated by William Jaffé. Homewood, IL: Richard D. Irwin.

Weingast, Barry R. 1979. "A Rational Choice Perspective on Congressional Norms." *American Journal of Political Science* 23:245–62.

——. 2002. "Rational-Choice Institutionalism." In *Political Science: State of the Discipline*, ed. Ira Katznelson and Helen V. Milner. New York: Norton, pp. 660–92.

——. 2005. "The Constitutional Dilemma of Economic Liberty." *Journal of Economic Perspectives* 19:89–108.

——. 2006. "Designing Constitutional Stability." In *Democratic Constitutional Design and Public Policy*, ed. Roger D. Congleton and Birgitta Swedenborg. Cambridge, MA: MIT Press, pp. 343–66.

Weingast, Barry R., and William J. Marshall. 1988. "The Industrial Organization of Congress; or, Why Legislatures, Like Firms, Are Not Organized as Markets." *Journal of Political Economy* 96:132–63.

188 : *References*

Weingast, Barry R., Kenneth A. Shepsle, and Christopher Johnsen. 1981. "The Political Economy of Benefits and Costs: A Neoclassical Approach to Distributive Politics." *Journal of Political Economy* 89:642–64.

Whelan, Jeff, and Josh Margolin. 2005. "How Tiff over Budget Turned into a Brawl." *Star-Ledger,* July 3, sec. 1, p. 15.

Wicksell, Knut. 1958. "A New Principle of Just Taxation." In *Classics in the Theory of Public Finance*, ed. Richard A. Musgrave and Alan T. Peacock. London: Macmillan, pp. 72–118.

Wilbanks, Charles H. 1990. "States News Service Wire Report." May 3.

Wildavsky, Aaron, and Naomi Caiden. 2004. *The New Politics of the Budgetary Process*. New York: Pearson-Longman.

Williams, Robert F. 1987. "State Constitutional Limits on Legislative Procedure: Legislative Compliance and Judicial Enforcement." *University of Pittsburgh Law Review* 48:797–827.

Wilson, Brian. 2001. "This Byrd Loves the Taste of Pork." *Fox Special Report with Brit Hume.* July 3.

Winerip, Michael. 2003. "Arm-Twister's Guide to School Finance." *New York Times,* February 26, A21.

Wittman, Donald A. 1995. *The Myth of Democratic Failure*. Chicago: University of Chicago Press.

Wolfensberger, Donald R. 2001. "Congress and the Politics of Pork." http://wilsoncenter.org (accessed December 15, 2005).

Wood, B. Dan, and John Bohte. 2004. "Political Transaction Costs and the Politics of Administrative Design." *Journal of Politics* 66:176–202.

Wooldridge, Jeffrey M. 2002. *Econometric Analysis of Cross Section and Panel Data*. Cambridge, MA: MIT Press.

Page numbers in italic type refer to tables or graphs.

Ackerman, Bruce, 129–30
Act 60 (Vermont), 38–39
agencies: delegation of regulatory authority to, 11, 56–57, 60, 61, 163n7; effectiveness of enforcement by, 34–35, 43, 56–57, 60, 124; rules for design of, 6–7, 161n4; transaction costs and design of, 6–7
agenda setter: balanced budget rule and, 14, 83; bargaining logic in closed rule model, 68–69; bargaining logic in open rule model, 69–70; in the baseline model, 48, 49, *49*, 50; behavior in closed rule model, 67, 143–44; behavior in open rule model, 67–68, 151–52, 154, 155; effects of court/agency enforcement of rules, 57; impact of constituency costs on behavior of, 58–59, 147–48, *149*; impact of open/closed rule on project size/net benefits, 71, *72*, *73*, *74*; impact of size of coalition required for legislation to pass, 79–80, 168nn9–10; incentive to abide by spending limits, 62–63, 75–76, 77, 79–80; legislature's constraint on, 159–60; net benefits to under open/closed rule, *74*; 90 percent rule and, 119–20;

in numerical example, 51; power of, 50, 71; preference for closed rule, 64, 74, 80; selection of, 67, 142; spending limits and, 52–53, 63, 64, 75–76, 144, 145; supermajority voting rule and, 54, 55; unanimity rule and, 51–52
Akerlof, George, 28
Alabama, 85
Alaska, 169n10
amendment procedures: bargaining logic and, 69–70; Baron-Ferejohn model (in Congress), 167n3; budget process and, 65–66; budget rules tied to, 62–81; stability of, 75; use of the term, 63. *See also* closed rule; constitutional amendment; open rule
Arctic National Wildlife Refuge (ANWR), 7–8
Armey, Dick, 11
Arnold, Douglas, 10
Article 1, section 5 (U.S. Constitution), 39–40
audience costs, 166n20

balanced budget amendment. *See* balanced budget rule; constitutional amendment

balanced budget rules: challenges to federal adoption of, 105, 106, 127–30; circumvention of, 118; constitutional enforcement of, 4; constraints of, 163n10; diversity of design and enforcement, 82; effectiveness of, 96, 103, 104, 124; effect on spending in states, 87, 88–97, 99, 103, 104, 124; enacted by states, 4, 5; enforcement of, 41, 85–86, 87, 168nn3–4, 169nn6–8; in European Union, 130–31; on federal level, 115–18; interaction with supermajority rules, 162n15; limitations on deficit spending, 22, 107; long-term fiscal restraint/short-term spending tensions and, 9–14; 90 percent rule, 118–21; no-carryover rule and, 84–85, *90*, 93, *94*, 96, 98–99, 103, 170n14; public view of, 10, 83; response to revenue increases, 98–99; shutdown rule and, 4, 19, 83, 101–3, 126, 136; spending levels and, 83–85, 168n1; supermajority voting rules and, 14, 116, 118–21, 162n12; types of, 84–85. *See also* budget rules; spending limit
Barbera, Salvador, 35
Baron, David P., 47, 66, 74, 80, 165n8, 173nn1–2
baseline model. *See* closed rule distributive politics model
Basinger, Scott J., 166n20
BEA. *See* Budget Enforcement Act (1990)
Bednar, Jenna, 35
Bernanke, Ben, 105
Besley, Timothy, 43
bicameralism, 13
Binder, Sarah A., 138, 161n1
Blackstone, William, 108
blue slip, 32–33
Bohn, Henning, 85, 99
Bowsher v. Synar, 110–11
Boxer, Barbara, 61
Bridges to Nowhere, 46

Briffault, Richard, 128, 129
Buchanan, James M., 18, 46
Budget and Accounting Act (1921), 106
budget deficit: carryover rules and, 84–85; Excessive Deficit Procedure and, 131–33,173nn6–7; Family Budget Protection Act and, 19–20; Gramm-Rudman-Hollings Act and, 108–10, *112*; Keynesianism and, 18–19; no-carryover rule and, 84–85, *90*, 93, *94*, 96, 98–99, 103, 170n14; politics of, 18–19; shutdown rule and, 4, 19, 83, 101–3, 126, 136; of the United States, 106, *112*, 173n9; variation among states, 4, 82, 126
Budget Enforcement Act (1990), 22, 107, 111, 113–14, 125
budget process: agenda control and, 32; amendments and, 65–66; Congressional Budget and Impoundment Control Act and, 106; government organization and, 12–14; institutional design and, 40–41; institutional environment and, 9–14; Keynesianism and, 18–19; long-term fiscal restraint/short-term spending tensions of, 9–14; multidimensionality of, 40, 65–66, 107–8; power of on-time budget, 99–101; untouchable categories, 3, 110, 113; of U.S. House of Representatives, 80; of U.S. states (*see* U.S. states)
budget reform: Budget Enforcement Act (1990), 22, 107, 111, 113–14, 125; challenges to, 22, 133–37; constituency costs and, 99–101, 103–4, 125; failure of federal attempts at, 3, 5, 105–15, 125; Gramm-Rudman-Hollings Act, 3–4, 22, 107, 108–13, *112*, 125; long-term/short-term and tensions of, 107, 110–14, 122; majority rule and, 106–8; policy-related/process-related, 107; nature of in states, 82; political compromise and, 122; of the twentieth century, 106–8
budget rules: challenges to design and en-

forcement of, 105–6, 114–15, 133–37; as constraint on behavior, 123; delegation of specific decisions, 11; design and enforcement of, 3–5, 40–41; design of as a political process, 4–5, 41, 60, 104, 105, 127; difficulty of design of, 80–81; enactment and effectiveness, 5, 96, 103, 104, 124, 137; enforcement of (*see* endogenous enforcement; enforcement; exogenous enforcement); environment of, 5–13, 60, 80, 102–3, 123; impact on spending patterns, 102–4; incentives for designing inefficient rules, 19–20; institutional interactions and, 14, 16, 31–33, 54–55, 86, 102–3, 162n12; interests and, 40–41; long-term/short-term and micro/macro tensions of, 21, 40, 110–14, 122, 126; malleability/stability of, 7–9, 63–64; metainstitutional interactions and, 162n12; prospective/retrospective, 84; question concerning design and evaluation of, 133–37; success of, 22; transaction costs and, 5–7; tying to stable aspects of the organization, 5, 36–37, 61–63, 64, 122, 126–27. *See also* balanced budget rule; no-carryover rule; shutdown rule

Bumpers, Dale, 46
Bureau of the Budget (BOB), 106, 172n4
Byrd, Robert, 7–8, 46, 138
Byrd-Grassley law, 109

Caiden, Naomi, 57
Calvert, Randall L., 35
cartel behavior model, 34
central planning, 163n2
checks-and-balances system, 42
Cheung, Steve, 38
Cho, Seok-ju, 167n2
citizen initiative, *90, 94,* 96, 164n22
Citizens Against Government Waste, 44, 46
Clement, Robert, 42

closed rule: agenda setter's preference for, 74, 80; elimination of delay and, 66; with endogenous enforcement of spending limit, 76–77; gatekeeping power and, 31–32, 164n12; as incentive for agenda setter to abide by spending limit, 75–76, 125; open rules vs., 65; outcomes under, 125, 167n2
closed rule distributive politics model: actors in, 49, 141–42, 165n10, 165n11; assumptions of, 49; bargaining logic under, 67–68; baseline outcome of, 50–51, 142–44, 165n10; with constituency costs, 57–59, 144–49; with delegated regulatory enforcement, 56–57; with endogenous enforcement of spending limit, 74–80, 144–47; equilibrium concept of, 49, 71, 142, 165n10, 174nn4–6; with executive veto authority, 54; game structure, 49, *49,* 142; game theory, 43; incorporation of enforcer preferences in, 56–59; legislative organization of, 142; lessons derived from, 60, 80–81; majority-rule version, 165n8; progress of play, 66–67, *67;* with quota rule, 143–44; results compared to open rule results, 70–80, *72;* results with endogenous enforcement, *72–73;* size and efficiency of projects, 70, 71; with spending limits, *52,* 52–53, 144–45; with supermajority voting rule, 53–54, 144–47
coalitions: maintenance in parliamentary democracies, 36; net benefits to under open/closed rule, *74;* size of and delay, 168n8; size of and implementation of spending limits, 78–79, 80, 168nn9–10; size of under open vs. closed rule, *72. See also* minimum winning coalitions; supermajority coalitions
Coase, R. H., 5
Coate, Stephen, 43
Codey, Richard, 101
collective action problems, 38–39
Committee of the Whole, 167n3

committees: blocking power of, 6, 161n5; effect of closed rules on, 65; gatekeeping power of, 31–32; proposal power of chairs of, 45

comptroller general, 110–11

Congress. *See* legislators; legislature; U.S. House of Representatives; U.S. Senate

Congressional Budget and Impoundment Control Act (1974), 106

Congressional Budget Office, 106, 114

Congressional Pig Book, 44

constituency costs: budget reform and, 99–101, 103–4; constitutional balanced budget rule and, 115, 118; for delay, 171n25; effectiveness of on federal level, 33, 60, 61, 122, 166n22; effect on state budget reform, 82, 99–101, 128; for elimination of balanced budget, 85; as external enforcer, 56, 124–25; GRH violations, 112; impact on spending, 43, 57–59, 147–49; for state legislatures, 128; use of term, 166n20. *See also* public

constitutional amendment: effectiveness on federal level, 4, 106, 108, 115–18, 122, 127–30; effectiveness on state level, 4, 86, 125, 128, 168n4, 169nn6–8; enforcement of, 33, 35; enforcement options, 22, 37, 41, 116, 127–30; feasibility of, 4, 19; impact on bargaining, 140; institutional interactions and, 128–29; interpretations of the Constitution and, 173n2; as product of compromise, 115, 116, 128; proposed in 1995, 115, 116, *117*, 118, 173n13; state vs. federal use of, 85, 106

constitutional balanced budget rules, 4, 41, 62, 127–30, 164nn18–19. *See also* balanced budget rule; constitutional amendment

constitutional convention, 129–30, 173n3

constitutional tax and expenditure limits. *See* tax and expenditure limits (TELs)

Constitution of the United States: Article 1, section 5, 39–40; checks-and-balances system and, 42; difficulty/effectiveness of amendment process, 106; stability of, 164–65n1; state constitutions vs., 85. *See also* constitutional amendment

constitutions, fragility of, 139–40

constitutions of states: amendment process, 85; provisions for legislative behavior, 39–40; U.S. Constitution vs., 85

continuing resolution, 101–2

contracts, 5–6, 15, 25–26

Corzine, Jon, 102

costs: analysis of enforcement and, 42; of enforcement, 34; institutional costs of rule changes, 36–37, 40, 62, 65, 76; of violating rules, 36–37, 40. *See also* constituency costs; transaction costs

courts: constitutional balanced budget rules and, 118, 173n13; effectiveness as enforcers, 33, 43, 56–57, 60, 86, 87, 103, 124, 129, 168n4, 169nn6–8; as external enforcer of constitutional rules, 35, 85; resistance to delegation of authority to, 61; ruling on enforcement for GRH, 110–11; selection procedure of justices, 86, 91, 93, 96, 103, 126, 169n5, 170n13

Cox, Gary W., 34

Crain, W. Mark, 87, 99

credibility: of central government, 13; of enforcement procedures, 5, 20–21, 31, 76, 123–24; of exogenous enforcement, 35, 57; of Gramm-Rudman-Hollings enforcement, 110, 111–12, 114, 126; of internal enforcement, 136–37; of leadership, 30; of veto threats, 59

Danforth, John, 109

de Figueiredo, Rui J. P., Jr., 13, 35

delay: constituency costs for, 99–101,

171n25; under open vs. closed rule, 70, 71, 73; rules governing, 101–3; shutdown rule and, 4, 19, 83, 101–3, 126, 136; size of coalitions and, 168n8. *See also* discount factor; patience

delegation of regulatory authority: by Congress to agencies, 43, 163n7; definition of, 56; outcomes and, 11, 56–57, 60

Democratic Party: filibusters and, 37, 62; spending and, 96, 171n22; veto override and, 92

Denzau, Arthur T., 31

discount factor: delay and, 102; implementation of spending limits and, 79, 79, 168n10; legislator patience and, 48, 50, 51, 142, 165n13. *See also* delay

distributive politics: closed rule model, 40–41, 47–51, 66–67, 67, 68–71, 72–73, 73–80, 74, 74–80; efficiency of, 124; inefficiency and size of spending, 134; open rule model, 7, 67–80, 68, 72, 73, 74; public view of, 44, 58; supermajority voting rule and, 53–54, 60; unanimity rule and, 51–52

district-specific projects: determining size of, 44–45; effects of inefficiency of, 66; models of distribution of, 47–51, 66–81, 141–42; multidimensionality of, 65; optimal spending for, 43–44; outcome of model, 51; paid by common tax pool, 43–44; public view of, 58; rules shaping choice of, 45; size and efficiency of under open/closed rule, 71, 72, 73. *See also* efficiency

Downs, Anthony, 162n16

Duggan, John, 167n2

earmark reform, 88, 169n9

EC. *See* European Commission (EC)

ECB. *See* European Central Bank (ECB)

ECM. *See* error correction model (ECM)

Economic and Financial Affairs Council of European Union (ECOFIN), 131–33

EDP. *See* Excessive Deficit Procedure (EDP)

efficiency: bargaining over single policy and, 162n17; as benchmark for evaluating outcomes, 17, 45; definition of, 48, 66, 71; distributive politics and, 40, 43; executive veto authority and, 54; norm of universalism and, 46–47; under open vs. closed rule, 71, 72, 73, 74; Pareto optimality and, 48; under perfect exogenous enforcement of rules, 50–51, 61; of pork-barrel projects, 45–46; preference for open rules and, 66; of projects under open rule, 70; relationship to spending, 55; rule design and, 4, 30–33; social welfare and, 165n9; spending limit and, 53, 54–55; supermajority voting rules and, 54–55

EMU. *See* European Monetary Union (EMU)

end-of-game effects, 48

endogeneity, 90–91, 170n13

endogenous enforcement: of Budget Enforcement Act, 114–15, 125; credibility of, 136–37; effectiveness of, 33, 63–64, 125; external vs., 4, 5, 6, 9, 20, 34, 39, 40; of Gramm-Rudman-Hollings Act, 110–12, 122, 125, 126; incentives for implementation of, 136; methods of, 61; of norms, 31; offer of closed rule to agenda setter and, 75–77, 125; Prisoner's Dilemma and, 26; repeated play and, 124; requirements for success of, 21, 34, 36; rule effectiveness and, 9; of Stability and Growth Pact, 131–33, 173nn6–7; tying rules to stable aspects of the organization, 34, 36–37, 61–62, 64, 75–76, 125, 126–27

endogenous enforcement model: bargaining logic, 68–70; comparative statistics of, 70–71, 72–73, 73–74; progress of play, 66–68, 67, 68, 77; spending limits and enforcement, 74–80 enforcement: analysis of rules and, 21, 31; assumed perfection of in baseline model, 42, 47–51, 60; of balanced budget rules, 82, 85–86, 87, 115, 122, 168n3; of Budget Enforcement Act, 113, 125; challenges to, 105–6, 164n17; checks-and-balance system as, 42; committee blocking power and, 6, 161n5; constituency costs as (*see* constituency costs); of constitutional amendment, 34–35; of constitutions, 139–40; of contracts in free markets, 25; costs of, 34; by courts (*see* courts); credibility of, 31, 35, 57, 110, 111–12, 114, 126, 136–37; delegation of to courts or agencies, 43, 56–57, 60, 61, 124, 163n7; design of, 28, 33–37, 39; effectiveness of, 33, 125, 168n4, 169nn6–8; effectiveness of rules and, 4, 21, 123–24; effects of imperfect forms, 55–59, 60; endogenous vs. exogenous, 4, 5, 6, 9, 20, 24, 34–35, 39–40; for enforcement of BEA, 113; for enforcement of GRH, 110–12; executive veto authority, 54, 60; failure of 1985 budget rules and, 125–26; of federal rules, 105–6; free rider problem and, 38–39; of Gramm-Rudman-Hollings Act, 110–12, 114, 122, 125–26; incentives for implementation of, 29, 34, 36–37, 40, 136; informational problems and, 34; inheritability and, 8–9, 36; institutional interactions under perfect enforcement, 54–55; of internal rules, 137–38; legislative rules and, 39–40; long-term fiscal restraint/short-term spending tensions of, 9–14; mechanisms for, 20, 39–40; of norms, 31; requirements for success of, 21; self-enforcing constitutions, 163n8; spending limits and, 52–53; of Stability and Growth Pact, 131–33, 173nn6–7; of states' balanced budget rules, 82, 85–86; supermajority voting rules and, 53–54; time inconsistency and,

12, 30; transactions and, 5–6; for truthful reporting of preferences, 27–28; tying budget rules to amendment rules, 62–81; tying rules to stable aspects of the organizations and, 34, 36, 61–62, 64, 75–76, 125, 126–27; unanimity rule and, 51–54. *See also* constitutional amendment; endogenous enforcement; exogenous enforcement

entitlements, 161n3

entrenchment, 39–40, 108

Environmental Protection Agency, 163n7

equilibrium, 35–36, 88, 142, 143, 144–47, 151, 165n10

error correction model (ECM), 97–99, 156–57, 170–71n15, 171nn19–23

European Central Bank (ECB), 130–31, 133

European Commission (EC), 131

European Monetary Union (EMU), 130

European Union (EU), 130

Evans, Diana, 44

ex ante expected values, 71, *72*, *75*, 77–79, *78*, 167n6

Excessive Deficit Procedure (EDP), 131–33, 173nn6–7

executive budget proposal, 106

executive veto authority: checks-and-balances system as, 42; distributive politics bargaining and, 124; Family Budget Protection Act and, 19; impact on federal spending, 43, 54, 59, 134, 166n16; spending limit and, 86, 87–88; state spending and, 87–88; study of, 87–88, 169n8; use of, 167n23

exogenous enforcement: assumption of perfection in model, 42, 47–51; checks-and-balances system as, 42; courts and agencies as, 43, 56–57, 60, 61, 124, 163n7; credibility of, 35, 57; effectiveness of, 33, 60, 124; effects of imperfect enforcement, 55–59; executive veto authority with perfect enforcement, 54; incentives for implementation of, 29; institutional interactions under perfect enforce-

ment, 54–55; internal vs., 4, 5, 6, 9, 20, 34–35, 39, 40; legislative resistance to, 61; spending limits and, 52–53; success of, 21, 41; supermajority voting rules with perfect enforcement, 53–54; unanimity rule and, 51–54. *See also* constituency costs; constitutional amendment
external enforcement. *See* exogenous enforcement

Family Budget Protection Act, 19–20
Fearon, James D., 166n20
feasible generalized least squares (FGLS) technique, *90*, 90–97, *92–93*, 156, 170n14, 170–71n15
federal aid, *90*, 93, *94*
federal balanced budget amendment, 85
federal government: enforcement of legislative rules, 9; failure of budget reform efforts, 3–4, 22, 105–15, 125; funding of local public works projects, 44; solution to deficit spending, 105. *See also* Constitution of the United States; legislature; president; U.S. House of Representatives; U.S. Senate; U.S. Supreme Court
federalism, 13–14, 35
Federalist 51, 23
federal spending levels, 1, *2*, 3, *3*. *See also* spending
Feingold, Russell, 8
Ferejohn, John A., 47, 66, 74, 80
FGLS. *See* feasible generalized least squares (FGLS) technique
filibuster: nuclear option and, 37, 62, 164n14, 164n19; senatorial courtesy and, 32–33; stability of, 4, 122, 126, 139; supermajority voting rule and, 172n6
filibuster pivots, 32–33
Fiorina, Morris P., 165n7
fiscal federalism, 17
fixed proposal power, 32, 164n13
Fletcher v. Peck, 108
focal points, 35

folk theorem, 35, 46
France, 132, 133
free rider problem, 14, 38–39, 130

game theory, 15–16, 42, 47, 135–36. *See also* closed rule distributive politics model; open rule distributive politics model
Garrett, Elizabeth, 64
gatekeeping power, 31–32, 164nn11–12
General Accountability Office (GAO), 110–11, 173n12
Germany, 132, 133
Gilligan, Thomas, 65, 96
Gilmour, John B., 64
Glorious Revolution (England), 30
Golden Fleece Award, 44
government: increase in entitlements, 161n3; optimal operation of, 23; provision of public goods, 27–28, 163n4. services provided by (*see* public goods); shut down in absence of budget agreement, 101–2; untouchable services, 3, 110, 113. *See also* federal government; U.S. states
governor: constituency costs for delay, 102–3, 171n25; ideology and spending trends, 87–88, 91–92, *95*, 96; veto authority, 102, 172n28
Gramm, Phil, 109
Gramm-Rudman-Hollings Act (GRH): adoption of, 3–4, 108–10; enforcement mechanism of, 110–12, 122, 125; failure of, 22, 111–12; focus of, 107; premise of, 63; projected deficits of, *112*
Grassley, Charles, 105, 109
Great Society reforms, 161n3
Green, Edward J., 34
GRH. *See* Gramm-Rudman-Hollings Act (GRH)
grim trigger strategy, 35

Hadi, Ali S., 169n10
Hallerberg, Mark, 166n20
Hatfield, Mark, 115

Hayek, F. A., 23, 36
Hollings, Ernest, 109

ideology: effectiveness of constituency
    costs and, 58–59, 60, 61; effectiveness
    of executive veto authority and, 54, 59;
    effects on state spending, 87–88, *90*,
    90–92, 96–99; measurement of, 91–92
Illinois, 85, 101
IMF. *See* International Monetary Fund
    (IMF)
incentives: for agenda setter to abide by
    spending limits, 75–76; approval of
    deficit spending and, 10; to change
    terms of a bargain ex post, 6; to
    change rules, 8–9; to design
    inefficient budget rules, 19–20, 106;
    electoral environment and, 12–13; free
    rider problem and, 38; for implemen-
    tation of rule enforcement, 29, 34,
    36, 56, 80, 81, 136, 163n8; importance
    of, 41; to keep spending down, 62–63;
    maintenance of federalism and, 13–14;
    to misrepresent preferences, 24, 26–
    28, 163n4; for not enforcing rules, 21,
    25; prospective budget rules and, 84;
    public finance models and, 17; suc-
    cessful implementation of policy and,
    11–12; transaction costs and, 6
infinite horizon bargaining models, 65,
    164n13
information: asymmetries in bargaining,
    26, 28–29; central planning and,
    163n2; enforcement and, 6, 34; free
    market and, 25; incentives to misrep-
    resent preferences and, 26–27;
    ineffectiveness of exogenous enforce-
    ment and, 60; principal-agent prob-
    lems, 26, 29; transactions and, 5–6
inheritability, 8–9, 36, 137
Inman, Robert P., 85, 99
institutional environment: budget rule
    design and, 123; electoral environ-
    ment and legislative incentives, 12–13;
    government organization, 12–14; im-

plementation of enforcement of rules,
    80; interactions of institutions (*see* in-
    stitutional interactions); long-term
    fiscal restraint/short-term spending
    tensions of, 9–14, 21, 40, 110–14, 122,
    126; malleability/stability of rules and,
    7–9; shutdown provisions and, 102–3;
    time inconsistency and, 11–12, 15, 30,
    123; transaction costs, 5–7
institutional interactions: agenda control
    and voting on budget, 32; amendment
    design and, 128–29; under Family
    Budget Protection Act, 19–20; gate-
    keeping power and open/closed rules,
    31–32; importance of, 54–55, 86; un-
    der 90 percent rule, 119–21; rule anal-
    ysis and, 16, 31–33; rule design and, 14,
    133–34; senatorial courtesy and fili-
    busters, 32–33; shutdown provisions
    and, 102–3
institutions: budget process and, 40–41;
    definition of, 23; design of rules and
    enforcement, 30–37, 40–41, 80, 133–
    34; effectiveness of, 123–24; fragility
    of, 139–40; functions of, 23; informa-
    tion and design of, 26–29; laissez-faire
    economic market and, 25–26; mainte-
    nance of, 35; repeated play and, 35–36;
    self-interest and, 24–26; state spend-
    ing and, 93. *See also* budget rules; en-
    forcement; mechanism of enforce-
    ment; rules
INS v. Chadha, 111
interests: amendment design and, 128;
    budget reform failure and, 105–6, 127;
    design of rules and enforcement, 4–5,
    31, 41; legislative preferences and, 60.
    See also preferences; self-interest
internal enforcement. *See* endogenous
    enforcement
internal rules, 137–39
international agreements, 130–33
International Monetary Fund (IMF), 131,
    133
Ippolito, Dennis, 84

Jackson, Matthew O., 35

Johnsen, Christopher, 46

judges: effectiveness as enforcers, 33, 60, 86, 87, 103, 124, 129, 168n4, 169nn6–8; elected/appointed, 86, 91, 93, 96, 126, 169n5, 170n13; as external enforcers of constitutional rules, 35, 56–57; presidential nominations of, 32–33, 37, 62, 139, 164n14; resistance to delegation of authority to, 61

Jung, David J., 86

Kettl, Donald F., 8, 82–104

Keynesianism, 18–19

Kiewiet, D. Roderick, 64, 169n10

Krehbiel, Keith, 65

Kydland, Finn E., 12, 30

laissez-faire economic market, 25–26, 28

legislative rules. *See* budget rules; rules

legislative welfare: in baseline model, 50, 141–42; budget rules tied to amendment procedures and, 62–63; executive veto authority and, 42, 54, 59, 124; impact of constituency costs on, 59; under open vs. closed rule, *72*; spending limit and, 42, 53, 54, 60, 124; supermajority voting rules and, 42, 54, 55, 60, 120, 124

legislators: bargaining logic in closed rule model, 68–69; bargaining logic in open rule model, 69–70; behavior under 90 percent rule, 158–60; design of suboptimal rules, 31; desire for reform of budget process, 100–101; enforcement of behavior of, 39; impact of constituency costs on behavior of, 58, 102, 148, 166n21, 171n25; impact of open/closed rule on project size/net benefits, 71, *72*, *73*, *74*; incentive to adhere to rules, 63–64; incentive to increase transaction costs, 6; long-term fiscal restraint/short-term spending tensions and, 21, 40, 110–14, 122, 126; model assumptions about,

15–16; net benefits to under open/closed rule, *74*; pork-barrel projects and, 44–46; position on amendments to distributive politics legislation, 64; preference for open/closed rules, 63, 64, 65–66, 74, 80; preference for types of revenue, 84; projects garnered under baseline model, 50, 51; proposal power of, 45–46; role in majority-rule model, 141–42, 165n11; role in open rule model, 67, 151, 152–53, 156; spending limits and, 144–45, 146; supermajority coalitions and, 55; unanimity rule and, 51–52. *See also* agenda setter; incentives; interests; proposer; self-interest; *specific legislators*

legislature: ability to alter rules with impunity, 39–40, 63–64, 108; ability to self-police, 111–13, 114, 115, 122; blocking power of committee system, 6, 161n5; checks-and-balances system and, 42; choice of budget size with endogenous enforcement, 76, 77; delegation of regulatory authority, 163n7; 90 percent rule and, 120; prerogatives of, 129; problems with deal making in, 6; rule design and, 31, 136–37; rule infringement by, 138; state spending and, *94*. *See also* U.S. House of Representatives; U.S. Senate

Levine, David L., 86

Lindahl equilibrium, 27

line-item veto, 134, 136

Lizzeri, Alessandro, 13

local spending, *2*, *3*, 3. *See also* spending

long-term fiscal restraint, 9–14, 21, 40, 110–14, 122, 126

loopholes. *See* political compromise

Maastricht Treaty (1992), 131

Machtley, Ron, 44, 165n4

Mackay, Robert J., 31

Madison, James, 23

majoritarian systems, 13

majority-rule model, 47–51
Makinen, Amy K., 173n1
malapportionment, 162n11
Mann, Thomas E., 138
market for lemons, 28–29
Marshall, John, 108
Marshall, William J., 6
Maryland, 171n27
Mason's Manual for Legislative Procedures,
    39
Matsusaka, John G., 96, 170n13
McCain, John, 44–45
McCarty, Nolan, 161n1
McCubbins, Mathew D., 64
McGinnis, John O., 118
McManus, John C., 38
Medicare, 110, 113, 161n3
metainstitutional interaction, 162n12
Michigan, 85
Milesi-Ferretti, Gian Maria, 13
Milgrom, Paul R., 56
military base closures, 11, 64
minimum winning coalitions: for budget
    reform, 105; formed in closed rule
    model, 50, 68, 144, 147; formed in
    open rule model, 69–70; implementa-
    tion of spending limits, 79, 168n9;
    norm of universalism and, 46; as out-
    come of baseline model, 50
Minnesota, 101, 102, 169–70n10
models: advantages of, 16; basic compo-
    nents of, 4; real-world politics and,
    123–24, 140. *See also* cartel behavior
    model; closed rule distributive poli-
    tics model; endogenous enforcement
    model; error correction model
    (ECM); generalized least squares
    model; infinite horizon bargaining
    models; majority-rule model; open
    rule distributive politics model;
    public finance models
Moe, Terry M., 106
Morton, Rebecca B., 16
moving the previous question, 67,
    167n3

Nebraska, 169–70n10
new economics of organization, 30–37
New Hampshire, 101
New Jersey, 101–2, 171n26
New York state: budget procedures in,
    171n27; budget reforms, 82, 99–101;
    dysfunctional legislature of, 1; late
    budget passage in, 99–100, 171n24
90 percent rule, 118–21, 122, 158–60
no-carryover rule: effect on spending,
    84–85, *90*, 93, *94*, 96, 103; FGLS
    specification for, 170n14; response to
    revenue increases, 98–99. *See also*
    spending limit
Noll, Roger G., 165n7
normative analysis, 16–18, 31
norms: effectiveness as enforcement, 61,
    62; enforcement of, 31; function of,
    23; repeated play and, 35–36; success-
    ful establishment of, 46; of universal-
    ism, 46–47, 165n7; violations of, 138
North, Douglass C., 23, 30, 56
North Carolina, 39
nuclear option, 37, 62, 139, 164nn18–19

Oates, Wallace E., 13, 17, 43
Office of Management and Budget
    (OMB), 106, 111, 172n4
open rule: closed rule vs., 65; effect on
    agenda setter's power, 71; gatekeeping
    power and, 31–32; legislature prefer-
    ence for, 74, 80; size and efficiency of
    projects, 70, 71, *73*; spending limits
    and, 74–75; supermajority coalitions
    and, 168n9
open rule distributive politics model:
    bargaining logic under, 69–70; base-
    line of, 150–55; equilibrium concept
    of, 71, 155, 167nn4–5; expected net
    benefits of, 77; lessons derived from,
    80–81; progress of play, 66, 67, *68*; re-
    sults compared to closed rule results,
    70–74, *72–73*
organizations: definition of, 23; informa-
    tional problems and, 34; leadership

credibility and, 30; principal-agent problems of, 30; tying rules to stable aspects of, 36–37, 40, 61–62

Ornstein, Norman J., 138

Pareto optimality: bargaining over single policy and, 162n17; as benchmark for evaluating outcomes, 17; of free market with complete contracting, 25; maximization of social welfare and, 48; Prisoner's Dilemma and, 26; relationship of discretion/commitment to, 30. *See also* efficiency

pay-as-you-go procedures (PAYGO), 113–14, 122

Perotti, Roberto, 13

Persico, Nicola, 13

Persson, Torsten, 13

point of order, 7–8, 37, 113, 162n6

political actors: characteristics of, 15, 18, 23–24; influences on behavior of, 16; self-interest of, 24–26. *See also* agenda setter; legislators

political compromise: constitutional amendment as product of, 115–16, 129; failure of budget reform and, 115, 116; failure of Gramm-Rudman-Hollings Act, 109; institutional interactions and, 133–35; loopholes in PAYGO from, 113; means to eliminate, 129–30, 136–37; suboptimal rule design and, 4–5, 41, 105, 113, 115, 121–23, 124, 135; supermajority coalition building and, 128

political economy approach: assumptions of, 6; foundations of, 15–16; illustrations of, 18–20; normative and positive analysis, 16–18

political parties: distributive politics, 171n22; executive veto authority and, 54, 59, 87–88; preference polarization, 4–5, 161nn1–2; state spending and, 87–88, 91–92, *94–95*, 96–99. *See also* Democratic Party; ideology; Republican Party

Poole, Keith, 161n1

population growth, *94*

pork-barrel projects, 44–46

Porter, Robert H., 34

Portugal, 132

positive analysis, 17–18

Poterba, James M., 170n13

preferences: of agenda setter for closed rule, 64, 74, 80; aggregation of, 23; budget rules as constraint on, 123; collective choice and, 46–47, 165n6; deficit reduction and, 110; evolution of rules and, 138–39; incentives to enforcement of rules and, 29; incentives to truthful reporting of, 24, 39; for inefficient district-specific projects, 44–46, 48; inheritability problem and, 8–9; of legislators for an open rule, 63; long-term fiscal restraint/short-term spending tensions and, 9–12, 21, 40, 110–14, 122, 126; polarization of, 1, 161n1; rule design and enforcement and, 4–5, 30–31, 41, 60, 104, 105–6, 122, 134; social welfare maximization and, 165n9; state spending as reflection of, 90; violations of PAYGO and, 114. *See also* interests; self-interest

Prescott, Edward C., 12, 30

president: budget proposal authority, 106; checks-and-balances system and, 42; ideology of and executive veto authority effectiveness, 54, 59, 87–88. *See also* executive veto authority; veto

President's Advisory Panel on Federal Tax Reform, 162n8

Primo, David M., 102, 165n8

principal-agent problems, 26, 29, 30

Prisoner's Dilemma, *26*, 26, 35, 38

proportional representation (PR) systems, 13

proposal power, 32, 45–46, 50

proposer, 32, 45. *See also* agenda setter

Proxmire, William, 44

public: effectiveness of enforcement by, 39, 60, 136; as external enforcer, 33, 43, 56, 57–59, 166n20; power of sanctions on rule violators, 16; view of long-term/short term budgetary goals, 10. *See also* constituency costs
public goods, 13, 26–28, 163n4

Qian, Yingyi, 17

rainy day funds, 99
random proposal power, 32
Rappaport, Michael B., 118
Reagan, Ronald, 3, 11, 109, 125–26
repeated play, 25, 35–36, 61, 62
Republican Party: balanced budget rule and, 84; filibusters and, 37, 62; rule infringements by, 138; spending and, 171n22; veto override and, 92
reversion budgets, 19–20, 22, 101–3, 136, 171nn25, 172n28
Riker, William H., 8–9, 36, 46, 137, 165n8
risk-neutrality, 163n6
Rodden, Jonathan, 13, 165n8
Romer, Thomas, 102, 126
Roosevelt, Franklin Delano, 106
Rosendorff, B. Peter, 133
Rosenthal, Alan, 40
Rosenthal, Howard, 102, 126, 161n1
Rostagno, Massimo, 13
Rudman, Warren, 109
Rueben, Kim S., 164n22, 170n13
rule design: for balanced budget rules, 82; budget deficits and, 3–4; components of, 20–21; difficulties of, 80–81; effectiveness and, 20–21, 30–33; institutional environment and, 123; institutional interactions and, 31–33; leadership credibility and, 30; as political process, 4–5, 41, 60, 104, 105, 127; questions concerning, 24, 134–37; for reversion budgets, 101–3; self-interest and, 24–26, 31, 41; of Stability and Growth Pact, 132–33; time inconsistency and, 11–12, 15, 30, 123;

transaction costs and, 5–7; use of norms as enforcement, 62; without possibility of exogenous enforcement, 61
rules: analysis of, 31–38, 42; for budgetary policymaking, 1; classifications of, 167n1; components of, 20; design and enforcement of, 3, 4; design and impact to reversion budgets, 101–3; design of enforcement for, 31, 33–37; enforcement by constituency costs, 57–59, 60; enforcement by courts or agencies, 56–57, 60; environment and, 5–13, 54, 60; formality/informality of, 31; free rider problem, 14, 38–39, 130; function of, 26–28, 30–31, 163n10; general legislative rules, 5; governing budget delays, 102–3; government organization and, 12–14, 21; impact on reversion budgets, 101–3; importance of, 140; incentives to enforcement of, 29; inheritability and, 8–9, 36, 137; institutional interactions and, 14, 31–33, 54–55; institution's relationship to, 23; legislature as designer of, 31, 136–37; long-term/short-term and micro/macro tensions of, 9–14, 21, 40, 110–14, 122, 126; malleability/stability of, 5, 7–9, 21, 34, 63–64; nuclear option and, 164nn18–19; open vs. closed, 65; reasons for failure of, 33, 60, 164n16; spending limits, 46; stability of, 39–40; time inconsistency and, 11–12, 15, 30, 123; transaction costs and, 6, 21; tying to stable aspects of the organization, 34, 36–37, 40, 61–62, 64, 75–76, 125, 126–27; voting procedures on changes to, 108, 172n6. *See also* balanced budget rule; budget rules; closed rule; executive veto authority; institutions; open rule; spending limits; supermajority voting rules

Samuelson, Paul A., 28
Schaps, Ronald, 165n8

Schelling, Thomas C., 35

Schick, Allan, 63, 107–8

Schoenbrod, Angus Macbeth, 86

school funding, 38–39

self-enforcing constitutions, 163n8

self-interest, 24–26, 28–29, 32, 60. *See also* incentives; interests; preferences

self-stable constitutions, 35

Sellers, Patrick J., 166n19

senatorial courtesy, 32–33

sequestration of funds: under Budget Enforcement Act, 113; under Gramm-Rudman-Hollings Act, 110–12, 125; 90 percent rule and, 119

SGP. *See* Stability and Growth Pact (SGP)

Shepsle, Kenneth A., 30, 46

shutdown rule, 4, 19, 83, 101–3, 126, 136

simple majority rule: implementation of endogenous enforcement with spending limits, 78, 125; implementation of spending limit and, 78, 80; spending with spending limits and, 92; tying budget rules to stable aspects of the organization and, 64

Smith, Adam, 25

Snyder, James M., 165n8

social net benefit function, 141, 174n3. *See also* legislative welfare

social planners, 24, 25, 163n4

Social Security, 110, 113, 116, 161n3

social welfare: consistency in government policy and, 11–12; efficiency and, 165n9; model definition of, 48; spending on in European countries, 173n1; time inconsistency and, 11–12. *See also* efficiency

sources of data, *91*

spatial model of spending, 120–21, 160

spending: agenda control with spending limits and, 32; balanced budget rule and, 83–85; in baseline model, 51; citizen initiatives and, 96; competing approaches to, 46–47; constituency costs' impact on, 58–59, 60; decentralized vs. centralized, 43–46; delegated enforcement's impact on, 56–

57; executive veto authority's impact on, 43, 54, 59, 86, 166n6; exogenous enforcement of rules and, 41, 60; federal aid's effect on, 93; imperfect enforcement of rules and, 55–59; increases in post-World War II era, 1, *2*, 3, *3*; institutional interactions and, 54–55, 86, 102–3, 124; majority-rule model of, 47–52; 90 percent rule and, 119–21, *159*; norm of universalism and, 46; under open vs. closed rule, 66, 71, *72–73*; party affiliations' effect on, 96–99; percentage of GDP, *3*; personal income's effect on, 93; public view of, 57, 166n19; relationship to efficiency, 55; revenue increases and, 98; shutdown provisions and, 4, 101–3, 126; spending for local projects, 170n11; spending limit's impact on, 42–43, 52–53, 54, 60, 86, 88, 93, 124; of state/local governments, 1, *2*, *3*, 3, *94–95*; states' balanced budget rules and, 3, 4, 82, 126; sunset provisions and, 19–20; supermajority voting rule's impact on, 14, 43, 53–55, 60, 86, 115, 116, 118–21; tax and expenditure limits and, 96, 103, 104, 124; taxing and, 3–4; unemployment's effect on, 93. *See also* outcomes

spending limit: balanced budget rules and, 118; definition of for states, 170n12; distributive politics bargaining and, 124; effect of tax and expenditure limits, 96; endogeneity and, 90–91; enforcement problem and, 74–80, 167–68n7; executive selection of, 166n15; feasibility of endogenous enforcement of, 62–65; impact on preference for open/closed rules, 65; impact on spending, 42–43, 52–53, 60, 86, 88, 93, *94*; implementation of, 77–80; interaction with agenda control, 32; malleability/stability of, 63–64; no-carryover rule and, 93, 96; operationalization of, 87; revenue increases and, 98–99, 171n23; rise of in

spending limit (*cont.*)
states, 85; selection procedure of justices and, 86, 91, 93, 96; shutdown
provisions and, 102–3; state debt and,
93; of states, *90*; in states with no-
carryover rule and elected courts, 88–
89; states with/without, 89; supermajority coalitions and, 54–55. *See also*
balanced budget rule; tax and expenditure limits (TELs)
spillover projects, 43
Stability and Growth Pact (SGP), 130–
33, 173nn6–7
Stevens, Ted, 7–8, 45–46
St. Germain, Fernand, 44, 165n4
sunset provisions, 19–20
supermajority coalitions: amendment
passage and, 128; attractiveness of
open rule and, 168nn9–10; balanced
budget rule and, 14; impact on spending, 54, 60; implementation of spending limits and, 79, 80; influence on behavior of legislators/agenda setter, 55;
90 percent rule and, 119; spending
with spending limits and, 92
supermajority veto override coalitions,
92
supermajority voting rules: distributive
politics bargaining and, 124; in federal
balanced budget amendment proposal, 116, 118–21; impact on spending, 14, 43, 53–54, 60, 86, 116, 118–21;
interaction with budget rules, 21–22,
54–55, 162n15; 90 percent rule and,
118–21, 159; tying budget rules to
stable aspects of the organization and,
64
Szakaly, Kristin, 169n10

Tabellini, Guido, 13
tax and expenditure limits (TELs): effectiveness of, 41, 103, 104, 124; era of
adoption of, 87; rise of in 1980s and
1990s, 85; state spending and, *90*, *94*,
96
taxation: balanced budget rules and, 83–

84; effect on consumer spending,
162n9; exploitation of districts with
no projects, 50, 51; for public goods,
27–28, 163n4; spending and, 3–4;
spending limits and, 87
tax code simplification, 11, 162n8
Thurber, James A., 112
Tiebout, Charles M., 13
time inconsistency, 11–12, 15, 30, 123
transaction costs, 5–7, 21, 23, 28
Tullock, Gordon, 46

unanimity rule, 51–52, 54, 163n10,
166n14
unified political parties, 165n8
U.S. House of Representatives: budget
process of, 80; illustration of equilibrium of model in, 51; illustration of
impact of spending limits, 53; rule infringements by, 138. *See also* legislators; legislature
U.S. Senate: filibuster, 4, 32–33, 37, 62,
122, 126, 139, 164n14, 164n19, 172n6;
rule infringements by, 138; Senate
Rule 28, 7–8. *See also* legislators; legislature
U.S. states: analysis of data on spending,
88–99; balanced budget rules and
spending, 82–85; balanced budget
rules of, 5; borrowing power and
spending, 13; budget process of, 80;
constituency costs and budgetary reform, 99–101; constitutional provisions for legislative behavior, 39–40;
design and enforcement of budget
rules, 4–5; effect of no-carryover rules
and elected justices on spending, 93,
96; effect of party affiliations on
spending, 96–99; effect of personal
income on spending, 93; effect of tax
and expenditure limits on spending,
96; effect of unemployment on
spending, 93; enforcement of balanced budget rules, 9, 85–86, 87; federalism and spending, 13; free rider
problem, 13–14; impact of citizen ini-

tiatives on spending, 96; incentives to balanced budgets, 128; influence of financial aid and debt on spending, 93; institutional effects on spending, 93, 96; operationalization of balanced budget rules, 87; response to revenue increases, 98–99, 171n23; seats in upper and lower legislative houses and spending, 96; spending for local projects, 44, 170n11; spending levels, 1, *2*, 3, *3*, *90*; spending limits and income, 98–99, 171n23; spending with effective budget rules, 3, 82; statistics for analysis, *90*, *92–93*; variation in budget deficits, 4, 82, 126; with/without spending limits, 89

U.S. Supreme Court: checks-and-balances system and, 42; as enforcer of the Constitution, 139–40; as exogenous enforcer, 35; opinion on entrenchment, 108; ruling on enforcement for GRH, 110–11. *See also* courts; judges

Vermont, 38–39
veto: checks-and-balances system and, 42; Family Budget Protection Act and, 19; governors' authority, 102, 172n28; impact on spending, 43, 54, 59, 166n16; unanimity rule as, 51–52; use in model, 48. *See also* executive veto authority

Vickrey-Clarke-Groves procedure, 27–28

Virginia, 171n27
voluntary fund, 38–39

Wagner, Richard E., 18
Wealth of Nations, The (Smith), 25
Weingast, Barry R., 6, 13, 17, 30, 35, 44–46, 56, 139, 163n8
Wicksell, Knut, 166n14
Wildavsky, Aaron, 9, 57
winner-take-all systems, 13
Wolf, Scott, 165n4
World Trade Organization (WTO), 133
WTO. *See* World Trade Organization (WTO)
Wyoming, 169–70n10

Young, Don, 45–46

zero-sum bargaining, 46